16650

CHRISTIANITY AND SCIENCE.

A Series of Lectures

DELIVERED IN NEW YORK, IN 1874, ON

THE ELY FOUNDATION OF THE UNION THEOLOGICAL SEMINARY.

BY

ANDREW P. PEABODY, D.D., LL.D.,

PROFESSOR OF CHRISTIAN MORALS IN HARVARD UNIVERSITY.

NEW YORK:
ROBERT CARTER AND BROTHERS,
530 BROADWAY.
1875.

Entered according to Act of Congress, in the year 1874, by
ROBERT CARTER AND BROTHERS,
In the Office of the Librarian of Congress, at Washington.

Cambridge:
Press of John Wilson and Son.

PREFACE.

THIS series of Lectures was delivered, by appointment, as the third course on the foundation established in the Union Theological Seminary by Mr. ZEBULON STILES ELY, of New York, in the following terms: —

"The undersigned gives the sum of ten thousand dollars to the Union Theological Seminary of the city of New York, to found a Lectureship in the same, the title of which shall be 'THE ELIAS P. ELY LECTURES ON THE EVIDENCES OF CHRISTIANITY.'

"The course of Lectures given on this foundation is to comprise any topics that serve to establish the proposition that Christianity is a religion from God, or that it is the perfect and final form of religion for man.

"Among the subjects discussed may be, —

"The Nature and Need of a Revelation;

"The Character and Influence of Christ and his Apostles;

"The Authenticity and Credibility of the Scriptures, Miracles, and Prophecy;

"The Diffusion and Benefits of Christianity; and

"The Philosophy of Religion in its Relation to the Christian System.

"Upon one or more of such subjects a course of ten public Lectures shall be given at least once in two or three years. The appointment of the Lecturer is to be by the concurrent action of the directors and faculty of said Seminary and the undersigned; and it shall ordinarily be made two years in advance.

"The interest of the fund is to be devoted to the payment of the Lecturers, and the publication of the Lectures within a year after the delivery of the same The copyright of the volumes thus published is to be vested in the Seminary.

"In case it should seem more advisable, the directors have it at their discretion at times to use the proceeds of this fund in providing special courses of lectures or instruction, in place of the aforesaid public lectures, for the students of the Seminary, on the above-named subjects.

"Should there at any time be a surplus of the fund, the directors are authorized to employ it in the way of prizes for dissertations by students of the Seminary, or of prizes for essays thereon, open to public competition.

"ZEBULON STILES ELY.

"NEW YORK, May 8th, 1865."

TABLE OF CONTENTS.

CHRISTIANITY AND SCIENCE.

LECTURE I.

SCIENCE AND CHRISTIANITY DEFINED. — THEIR SOURCES OF EVIDENCE. — I. TESTIMONY. — DEPENDENCE OF SCIENCE ON TESTIMONY. — ANTIQUITY OF THE GOSPELS.

THERE is no scriptural type oftener reproduced than that of Uzzah, who thought that the ark of the Lord would be overturned because the oxen shook the cart. Good men, in every age of unfettered thought and bold investigation, have been afraid for the truth, and afraid of the truth; unwilling that inquiry and research should have free course, lest their results should unsettle verities which they yet profess to believe divine and eternal, or throw discredit on records which they yet maintain to have been written by the inspiration of God. The supposed antagonism varies with the spirit of the times; each and every department of learning and liberal study, when in the ascendant, having been regarded as of ill omen to religious faith and piety. Apprehensions of this kind are virtual infidelity. They who entertain them have not the firm belief which they profess, and their fears do more injury to their cause than can be done by open and bitter enmity. While they mean to be loyal, they play the part of Judas, and betray the Master whom they love.

The chief cause of alarm at the present time is found by timid Christians in the progress and tendencies of physical science, as hostile to the authority and prestige of the Gospel. That speculations and hypotheses which seem opposed to Christianity are rife in certain quarters cannot be denied ; but that actual and ascertained results of scientific inquiry are repugnant to aught that God has revealed or Jesus Christ has taught, is an assumption as baseless as the most absurd of those made in the opposite camp. True science and Christianity, if it come from divine revelation, cannot by any possibility contradict each other : they must coincide as far as they cover the same ground ; and it cannot but be that at numerous points each should confirm the other. If God is, he must have put his signature on his whole creation no less than his impress on his manifested or written Word. The hieroglyphs of nature must needs correspond to the alphabetic writing of revelation, which may interpret and supplement, but cannot supersede or falsify them.

But what are the science and the Christianity which we may expect to find thus coincident and harmonious ? This question let us answer with due care and caution ; for we cannot extend our statement to whatever any sciolist or erratic student of nature may choose to term science, nor yet to whatever any enthusiast or bigot may claim as Christianity.

In the first place, we use science in the literal sense of the word; for in this sense only can scientific men claim for science the respect and deference of Christians. Science is not speculation, but knowledge; not half-truths, but whole truths; not hypotheses which may explain the phenomena of nature, but principles which do explain them, and at the same time are verified by them. There is, as you well know, such science. There are truths appertaining to the material universe, of which there is no more doubt than of the laws of number and proportion; and I have yet to learn that there is any repugnancy between science thus defined and Christianity. But all is not science that demands to be so called. This name is wholly inapplicable to theories which include only a portion, and ignore a portion, of the facts or phenomena within their scope, to those which from their very nature do not admit of proof or verification, and to those which are of too recent origin to be fully verified. The opinions of scientific men, however plausible, nay, however probable, are not science, — not, even though they prevail so generally as to make dissent from them seem a mark of an illiberal and narrow mind. There have been many such opinions thus dominant at former periods, but now obsolete, and even objects of ridicule. There have been such opinions inconsistent with all received religious verities, which have shown open fight, and have threatened the very existence of Christianity, but which passed into an early and unhonored grave, while the religion that they assailed survived unharmed.

I do not regard the theory of development or evolution, now so generally received among scientific men, as necessarily hostile to religious faith ; for there are among its most intelligent and able adherents some earnest and devout Christian believers. Moreover, there are certain aspects in which this theory is peculiarly attractive on religious grounds. If specific creation implies creative wisdom, much more is it implied in the endowment of primeval atoms or monads with the power of development into all the various and unnumbered forms of organized, sentient, intelligent, moral, spiritual being ; and we have thus presented to us, were it possible, even a more sublime significance for the opening words of the Hebrew Scriptures, "In the beginning God created the heavens and the earth." Then, too, were we constrained to trace our descent from an ancestry of apes or frogs or infusoria, we could look with no little complacency on our humble origin, from which we might anticipate further development in a posterity of angels and archangels, as far superior to ourselves, as we are to the brutes or animalcules from which we sprang. When we compare the alleged beginnings of our race with its present condition, there is no limit to what it may become, and the brightest visions of prophecy may be transcended by the history that shall be written. Then, again, when we are told that the individual human being actually passes through the various forms of his lower ancestry, why may he not in his own person pass successively through all the higher forms of which finite being is susceptible ? But while we have no reason, as the friends of religion, to fear these speculations, we are not called upon to make concessions to them or compromises with them: for they are mere hypotheses, are entirely unproved, have no claim to be regarded as science, and have not as yet complied with the first condition of science; namely, the production of evidence which points conclusively in their direction. From the nature of the case, it may be doubted whether they admit of such evidence; and if not, however strong, however well grounded may be the bias of the scientific mind in their favor, they can have no argumentative value against truths or facts which purport to rest on direct evidence.

We now ask, What is the Christianity for which we can claim and hope to establish equal validity with that of the accredited truths of science? I answer, Simply and solely, the genuineness of the divine mission of Jesus Christ; that is, not of any Christ of one's own special shaping or fancy, but of the Christ of history, of the Gospels, of the Church,—including, of course, the substantial authenticity of the evangelic narrative of what Jesus was, said, did, and suffered. This narrative has come down to us in human language, and is intimately connected, in the faith and reverence of Christians, not only with contemporary writings that may illustrate and confirm it, but with writings of a much earlier date, which contain large sections of biography and history, numerous details of dates and incidents, and frequent references to opinions of their times. But chronology, secular history, ethnology, cosmogony, names and dates, genealogies, unscientific opinions, are not religion, can have formed no part of a divine revelation, and do not need to be verified in order to substantiate a revelation. "We have this treasure in earthen vessels;" they look to me, indeed, like vessels which never could have been fashioned on a potter's wheel, had not the spirit of God been in the wheel; but, supposing it were not so, our concern is not with the vessels, but with their contents. I grant that the vessels — whatever of the divine handwork may or may not be discoverable in them — are by no means masterworks in their human aspect, and, especially, that the Gospels are singularly unelaborate. I rejoice that this is the case. If the life and teachings of Jesus had been transmitted to us in such an artistical form as would elude all cavil, their very perfectness would prove that these records were not written by the peasants and fishermen whose names they bear, but that they were concocted at some later day when there were in the Church learned men and practised writers. That the wonderful story is told with precisely such omissions, repetitions, inadvertencies, and discrepancies, as ignorant men and unskilled writers could not avoid, is to every candid inquirer among the foremost tokens of its genuineness, and guarantees for its authenticity. It is Christianity thus defined and limited — the Christianity contained in, identical with, the historical Christ, and this alone — that I shall, in the present course of lectures, attempt to verify as pre-eminently worthy of belief and acceptance.

Before I go farther, permit me to state explicitly what I do not intend to do, and to give my reasons for thus limiting the discussion.

I shall omit, as far as possible, all reference to the dogmatic contents of the Christian revelation. I shall exclude them from consideration, not because I occupy with regard to them a different position from those by whose invitation I am here; for the same catholic spirit which gave the invitation would, I am sure, extend itself to the expression — were it pertinent — of any opinions of mine that diverge from theirs. But, while I do not deem the differences of belief among Christians unimportant, all questions of interpretation are justly thrown into the background in comparison with the fundamental question, Have we a record of revelation that needs and craves to be interpreted? If we have no such record, then we are left, in the battle of life and in the chances of the unknown future, to stand or fall, to sink or swim, as we may: we owe no allegiance; we can look for no help or quarter; our own right arm must work out our salvation, whatever that salvation be; our only alternative is defiance or despair. But if from the parted heavens a voice from on high has broken the eternal silence; if "the mighty God, even Jehovah, hath spoken, and called the earth from the rising of the sun unto the going down thereof," — then are we no longer orphans, abandoned to our miserable self-help; the everlasting arms are beneath and around us; there is room for faith, submission, religion; the union of the human spirit with the divine, before inconceivable, becomes possible. In fine, the very dispositions of mind and heart implied in accepting a revelation — the abnegation of all self-dependence, and the felt need of redemption and salvation from God alone — are precisely those which the contents of the Christian revelation demand and cherish. These are the two poles of the religious life, and those who are within the sphere of their attraction must of necessity differ so much less from one another than from their unsphered brethren that their very differences are unity. I want, then, in the discussion before us, to omit these differences on the same principle on which the mathematician, in working out the equation of some great cosmical law, drops remainders and eliminates factors which would be of essential import in a problem of more limited scope.

In the next place, I shall take no note of specific theories of inspiration. The kind and degree of inspiration that may be claimed for the Bible or for portions of it is a question for Christians among themselves, not between Christians and unbelievers; and it is at best a matter of secondary moment. The prime, all-important question is that of authority, trustworthiness, infallibleness. Have we a record of divine truth which cannot mislead us? To this inquiry we have an affirmative answer when we have established the genuineness of the Gospels; for, first, it is impossible that, if the Author of our being has revealed the way of salvation, he should have confined the knowledge of that way to the contemporaries of Christ, and left all coming generations to records which cannot claim their confidence; and, secondly, if the gospel narratives are genuine and true, there must have been in the apostolic circle, whence the Gospels emanated, a fulfilment of the promise, "The Holy Spirit shall teach you all things, and bring all things to your remembrance, whatsoever I have said unto you." The Bible, from Genesis to the Apocalypse, is all along ablaze with light never kindled in our lower sphere. But it is the best, I would even say the only, evidence for its own inspiration. God's Spirit in the soul of man bears unanswerable testimony to his Spirit in the written Word. Inspiration is therefore to be discerned and felt, rather than proved *ab extra;* while genuineness and authenticity may be proved in accordance with the established laws of evidence.

One more omission. I shall say little or nothing of Judaism and of the Old Testament. It seems to me to have been a very damaging error in the defenders of the Christian faith, to blend Judaism with Christianity; to put on the same level of credibility the obscure traditions of the earliest ages and the gospel narratives with their transparent simplicity and self-evidencing truthfulness; to make the reality of Christ's mission from heaven depend on verifying the capacity of Noah's ark, or reconciling the genealogies in the Chronicles with the various passages where the several names occur. I have no fault to find with these learned exercitations on the Old Testament. There is no portion of the records of remote antiquity so well deserving and so richly rewarding research. I believe in the divine mission of Moses, in the divine origin of Judaism, in the miracle and prophecy which attested and attended it. But Judaism is superseded. It is no longer, as once, the avenue to the Christian Church. We are not to become Jews, in order to become Christians. What wonder then is it, that Providence should permit here and there a broken arch or a tottering wall in those once appointed, now disused, forecourts of heaven? That the evidence for Judaism was, in its own time, as clear and full as can have been needed or desired I cannot doubt. That it should be less obvious and attended with greater difficulties at the present day, is precisely what we should expect to find, if its age has passed and its mission has terminated. Instead of coming to Christ through Moses, our way evidently is to go to Moses through Christ. Independently of the New Testament, I see in the Old, along with numerous tokens of divinity which I cannot ignore or explain away, a great deal which I cannot understand, and know not how to appreciate. But Christ's full and emphatic recognition of Moses and the prophets constrains my own. My belief hangs on his knowledge. My ground, then, is that the evidences of Christianity carry Judaism along with Christianity; while Judaism, being so much more ancient, obscure, and open to cavil than Christianity, cannot essentially subsidize the Christian evidences. It must be remembered that the strength of a chain of evidence is precisely that of its weakest link; and so far as we put in the same category, and attempt to prove by the same line of argument, the swimming of the prophet's axe and the resurrection of Jesus Christ, we attach to the latter event whatever of suspicion or incredulity may cling to the former. While I can admit both as credible, I can imagine a condition of mind in which the former would seem to me a legend, the latter a glorious reality; and I am sure that our course of reasoning with regard to the one should be such as should not clog it with the doubts and misgivings that might innocently exist as to the other. Concentrate your forces in the citadel, and from it you can defend the outworks. Divide and scatter your forces through a long array of antiquated and half-dismantled outworks, both outworks and citadel will suffer detriment from your feeble defence.

So much as this it was necessary to say, in order that my omissions may be charged, not to my own lack of faith, but to my proposed course of argument.

The proposition which I hope to maintain is, that science and Christianity, as I have defined them, so far from being mutually hostile, and from excluding and negativing each the other, in fact rest upon the same foundation, and must stand or fall together. They appeal to precisely the same sorts of evidence, and there is no principle on which these can be admitted in behalf of science, and set aside in the case of Christianity. Science and Christianity have, in common, three sources of proof or evidence, — testimony, experiment (or experience), and intuition. We will consider these successively; though the first of the three, as demanding more detail of statement, will occupy the greater part of the course.

Under the head of testimony, it is incumbent on us to show that human testimony is as essential to the establishment of scientific truth as to the verification of Christianity, and that the testimony in behalf of Christianity is not inferior in completeness and credibility to that which underlies the truths of science.

Scientific truth rests wholly on a basis of transmitted and accumulated testimony. In no department has any one man, or have the men of any one generation, gone over the whole ground; but observed facts have been collected from various and distant localities, and freshly observed facts have been collated with those that have come down from former times, and often from a very remote antiquity. Thus, in establishing the relations and the laws of the heavenly bodies, not only have astronomers in every zone contributed their observations; but these have been compared with data derived in some instances from sources reaching back thousands of years. Indeed, there are some secular variations in planetary and stellar motion, infinitesimal in amount, yet of prime importance in theory, which cannot be verified without resort to the testimony of Hipparchus and other astronomers who flourished long before the Christian era. In geology, explorations have been made all the world over, and very important conclusions have often been drawn from or modified by the testimony of a single witness, — the journal of a first explorer of a previously unknown region. Moreover, as regards gradual changes on the earth's surface, the alterations of coast-lines, local elevations and depressions, traces of volcanic agency, testimony from the very birth of history to the present time has been sought, received as authentic, and built upon as furnishing a solid ground for scientific inferences of the most comprehensive character. Nor have the acknowledged misapprehensions, errors, and puerile theories of the ancient writers been regarded as invalidating their testimony as to facts that came properly within the sphere of their knowledge. Herodotus was grossly credulous ; Aristotle and Pliny maintained the most absurd opinions about the natural objects and phenomena that they describe : yet no one doubts their trustworthiness as to what they had themselves witnessed, or had received from witnesses worthy of credit. I am especially impressed by the intense stress which the advocates of the development-theory lay on even obscure and second-hand testimony, on the mere rumor of the creation of *acari* by artificial heat, or of some anticipative dawning of human intelligence or sensibility in dog or ape, bee or beaver. In fine, what now calls itself natural *science* a quarter of a century ago did not aspire to that name, but was merely natural *history;* and now, so far as it is science, it rests wholly on natural history, much of it very ancient history ; but natural history, like all other history, is nothing else than human testimony.

Christianity, equally with science, has an historical basis, and thus far depends on testimony. It has its historical records, to which it appeals for the life and the teachings of its Founder. There has been of late, in the theological world, almost a mania for discrediting the genuineness and authenticity of these records, just as a generation earlier it was the fashion among classical scholars to deny the authorship of the Iliad by Homer, or by any one man or generation, and as there has appeared more recently in some quarters a tendency — not without a plausible show of argument — to maintain that Shakespeare did not write the plays called his. Meanwhile, the really great biblical scholars — such men as Tischendorf, who has no pietistic prejudices to warp his critical judgment — have seen no cause to change their belief in the genuineness of these writings. As for Strauss, he may be fairly set aside as of no authority as to a question of fact; for he expressly admits that he shapes his chronology to suit his theories; and, during his last ten years, he changed his chronological base more than half a century, solely because he found that the dates which, on documentary evidence, he had assigned to the composition of the Gospels in the earlier editions of his "Life of Jesus" were utterly incompatible with his mythical hypothesis. Renan's "Life of Jesus," on the other hand, manifests no more noteworthy trait than the author's proclivity to give to and claim for the authenticity of the Gospels the fullest credit, wherever their narratives come within the limits which he, in his assumed omniscience, knows that the divine Providence can never have transcended.

Our first inquiry under the head of testimony must be as to the genuineness of these Gospels; that is, their authorship by the men whose names they bear. The inquiry embraces many considerations that apply to the four Gospels; some which are peculiar to the first three; some which belong to the fourth Gospel only, the genuineness and remote antiquity of which are denied by not a few critics who admit that the other three were written in the apostolic times and by their reputed authors. With reference to the Gospels, collectively and individually, the stress of the question rests mainly on their antiquity; for, if we can trace them back to the lifetime of the men whose names are attached to them, it can hardly be maintained that they are either of spurious origin or of gradual growth.

In behalf of the antiquity of these books, the most conclusive argument is that furnished by the quotations from them and the coincidences with them in the writings of the early Christians. To appreciate this argument, let us take a closely parallel case. Suppose that of the many narratives of our late civil war that have been or will be written, there are four, and but four, by men personally conversant with the whole series of events, and worthy of being regarded as of conclusive authority, — we will say by A, B, C, and D, — and that these four will become the great historical monuments of this era of our history. What will take place as to quotations from these books? In the lifetime of the present generation they will not be quoted or referred to by name; for the events they record will be so recent, that all who make mention of them will write from their own memory, or from such memoranda or fugitive documents as they may have on hand. There will thus be coincidence with these authorities, but no quotation. In the next generation they will be quoted, but seldom and informally: for the men of that generation will have talked with the actors in the events described; there will remain a multitude of floating traditions and loose documents, and many of the events will still be too familiarly known to need the citation of authorities; while, the want of a standard history being not yet felt, those four histories, though known to be authentic, will not have assumed in the public esteem the paramount distinction as standard works which will afterward be accorded to them. There will, therefore, be in the writings of this next generation coincidence with our supposed histories, but few quotations from them and very scanty reference to them. But, with every successive year after the second generation shall have passed away, miscellaneous sources of information will fail; narratives of secondary value will disappear; these four histories will be more and more relied on as of sole authority; the quotations from them will grow more and more frequent, till at length they are appealed to by name whenever any subject of which they treat is recalled. Now suppose that, two thousand years hence, there will be historical sceptics who will say, "No, these books cannot have been the original works of A, B, C, and D, who, as we know, were contemporary with the events recorded in them. They must have been compiled a century or two later." Suppose that sound and reasonable critics take up the theme of inquiry thus started, what aspect will the mass of quotations from these histories bear? They will appear in the form of a pyramid, with a very broad base in the later ages, but always diminishing from century to century, growing very slender toward the middle, and tapering to its apex in the earlier half, of the twentieth century; beyond which there will be numerous close coincidences, but perhaps not a single quotation. The candid critic of the thirty-ninth century will then say, "There cannot be the slightest doubt that A, B, C, and D, who are known to have flourished in the middle of the nineteenth century, wrote these books. Had they been later works, or by other hands, they could not have been quoted as they were in the twentieth and twenty-first centuries. The quotations from them by name begin too early to leave any doubt as to their authorship. It is impossible that their real character as genuine compositions or otherwise should not have been known in the twentieth century; and, if they had been even doubted, they would have been quoted as probably, or as supposed to be, or as pretending to be, the writings of A, B, C, and D, not as actually their writings."

This precisely represents the case of the Gospels. The quotations from them form such a pyramid as I have described. After the first two or three centuries, we find them expressly quoted, and generally by name, whenever the events they record are referred to. As we go farther back toward the first century, we find them still quoted by name, but less and less frequently, till we come to writers that were contemporary with the Apostles, though their juniors, and they refer continually to the events described in the Gospels, sometimes in almost the very words of the evangelists, yet without citing them by name. This aspect of the Christian writings can be accounted for only by supposing the Gospels to have been written by the apostles and apostolic men whose names they bear. Had they been later, or forged, or mere compilations, they could not have been so early quoted as of undoubted authority. They could not, if on any score doubtful, have come into general use among Christians without disputes as to their origin ; and these disputes would have left ineffaceable traces of themselves in the early Christian literature.

There is yet another consideration which may determine, not only the age of the Gospels, but the kind of men to which their authors must have belonged. The Gospels are written in Hellenistic Greek, — a dialect created by the transfusion of Hebrew idioms into Greek forms. There is hardly a sentence that does not betray the Hebrew origin and culture of the evangelists, who must needs have been born Jews. But it is universally admitted that in the middle of the second century these books were received throughout the Christian Church as of paramount authority with reference to the life and teachings of Christ. Yet, even in the lifetime of the apostles, feuds, not destined to be reconciled, broke out between the Jewish and Gentile Christians ; and before the end of the first century there seems to have been between these portions of the Church an entire separation and a bitter enmity. It is absolutely certain that, at a later period than this, neither party would have received sacred books from the other as unquestionable and authori tative. Had the Gospels been written by post-apostolic Jews, they would have been either rejected by the Gentile churches, or received by them with marked suspicion and reserve. Of Jewish Christians, only the apostles and their coevals were recognized by Gentile converts as worthy of their entire confidence and fellowship. From this apostolic fraternity, then, the Gospels received by the Gentiles must have been derived.

We have another proof that these books were written by men who were contemporary with Jesus Christ, or who at least were conversant with Palestine before the destruction of Jerusalem, in their freedom from anachronisms, and from mistakes as to persons and places. The Gospels are, as you know, full of designations of time and names of places, and that, during an eventful period of Jewish history, when important political changes were continually occurring, when the tributary monarch of one year was likely to be the proscribed exile of the next, when even the names and boundaries of political divisions were undergoing frequent alterations. Of this whole period we have a detailed history by the Jew Josephus ; and we find no discrepancy between his narrative and the circumstantial references in the Gospels. This negative fact has a positive bearing of the highest significance. A writer who undertakes local details in a field with which he has had no personal acquaintance, never fails to betray his ignorance. Even elaborate histories — on sure ground while describing the march of grand events — when they undertake to portray scenes on a contracted theatre, always contrive to misplace some of the actors or the incidents; and conscientious historians, aware of this liability, have often prepared themselves for their task by minute personal investigation. There are also not a few fictitious works — novels, tales, series of letters — which have been written expressly as imitations of antiquity, in which by an antique style, and by carefully framed references to well-known historical personages, places, and events, it has been designed to maintain the illusion undisturbed in the reader's mind. Some of these books, like Barthélemy's "Travels of Anacharsis" and the English "Athenian Letters," have been written by men of pre-eminent classical scholarship. Yet you can find no work of this kind in which the writer does not sometimes blunder or forget himself, fall into an anachronism, or insert some incident out of place. Josephus knew the whole ground thoroughly, as no one could by any possibility have known it after the fall of Jerusalem. Had not the writers of the Gospels possessed the same conversance with Palestine while Jerusalem was still standing, it is a literary impossibility that, even with the history of Josephus in their hands, they should not have left traces of their ignorance of the country, which lynx-eyed criticism would long ago have detected and laid bare. The minute and manifold coincidences with history, as illustrated and confirmed by modern research, show that the evangelists in describing transactions and events in Palestine were on their own ground; that is, must have been Jews in Palestine before A.D. 70.

In addition to this absence of discrepancies, it would be easy to trace not a few latent and manifestly undesigned coincidences between the Gospels and exterior history. One must suffice. The word constantly employed by the evangelists, and in the New Testament generally, to denote a soldier, is a noun which may signify a man under military orders, whether in active service or not.* Once only occurs the participle used to designate not merely soldiers, but soldiers in active service.† This is in Luke's Gospel, where he speaks of the soldiers that resorted to the preaching of John the Baptist. It is a common belief that the period of the Saviour's lifetime was an era of universal peace. Moreover, that desert region on the banks of the Jordan was not a place where soldiers on garrison duty, or belonging to a peace establishment, were likely to be found. Thus the presence of persons who could be designated by the noun referred to was improbable, much more that of soldiers on actual military duty, to whom the participle evidently points. But we learn from Josephus that there may have been soldiers in active service passing down the valley of the Jordan at that very time. It must have been about this time that Herod Antipas, of Galilee, repudiated his wife, the daughter of Aretas, a petty Arabian king, in order to marry Herodias, to whose hatred John fell a victim. There had been previously hostile passages about

* Στρατιωτής.

† Στρατευόμενοι.

boundaries between Herod and his father-in-law. Herod sent against Aretas a small army, which was betrayed and destroyed. This catastrophe, it seems most probable, took place a year or two later, after the death of John the Baptist; but a desultory warfare had then been going on for some length of time between Herod and Aretas, and any military expedition of Herod against his father-in-law would have taken John's preaching-ground on its way.*

The proofs that I have adduced are conclusive in behalf of the authorship of the Gospels in the age when they purport to have been written, and by men belonging, if I may so speak, to the apostolic circle; no mean witnesses, as regards their credibility, even if they were other than Matthew, Mark, Luke, and John.

One word only in conclusion. In my reasoning thus far — and I shall endeavor to adhere to the same rule through my whole course — I have taken and claimed no advantage for the Gospels because they are sacred books, and seem to me of vital importance. I have reasoned as I would about books of contested origin that had come down to us from the ancient times of Athens or of Rome. I think that I have, and I shall endeavor to give you, as good reasons for my belief in the genuineness of the Gospels as I have for that of Plutarch's Lives or of Virgil's Æneid.

* See Appendix, note A.

LECTURE II.

GENUINENESS OF THE GOSPELS. — TESTIMONY OF CHRISTIAN FATHERS. — OF HERETICS. — OF ENEMIES. — RULES OF EVIDENCE. — AUTHENTICITY OF THE GOSPELS. — THEIR AUTHORS COMPETENT WITNESSES. — THE GOSPELS COMPLEMENTING AND INTERPRETING ONE ANOTHER.

IN my last Lecture I sought to prove the antiquity of the Gospels. I showed you that we have reason to believe that they could not have been written later than the apostolic age; that is, that they are undoubtedly works of the first Christian century. We will now consider the proof that they were written by the men whose names they bear.

The first question that suggests itself is, Why should we not believe that the Gospels were written by these men? We have precisely the same reason for so believing that we have for our belief in authorship generally. When we find an author's name attached to a book with the earliest mention of it, and that name remains so attached from generation to generation without its rightful use being once called in question, the probability is little less than certainty that the name properly belongs to it. Thus, although there is no quotation or mention of the "Theogony" or of the "Works and Days" until some four hundred years from the time when they were written, because when mention of them is first found they are spoken of as Hesiod's, and no doubt is expressed as to their authorship in the age when such reasons for doubt as there might have been could not have grown obsolete, classical scholars have consented to call them Hesiod's, with a unanimity broken only by certain extremists of that class of critics whose fundamental canon is that "things are not what they seem." The Histories of Herodotus and Thucydides are known to be theirs only on this ground; and the case is the same with most books, modern no less than ancient. We have no detailed account of their inception, writing, and publication. All that we know is, that a certain book appeared under a certain name, and that no one ever gainsaid that name, or suggested that another name ought to have taken its place. Now, these four Gospels of ours are called the Gospels of Matthew, Mark, Luke, and John, as early as we can find any traces of their existence: they were never called by the names of any other men; nor, so far as I know, till the last century, did any one ever deny or doubt that they were written by these men.

But we are not left to this general consideration. We can, with entire distinctness and confidence, trace the very four Gospels that we now have as not only in existence, but universally received in the Church, under the names which they now bear, at a period so early that a false theory as to their origin could not by any possibility have obtained undisputed currency. In this line of argument I need but two names. There is, indeed, a cloud of witnesses that might be adduced;

and the Christian apologist finds his only embarrassment, not that of penury, but that of superabundant wealth. The voluminous testimony of the first four centuries is invaluable: there is ready access to it in Lardner's great work and in other less complete collections; but there is no subject to which we might apply with more literal truth than to this the scriptural saying, "Out of the mouth of two or three witnesses the whole matter shall be established."

My chief witnesses are Origen and Irenæus. Origen was born about A.D. 185, and was known as a scholar and a writer till after the middle of the third century. He was, perhaps, the most learned man of his time, and realized more fully than any other person in classic or Christian antiquity the idea which we attach to the designation of a critical scholar. He prepared with great skill and care what would now be called a critical edition of the Septuagint, collated with other Greek versions of the Old Testament. He was a zealous collector of manuscripts, having by his spiritual services secured for his literary pursuits the affluent aid of a man of large wealth. He, in his various books, quotes from our present Gospels so copiously that, were they lost, we could almost replace them from his quotations. He describes the four Gospels, and names their authors, giving the order of their composition precisely as they are arranged in our present Bible. He speaks of them as "the elements of the faith of the Church;" again, as "not rare books, read only by a few studious persons, but in the most common use;" still farther, as "received without controversy;" and yet once more, as "believed by all the churches of God." He was in the habit of comparing different copies of the Gospels, and commenting on the various readings which he found, which are in every instance identical with or similar to the various readings to be collected from now existing manuscripts. There is not the faintest indication that the Gospels which Origen used contained any thing that is not in our present Gospels; while the great number and variety of his quotations from them, his comments on their phraseology, his frequent analysis and exposition of single texts from them word by word, and his repeated mention of the various readings, render it absolutely certain that he had in his hands our present four Gospels substantially as they are now. As Origen was of Christian parentage, of liberal education, and a public teacher of religion from the age of seventeen, his testimony must of necessity cover the whole period embraced within his personal memory. The Gospels must have been regarded in his youth and childhood as he regarded them; else, whatever his own opinion of them, he could not have spoken of them as universally received without controversy.

Irenæus died about the time of Origen's entrance on public life. He was contemporary with Clement of Alexandria, who was Origen's teacher. He thus represents the generation from which Origen derived his knowledge of the Gospels and his reverence for them. He was a man of no little learning, very extensive travel, and high official standing. He is spoken of by Tertullian as "a diligent inquirer into all sorts of opinions." He was a native of Asia Minor, was for many years a bishop in Gaul, and had numerous correspondents in all parts of the world in which Christianity had gained a foothold. He, beyond a doubt, had received the very same traditions about the Gospels that were transmitted to Origen, and it is certain that he had in his possession precisely the same Gospels. He writes, "We have not received the knowledge of the way of salvation by any others than those by whom the Gospel has come down to us; which Gospel they first preached, and afterward, by the will of God, committed to writing that it might be the foundation and pillar of our faith." He then goes on to describe the four Gospels, the circumstances of their composition, and the precise view with which each was written. He cites the opening sentences of each of the four, which correspond verbally with the first sentences of our Gospels. He quotes frequently from the Gospels, and the passages quoted are in every instance to be found in our Gospels. He gives a detailed catalogue of the contents of Luke's Gospel, discriminating those portions which are peculiar to Luke from those which are common to him and one or more of the other evangelists. There cannot be the slightest doubt that he had the same Gospels that we have, and that he believed them to have been written by Matthew, Mark, Luke, and John.

Irenæus was a disciple of Polycarp, who had been a disciple of the evangelist John, and he tells of Polycarp's relating his conversations with John and others who had been with Jesus, and of his repeating what he had heard from these eye and ear witnesses about the preaching and the miracles of Jesus, all of which, he says, Polycarp described "in accordance with what is written," that is, in the Gospels. Irenæus must have been born a little before the death of John the evangelist. If the Gospels were of post-apostolic authorship, they must have been written during his lifetime. He was, as we have seen, familiar with the traditions of the apostolic times; and he records as among these traditions the names of the authors of the Gospels, the circumstances under which they were written, and the reasons for writing each of them. He knew whether Polycarp had these books, and held them in veneration. If he had never heard of them from Polycarp, it would not have been possible to palm them off upon him as apostolic writings, and to make him believe that they had come down as such without Polycarp's knowing any thing about them. Strauss (in his "Life of Jesus for the German People") and the Tübingen critics say that the Gospel of John could not have been written before A.D. 150, and they date those of Mark and Luke but about fifteen years earlier. In A.D. 150, Irenæus cannot have been much less than forty years of age, and had already been for some years a preacher of Christianity; yet, according to these critics, he was made to believe that brand-new books, of which he had never heard from his teachers or from his seniors in the Christian ministry, were really written by members of the apostolic company, and constituted, as he styles them, "the pillar and foundation of the Church which is spread over all the earth." It is perfectly evident that books of which Irenæus speaks so confidently could not have been written in his time, but must have been regarded by his venerable teacher and by Christians contemporary with him in the same light in which Irenæus himself regarded them.

Let us review the several stages of our argument. Origen's numerous quotations and textual criticisms enable us to identify the Gospels which he had with our own. He speaks of their unquestioned and universal reception and authority in his time as writings of the apostolic age. That reception and authority could not have begun to be in his lifetime; else it could not have been universal and unquestioned. Irenæus belonged to the generation from which Origen must have derived his Christian traditions. Irenæus gives accounts of the Gospels coinciding point for point with those of Origen, and quotes from them so copiously, and describes them so minutely, as to make it certain that he had the same Gospels. Irenæus received his Christian traditions from those who had been intimately acquainted with the apostles and their friends, and who could not have been mistaken as to the books purporting to have emanated from that circle.

I might close my argument here; but I will ask leave to dwell a little longer on the testimony of Irenæus, in connection with parallel testimonies of similar bearing. Contemporary with Irenæus in Gaul, were Theophilus at Antioch, Tertullian at Carthage, and Clement at Alexandria. They all quote, as from the Gospels, passages that are in our

Gospels ; they all speak of the Gospels as works of the apostolic age and of unquestioned authority ; and Tertullian and Clement give descriptions of them and of the circumstances and causes of their authorship closely resembling those of Irenæus. The first remark to be made on their testimony is, that it is not theirs alone. They were representative men, official personages, organs of Christian communities. They cite and describe the Gospels, not merely as histories which they receive, but as books approved and believed, received and read, by all Christian men. Their voice is that of the whole Church.

In the next place, Irenæus and his contemporaries, by their testimony, render it certain that these Gospels were generally and numerously diffused in every part of the Church ; that is, that there existed many thousand copies of them : and their quotations are sufficiently ample and various to show that they had not different but the same books under the name of Gospels in Gaul, at Antioch, at Carthage, and at Alexandria. Books were then multiplied and circulated with a slowness of which it is now hard to conceive. It must have taken a longer period than the lifetime of one generation to give these books the universal currency which it appears that they had in the latter part of the second century. Suppose them written (as Strauss and Baur maintain that they were) when Irenæus was a young man in Asia Minor, it is utterly impossible that, by the time he was established as a bishop in the heart of Gaul, they should have obtained such a circulation and prestige in every part of the empire as to make him forget that he had never seen them or heard of them in his youth, and imagine that they had been books of standard authority before he was born. This hypothesis trenches so far on the miraculous that we can hardly conceive of it as tenable in quarters where miracles are repudiated with scorn.

Irenæus is probably the earliest author who expressly mentions the four Gospels, and formally quotes from either of them; and this corresponds to what we should expect on the ground stated in my last lecture. As we recede nearer the apostolic age, we find in the Christian writers coincidence without formal quotation. There is one of these writers, however, who forms, as it were, an intermediate link between the epoch of express quotation and that of non-quotation; and who has often been adduced as a virtual witness against the antiquity and genuineness of the Gospels. I refer to Justin Martyr. It is urged as a conclusive argument for the non-apostolic and late origin of our Gospels that he does not once mention them; while yet, in his own words and way, he gives almost their entire contents, occasionally referring to what he calls "Memoirs by the Apostles," * and in one place, "Memoirs by the Apostles, which are called Gospels." † It is alleged that these Memoirs could not have been identical with our Gospels, inasmuch as Justin relates some, though very few sayings of Jesus and incidents in his life,

* Τὰ 'Απομνημονεύματα τῶν Ατοστόλων.

† Ἅ καλεῖται εὐαγγέλια.

which are not to be found in our Gospels.* As for his omission of the names of the evangelists, it must be remembered that his extant writings are chiefly apologetic, addressed to heathen emperors, and designed for heathen readers, to whom the names of those obscure Jewish writers would have been a matter of indifference. Then too, Justin, though not many years earlier than Irenæus, was born in Samaria, spent a large part of his life in Palestine, and must have had numerous sources of information by tradition or from the narratives of survivors of the apostolic age, entirely independent of the written Gospels, which then held by no means the sole and undivided place as repertories of knowledge about Jesus Christ which the next generation assigned to them, and were not read so constantly, and so absorbed word by word into the memory, as they were when the links of oral tradition became feeble and treacherous. Justin had, no doubt, heard a great deal more about Jesus than he had read. He had heard many of those things which, it is said in the sequel to the fourth Gospel, were too numerous to be written; and a few of them — probably authentic; for they are not in a single instance inconsistent in time, place, or character with our canonical Gospels — found their way into his treatises. He writes, as it seems to me, about the life of Christ very much as we should write about our late civil war for the information of foreign and unfriendly readers. We should have Abbot's, Greeley's, and other histories at hand, to refresh or verify our recollection; and we should

* See Appendix, note B.

be very likely to mention these histories collectively, "As we read in the histories of the time;" but we should hardly name them, seldom quote them, should, for the most part, tell in our own way what we had seen or heard at the time, or had learned afterward from those personally concerned in the events narrated, and should undoubtedly tell some things that are not recorded in the histories. I have no doubt that it is our four Gospels to which Justin so often refers; but, even were it otherwise, his testimony is none the less valuable, as it shows that there were afloat and on record, in the generation next succeeding the apostles, the same accounts of Jesus Christ that are contained in our Gospels, and no account of a different style or tenor.*

It is often alleged, in answer to the arguments for the genuineness of the Gospels, that the early Christian centuries were an uncritical age, when questions of authorship were not likely to be discussed, and when a false name might have easily become attached to any writing without protest or inquiry. We have, however, ample reason for the opposite opinion. I do not remember, indeed, any classic writing of those times, in which the specific question of the genuineness of a book is discussed; but there are treatises of Cicero and chapters of Quinctilian which are masterworks of critical skill and acumen, showing precisely that keen curiosity and close observation as to the details, conditions, and surroundings of literary composition, which constitute the art of the

* See Appendix, note C.

modern critic. Among Christian writers, Origen may be fittingly termed an eminently discriminating and skilful critical editor of the Septuagint; while his labors on the New Testament show a careful comparison of texts, and a clear recognition of the canons by which decision is to be made in doubtful cases. Then, as regards the special question of authorship, we have in a well-known passage of Eusebius, in the half-century next succeeding that in which Origen died, proof that the importance of the inquiry was fully understood, and that special care had been bestowed upon its answer. Eusebius was a man of very great learning. He undertook to write the history of the Church; and prepared himself for this work by extended study, travel, and correspondence, and by collecting, at great expense, from every portion of the empire such books as might aid him in his enterprise. His work shows manifest tokens of the most faithful research into the beginnings and early growth of Christianity, and a diligent and judicious use of all authorities extant. He divides the books in the hands of Christians into three classes, — those acknowledged as genuine,* among which are our four Gospels; books disputed,† though well known, and approved by many, among which are included most of the (so-called) Catholic Epistles; and those which are undoubtedly spurious.‡ He expresses doubt whether the Apocalypse belongs to the first or the third class; that is, whether the apostle John's name

* Ὁμολογουμέναι γραφαί. † Ἀντιλεγουέναι γραφαί.
‡ Νόθαι γραφαί.

had been truly or falsely connected with it. In a subsequent sentence, he speaks of some books as disputed, notwithstanding that they are recognized by most ecclesiastical writers. What could demonstrate more clearly than such language as this, that the authorship of the sacred books had been subjected to searching investigation, and that these Gospels of ours, as contradistinguished from books recognized by most, had been recognized by all Christian writers?

Nor let it be imagined that Eusebius was ready to accept testimony without challenging the witnesses. I know of hardly a finer specimen of the acute and skilled sifting of testimony than his chapter about Papias. He, in the first place, corrects a careless statement of Irenæus about Papias. Then, speaking of Papias as a man of limited understanding, he rejects certain traditions reported by him from unknown sources, but lays emphatic stress on such as he professed to have received directly from the companions of the apostles. From this same Papias he quotes a cursory mention of Matthew's and Mark's Gospels, and a statement which shows what I have already dwelt upon, that books like the Gospels, however genuine and authentic, could not be estimated at their full value, so long as oral tradition remained fresh and clear. "I do not think," Papias is quoted as saying, "that I derived so much benefit from books as from the living voice of those that are still surviving." *

I have thus far drawn testimony only from men who

* See Appendix, note D

were in the direct line of spiritual descent from the reputed writers of the Gospels; and though they had the best opportunities of knowing that of which they testified, it may be said that their subjective faith, which may have been the result less of evidence than of personal influence, made them partial witnesses for the reputed records of their faith. The same cannot be said, however, of the Gnostics, who had every possible motive to throw the Gospels into discredit, if they could have done so with any show of reason. The theology of the Gnostics was an incongruous and deformed hybrid of the Oriental Dualism and Christianity. All their mumerous sects were agreed in maintaining that the supremely good God of the New Testament was a different being from the God of the Old Testament, who was the creator of the world and the author of the Mosaic theocracy; and that Jesus descended from heaven, not in body, — for he had no body, — but in spirit, to reveal the supremely good God, and to put away the imperfection and evil that deformed the earthly domain of the Creator. Of these sects, the Marcionites received as of authority the Gospel of Luke, with some omissions of passages unfavorable to their views, and disavowed the authority of the other three, not because they questioned their genuineness, but for a reason which only bears added attestation to their genuineness, — because they were so thoroughly Jewish. The remaining sects of Gnostics received all four of the Gospels as genuine, and quoted them constantly in their controversial writings, garbling them, indeed, and putting text and text together, so as often to elicit from the two a meaning that can have belonged to neither. Irenæus and Tertullian are full of complaints about their methods of quoting the Gospels. Irenæus says, — and the sentence, for the indirect evidence it gives, is worth volumes of more direct testimony, — "There is such assurance concerning the Gospels, that the heretics themselves bear testimony to them, and every one of them endeavors to prove his doctrines from them."

Now it is certain that the Gnostics derived no countenance for their views from the Gospels. It would have been very much to their purpose to prove these books to be of late or doubtful origin, jottings down of floating traditions, or compilations by unauthorized editors. It cost them a vast amount of trouble, contradiction, and absurdity, to quote the Gospels as they persisted in doing; and their persistency is to be accounted for only on the ground that they believed the Gospels to have emanated from the apostolic circle. Moreover, as Gnosticism may be traced back to the very lifetime of the apostles, and as the Gnostics would have run counter to all known laws of belief and action, had they midway on their career accepted as of primitive authority books that then first came to hand, the conclusion is inevitable that the Gospels are as old as Gnosticism, and, if so, that they are in date and authority what they purport to be.

The early writers against Christianity may also be cited as witnesses to the genuineness of the Gospels. They quote very largely from the Gospels, assume their contents as the basis and substance of Christian belief, and refer to them as written by the immediate disciples of Jesus. Only one of these hostile writers lived early enough to be of importance as a direct witness to primitive tradition; namely, Celsus, who was contemporary with Irenæus. His book is lost; but we have Origen's answer to it, in which he constantly quotes the very words of Celsus. In these numerous extracts the author perpetually refers to narratives and sayings contained in our Gospels, so as to make it certain that he had these and no other written records of the faith which he assailed; and he speaks of the statements thus quoted as "written by the disciples," and, in one instance, as "your own writings, in addition to which we need no other testimony." These books cannot, therefore, have been just coming into circulation in the time of Irenæus; but must even then have been currently regarded, by enemies no less than by friends, as works of the primitive disciples. The other hostile writers who might be named, like Celsus, treat the Gospels as the undisputed records of what Jesus was believed by his disciples to have done and said; and they are of the same value as witnesses with such Christian writers as were contemporary with them respectively.*

I have thus shown you, in the last and in the pres-

* The testimony in behalf of Christianity, derived from the writings of its early Pagan and Jewish adversaries, is exhibited with equal thoroughness and candor, in the second volume of "Lowell Lectures on the Evidences of Christianity," by John G. Palfrey, D.D., LL.D.

ent lecture, that the testimony of orthodox Christians, heretics, and enemies, is unanimous and manifold in affirming the authorship of our Gospels in the apostolic age by primitive disciples, and, wherever names are given, by the men whose names are now attached to them. This authorship has been denied, not on the ground of the discovery of any new testimony, but on the score of the alleged inadequacy of that which has been cited. To me it seems more than sufficient, even had there been adverse opinions in the third and fourth centuries, of which we find not a vestige. Opinions of later times have no validity as evidence. We may apply here a principle of evidence recognized in all the courts of Christendom; namely, that involved in the statute of limitations, which is not a decree of arbitrary legislation, but a law of nature and a dictate of common sense. Permit me to illustrate its application here.* If against a claim openly made and maintained, there be valid adverse claims, it is morally certain that they will be presented while the evidence for them is fresh, the witnesses living, and the whole case capable of being carefully revised. Experience in different countries and ages can easily determine the extreme limit of time within which valid counter-claims are likely to appear. After this limit is passed, if adverse claims are presented, not only the legal, but the moral

* The author is indebted for the suggestion of this legal analogy, as also for a similar analogy introduced at the close of the third Lecture, to his friend Rev. Francis Wharton, D.D., LL.D., whose well-known legal acumen and learning are most happily employed in the defence and illustration of the Christian faith and its records.

probability is that they are fraudulent claims, set on foot for base ends, in reliance on the absence of original witnesses or the disappearance of original documents.

The first three Christian centuries were a period of perpetual conflict between Christianity and rival pre-established religions. During this whole time — of which we have many surviving literary monuments, not a few fragments of the writings of enemies, and, in the works of the Christian apologists, the precise moulds in which objections were cast (for the answers of course show what the objections were) — we have not the slightest trace of a doubt as to the genuineness of the Gospels. During this same period there were, also, in the Church heresies wild and strange, forms of belief so thoroughly extra-Christian in their origin and type, that we can hardly imagine how their disciples could have coveted and claimed the Christian name. Though one and another of these sects, on doctrinal grounds, disclaimed the authority of portions of this or that Gospel, and one of them set aside three of the Gospels, — just as Luther, without doubting that St. James wrote the epistle that bears his name, called it an epistle of straw, because he did not like its doctrines, — there is not on record a single instance in which any heretical sect or writer denied the genuineness of either of the Gospels. They would have been greatly relieved and comforted by such denial; that they did not make it proves that they could not make it. Now if with the means of establishing the spuriousness of these writings within reach; with the origins of Christianity familiarly known by intelligent and hostile Jews scattered all over the world, and by not a few of the cosmopolitan Roman officials of various grades, civil and military, who, for a time in Palestine, were subsequently dispersed through the empire, — if, I say, with these materials for sustaining the adverse charge, the early authorship of the Gospels by their reputed writers remained unquestioned, subsequent doubts might seem ruled out by a reasonable statute of limitations. If there existed actual grounds for such doubts, they would have been exhibited and urged in the primitive ages, when the materials for substantiating them still existed. Doubts that have sprung up almost in our own time might be fairly dismissed without examining their alleged merits, as we would dismiss, without examination, a legal claim which had been suffered to lie over for many years by those who had the strongest interest in maintaining it, if valid. It is not my intention, however, to leave these doubts unexamined. Those that relate to the testimony of the early centuries have been already considered. Others, based on the contents of the Gospels, will come before us in due time.

I have confined myself thus far to the question of the genuineness of the Gospels. Their authenticity will be a subject of future inquiry. But I will avail myself of the few moments that remain of the present hour to offer some preliminary considerations on this head.

In the first place, the genuineness of these writings

is of itself a strong argument for their authenticity. The authors had the best opportunities for knowing what they recorded. Matthew and John were the companions of Jesus for many months, and John took care of the mother of Jesus after her Son had departed from the earth. The house of Mark's mother was one of the rallying points for the Christians of Jerusalem shortly after their Master had left them; and there is, therefore, hardly a doubt that he and his mother had been disciples of Jesus during his lifetime. Moreover, uniform tradition assures us that Mark's Gospel was virtually Peter's, Mark having written what he heard from Peter; and there are in the Gospel strong marks of the fervid genius of Peter, especially in the preservation, in several instances, of the precise Syro-Chaldaic words used by Jesus under circumstances of peculiar interest. Such a mind as Peter's would have treasured up the mere sounds that fell from his Master's lips, and he would have been the very man to reproduce them even where they were unintelligible till interpreted. Luke was an intimate friend of the apostles: his name is found in some old lists of the seventy disciples,—lists, indeed, whose authenticity cannot be affirmed, yet which are from their very nature among the things least likely to be forged; and so graphic is his description of the walk to Emmaus, that I cannot resist the belief that he was the companion of Cleopas on that memorable occasion. These men had, then, the requisite knowledge.

Had they any motive for writing such narratives, if

they knew them to be false? We can conceive of none. On the other hand, it was for their earthly interest to suppress the whole marvellous story, or to leave it to take shape as it might, if they knew it to be true. They had nothing to gain, and every thing to lose, by writing and circulating such narratives as these books contain. For the cause in behalf of which they wrote, they and all their associates were sufferers, many even to death.

But might they not have been deluded? Their style is not that of madmen, or of men laboring under hallucination. They write very calmly. No one can talk about the events they describe with as little emotion as they manifest in writing about them. I know of no way of accounting for a style like theirs, except by supposing that they had become so much accustomed to experiences on a higher plane than that of common humanity as to be almost unconscious of their unique position, — just as natives of Switzerland might talk and write quietly and coldly about snow-peaks, glaciers, and avalanches, the very thought of which quickens our pulses, and as to which we are capable only of glowing and enthusiastic utterance.

It next claims our emphatic notice, that the relation of these four books to one another is such as to confirm the authenticity of each and all. The writers manifestly did not copy from one another. The resemblances and parallelisms of the synoptic Gospels will be a subject for distinct consideration hereafter, and may, I think, be fully accounted for. But that they were not copyists of one another's books is very manifest, both from the materials of transcendent interest peculiar to each, which no copyist would have been willing to omit, and from the frequent occurrence of just such unessential discrepancies as would naturally and necessarily be found in independent narratives. Then, too, in every instance in which a many-sided action is described, each writes as if he had regarded it from a different point of view. Thus, in the narrative of the resurrection of Jesus, while they all record the main fact and a very few of the accessory facts, each relates circumstances which may have escaped the notice or eluded the knowledge of the others, had they belonged to different groups of disciples, or lodged at different houses, or first became apprised of what was taking place at different moments of that eventful day.

There are also many cases in which one of the Gospels supplies what is necessary to the clear understanding of the others. For instance, in each of the first three Gospels we have a list of the twelve apostles. In Matthew and Luke the lists are given in pairs, "Simon and Andrew, James and John, Philip and Bartholomew;" but there appears no reason for so grouping them. In Mark's Gospel they are not thus grouped; but in that alone we are told that Jesus sent them forth to preach "by two and two."

Another case of the same kind may be found in the narrative of Christ's appearance before Pilate. According to Luke, he is charged with calling himself a king. Pilate asks if he is the king of the Jews, and on his admitting the charge, strangely enough for a Roman procurator, says at once, "I find no fault in him." This can be explained only by John's narrative, in which Jesus says to Pilate, "My kingdom is not of this world. To this end was I born, and for this cause came I into the world, that I should bear witness unto the truth. Every one that is of the truth heareth my voice;" that is, belongs to my kingdom. Pilate, thus convinced that as against the Roman sovereignty the alleged kingship has no significance, says very naturally, and in accordance with the fitness of his official position, "I find no fault in him."

These are specimens of numerous instances in which one evangelist, after the manner of an unartistic, inexperienced writer, tells but part of a story, omitting what alone could fully explain it, and the explanation is supplied by a like fragmentary statement of another of the four. In fine, the Gospels are full, not of superficial, obtrusive coincidences, which are always suspicious and always abound in falsified narratives, but of latent coincidences, such as reveal themselves only on close inspection and diligent study, such as could never have been invented or contrived, such as can be explained by no hypothesis other than the substantial truth of the several narratives.

We have lingered thus far, as it were, in the outer courts. In the next Lecture we will approach — may it be with profound and loving reverence! — the holy of holies, and consider Jesus himself, in the human and divine personality in which his historians present him, as the most conclusive argument for the authenticity of those biographies which enshrine the faith and hope of our race.

LECTURE III.

INTERNAL EVIDENCE OF AUTHENTICITY. — THE HUMAN VIRTUES OF CHRIST. — HIS ETHICAL AND RELIGIOUS TEACHINGS. — HIS INFLUENCE. — THE DIVINE SIDE OF HIS CHARACTER. — HIS SUPERHUMAN WORKS NEITHER IMPOSTURE NOR DELUSION. — ADMISSIONS OF EARLY ADVERSARIES OF CHRISTIANITY.

IN my last two Lectures I have endeavored to establish the genuineness and authenticity of our canonical Gospels, partly by adequate testimony, partly by their superficial characteristics and their relations to one another. The contents of a book have an important bearing on the question of its authenticity. There are books which cannot be believed. There are books which, unless they were true, could not have been written. No one could believe the Baron von Munchausen's narrative of his adventures, though it made its first public appearance under his own highly respectable name and authority. On the other hand, there was probably never a classical scholar so sceptical as not to give entire credence to Xenophon's Anabasis, — a story so coherent, so closely in accordance with all that is known of its time and scenes from other sources, and in portions so journal-like, equally in its minuteness and its vividness, that, were the book found now for the first time, without the author's name, the universal verdict would be that it was perfectly true throughout, and undoubtedly written by one who had borne part in some of the principal events recorded. The story, unless true, could not have been written.

The object of my present Lecture is to establish this same proposition as to our canonical Gospels. They could not have been written, had they not been true. To test this statement, let us take an inventory of their contents.

The character of Jesus Christ stands out alone, whether in fable or in history. Viewed in its human aspects, it is entirely unique. There is a blending, a harmonizing, of all seeming contrasts of moral excellence, — of traits, any one of which in equal lustre would have immortalized him in whom it shone forth among multiplied imperfections and foibles, — magnanimity and humility ; firmness and meekness ; uncompromising justice and unexhausted benevolence ; dignity and condescension ; the spirit of command and that of the lowliest service ; purity in which the most watchful hostility could detect no stain, and tenderness for the lowest, vilest types of depravity ; a walk with God so close that he seemed ever within temple-gates, and yet a walk with man so genial, friendly, loving, and helpful, that his eyes and thoughts might seem never lifted above the surrounding world ; a might stern and resolute, such as was never witnessed before or since in the conflict with evil, and a submission and resignation so serene and trustful, so gentle and kindly, as to call forth the admiration and sympathy of men whose lives had been passed in scenes of warfare and carnage.

This picture is presented under a kaleidoscopic diversity of aspects. We see Jesus in every condition of life: in moments of triumph, with the hosannas of adoring multitudes; in hours of rude buffeting, coarse jeers, and brutal insults, when Jew tosses him over with cruel scorn to Gentile mockery, and Gentile remands him scourged and lacerated to fresh Jewish outrage. We behold him, now at the marriage feast; now by the death-bed, the bier, the grave-side; in the evening with the friends at Bethany, to whom his advent is high festival; on the morrow among those who despise his claims and scoff at his teachings; then among disciples who misapprehend his words, misconceive his mission, annoy him by their paltry rivalries, disturb his serenity by their angry strife; then, again, among those who watch every word and gesture that they may find ground of censure and accusation; then among those who look to him for temporal benefits, but turn a deaf ear to his counsel and admonition. We are admitted even to his retirement. His heart is laid open to us. We learn that, as others by sleep, he by midnight devotion seeks strength for the burden of the day; and through the agony of prayer in Gethsemane comes to him the peace, the sweetness, the triumph of that awful, glorious death-scene on the cross.

In this entire picture of human virtue, we find no situation or incident out of keeping with any other, or out of harmony with the relations in which he stood to the institutions, life, and men of his time. It is not a compilation of excerpts from different lives; not like some of the stories of heroes in prehistoric times, and those in the hagiobiography of the early Christian ages, the heaping together under one name of anecdotes, events, and traditions, that evidently had at the outset various titles. The narrative is homogeneous; its contents belong together. The four Gospels manifestly present different sections — often parallel, and, when not so, mutually consistent and of like staple — of one and the same life, real or imagined. Even were it maintained that the longer discourses in the fourth Gospel differ essentially from those in the other three; still the human Jesus of John is precisely the same person with that of Matthew, Mark, and Luke, with not a trace or shade of difference as to the features of character or the style of incident. It is no more certain of the several biographers of Washington than of the evangelists, that they wrote the life of one and the same personage, or, if fictitious, of one and the same unreal character, whose fabulous history was equally known to them all.

As to the features of Christ's character, we may say, without fear of contradiction, that they have commanded the entire approval of persons of every age, condition, and culture, and the most cordially, of the confessedly greatest, wisest, and best. Whatever objections there are to the contents of the Gospels do not apply to the character of Jesus as a man. "We can find no fault in him," has been the verdict of his enemies from Pilate until now. Nor can we detect in

3

him the absence of any virtue or grace which enters into our highest ideal of human excellence.

His, too, is a character whose pre-eminent worth wins universal recognition. Though he is a Jew as to birth and surroundings, there is no Hebrew or Oriental element about him which interferes in the least with the appreciation of his moral supremacy by nationalities of the opposite stamp. The German, the Englishman, the Frenchman, is not constrained to make the slightest abatement or allowance in estimating his merits. He belongs equally to all ages. He has no secular parallax. In the darkest times he has been acknowledged as supremely perfect, and equally so at epochs of the highest culture, mental and moral. He is transcendently beautiful and glorious to the rudest aspirant after goodness ; and no less so to a Fénelon, a Martyn, an Oberlin, a Judson. The ignorant woman who can hardly spell out his story in her Bible can imagine no other being so lovely, so adorable ; and he seems no less the highest type of humanity to Milton, Newton, Locke, Bunsen, Faraday. In the galaxy of the greatly good, he is not a star a little brighter than the rest, but a sun in whose light the stars grow pale.

Such is the character which either grew under the pens of the evangelists, or was incarnated in the life of one of their coevals. The former hypothesis need detain us but a moment ; for probably hardly any one holds it now. Friendly and hostile critics will agree that the evangelists show neither the imagination, the culture, nor the capacity of authorship, which would have started them on the career of fictitious literature, or made their success in it even possible. They evidently used with no little difficulty the language in which they wrote. They exhibit no familiarity with any literature except the Hebrew Scriptures. Their style is literal, prosaic, unimaginative. The first three enter but imperfectly into the beauty and majesty of their own picture, — build better than they know, — describe a breadth and a tenderness of spirit with which, when they write, they have hardly come into full sympathy.

Then, too, the differences among the evangelists as to style and material render it certain that they were four men, not one man under four names. Now, were you to set the four most able and accomplished writers that can be found to write four fictitious stories about the same imaginary personage, in such a way that the events of the four can be combined into one story, and that there shall be nothing in the hero as described by either of the four that shall not be in perfect harmony with all that is related of him by the other three, it is inconceivable that, without more than human genius and vigilance, there should not escape here and there, from one or another of them, an expression out of keeping with the rest. Nay more, the hero himself, though intended to be the same, could not pass through these four different moulds without some variation of form and feature, discernible, if not to superficial view, on close inspection. The only alternative is that the character described by the evangelists actually existed in a person whom they all knew.

Here I am ready to join the company of unbelievers in maintaining that, in accordance with the recognized laws of human nature and development, such a man could not have sprung up and lived in that age and people. If you will look through the list of eminently good men in all times and nations, you will find, Jesus Christ alone excepted, not one who does not bear a perceptible relation to his antecedents and surroundings. Other good men have become illustrious by transcending by a very little the moral standard of their day, by ridding themselves of a few prevalent partialities or prejudices, by abjuring the most glaring faults of their contemporaries; in fine, by anticipating the next stage of progress. But none of them have lost the flavor of their native soil, or obliterated the date-mark of their birth. Socrates would not be received as an exemplary man anywhere in Christendom. Marcus Aurelius Antoninus would not satisfy a purist of our day. The saints worshipped by the Romish Church would, many of them, be excommunicated were they living now; and those of them who were truly holy men, often from conscientious motives, outraged all the decencies of common life. There were many things licensed among good men of the last century which would be utterly inconsistent with respectability, not to say piety, at the present time. Praying men commanded slave-ships and privateers. Ministers of the Gospel managed lotteries, and harvested their profits for the supposed interests of religion. As intelligence advances, even if the world does not grow better, Christians see more clearly what they ought to be, and each generation finds deficiencies and faults in the standard of all that preceded it. Christ alone does not fall under this law.

Do you say that he had before him the examples of the great men of the earlier dispensation, — patriarchs, psalmists, seers? I ask in reply, Fall they not into the same category with all other worthies of the early time? Abraham, Jacob, Moses, Samuel, Elijah, — is there one of these whom Jesus can have taken as a model for his character? Moses and Elijah are in the record (as I believe they were visibly on the mountain of transfiguration) placed side by side with him, — grand, glorious men for their times, well worthy to be captains in the Lord's host; but both of them men of violence and blood, implacably vindictive against the enemies of God, more prompt to curse than to bless. The Jewish type of virtue and piety was harsh and hard, narrow and exclusive, ungentle and stern, at the opposite pole from that of Christ. The Hebrews, like the classic nations, had no esteem for what we call the passive virtues, — to the whole ancient world not virtues, but weaknesses. These virtues had not even decent names in the language in which the evangelists wrote. The only names which they could find for humility meant (like the Latin *humilitas*) not a good quality, but a mean quality, — grovelling abjectly on the ground; and these words, for lack of better, the sacred writers had to pick up out of the dust, and to give them Christian baptism, to denote a habit of mind which in Jesus Christ was for the first time consecrated as a duty and a virtue, but which is now a gem second in lustre to none in the kingly diadem with which grateful generations have crowned him who unearthed it.

Jesus was, indeed, "a root out of a dry ground." He is not to be accounted for by any spiritual Darwinism, by any possible process of development. Do what you will with his character, you cannot bring him into line with his predecessors, whether Jewish or Gentile, or with the culture or standard of his age. These eighteen centuries of progress have not brought the advanced guard of humanity up to him. We can trace the rudiments of other pre-eminent characters, and show whence and how they grew. There is no human or earthly accounting for him. Yet he must have lived; if not, you have a still more marvellous prodigy, — an unprecedented, unequalled, and unaccountable creation of transcendent excellence, repeated fourfold in the imaginations of two fishermen, a tax-gatherer, and an obscure physician in Galilee.

But this is not all. There can be no doubt that Jesus taught no less than lived. Renan admits that the ethical teachings of the Gospels were for the most part handed down from his lips. And what are they? It is conceded by candid and virtuous unbelievers, it is asserted in every form of strong asseveration by Renan, that "never man spake like this man." We find no pre-arranged system in his words. They were suggested by the occasion, the scene, the casual surroundings, the incident of the moment. Yet when we put them together, we find no *lacuna*, no department of duty omitted, no question which the tender conscience can ask unanswered. While his Church has made but slow advances in the embodying of his precepts, and still falls far short of the fulness of his requirements, not one of them has been disallowed or outgrown or transcended ; nor has the keenest or the most malevolent criticism detected fault or flaw in the morality that flowed in his words and was incarnated in his life.

Here, again, we find him alone and unapproached. Socrates, Plato, Zeno, Cicero, Plutarch, Seneca, have been outgrown. Socrates gave a broad license in some portions of the moral code, and virtually sanctioned by acquiescence tantamount to approval, if not in his own practice, some of the worst vices of his age. In Plato's morals, with much that is pure and noble, there are some of the worst maxims that disgrace the phalanstery. The Stoics were in certain respects almost Christian ; but their philosophy gave scant honor to the gentler virtues, and recommended suicide as the wise man's avenue of relief from defeat, disappointment, incurable disease, and the infirmities of old age. The Hebrew morality, divine so far as it went, yet imperfect, needed at every point the "filling out," which neither sage nor prophet had conceived, but which Jesus gave at the very beginning of his ministry. His movement among the virtues was no less than revolutionary. The mountains were laid low ; the valleys exalted. The first were made last ; the last first. And the moral judgment of the Christian centuries has, point for point, sustained his decisions. That such a teacher, remote from all the great centres of intelligence, destitute even of such instruction as the rabbies of his nation might have given him, should have been nurtured and developed, by the might of his own genius, in that poor, starveling village in a despised corner of Palestine, is simply impossible. Yet that there was one such, if not four, is an historical fact as fully authenticated as is the fact that Augustus Cæsar was the Roman Emperor at the reputed era of his birth.

Yet more. There were other than ethical teachings. No one doubts that Jesus proclaimed the fatherhood of God as it had never been conceived before; that he declared the doctrine of a full and righteous retribution for the good and evil of men's lives, — a retribution reaching out into the depths of eternity; that he presented the divine clemency and forgiveness for repented sin, as to which there had been previously no clear assurance, and which had been tentatively, often despairingly, sought by bloody sacrifices, nay, by horrible self-torture, and, even in highly civilized communities, by the immolation of human victims, in lieu of all which he prospectively announced his own impending sacrifice on the cross as fully and for ever sufficient. Toward the last of these great truths, there had been in the later Hebrew prophets a certain negative tendency in the comparatively low esteem in which they regarded sacrifice; but even from this tendency the nation had retroceded into the merest ritualism. Immortality, dimly taught, if at all, in the Hebrew Scriptures, denied by the Sadducees, travestied by the Pharisees, had nowhere, either on Jewish or Gentile soil, been so received as to furnish motives for the government of the earthly life, comfort under its griefs, or a confident onlooking beyond its confines. As for the divine nature, its paternal aspect toward the individual worshipper or the Jewish people is recognized but sparingly, toward others than Hebrews in not a single undoubted instance, in their nationai Scriptures. Yet, without any intermediate stage of development, these truths come from Jesus Christ, clear, round, and full, so that there are no statements of them in human language so explicit and satisfying as his ; and, what is more, they take their start from him as motive powers of the intensest momentum and efficacy. The divine fatherhood, through his ministry extended to Canaanite and Samaritan, in John and Paul fructified into a universal brotherhood, which has been the soul of Christian propagandism and philanthropy until now. Immortality, from a vague conjecture, exhaled when most needed, through him became a conviction immovable as the consciousness of selfhood, with unexhausted energizing power both for brave endurance and for virtuous action. From him, too, the divine forgiveness — with precisely the agency which was first attributed, not by those who came after him, but by himself prophetically, to his own death — grew at once into a regenerating force, by faith in itself creating its own subjects in a line of succession which, commencing on the first Pentecost after his crucifixion, promises to last as long as sin shall endure. These revolutionary doctrines were enunciated, established, put into action by one who in training, position, and external advantages, possessed no prestige whatever, —

by one who was unlikely to be either highly intelligent or peculiarly spiritual, and still less likely to obtain extended or lasting influence.

There are some facts of a more comprehensive scope that belong essentially with the specific considerations which I have stated. Jesus Christ, whose actual existence, as I have shown, alone can account for the existence of the Gospels, was in every human point of view by far the most remarkable man of any age or race. Who else is there whose birth civilized man would ever have consented, or could without patent absurdity have proposed, to assume as an era from which to date our years? Yet this seems unnatural to no one; for his birth marks the intrusion among pre-existing forces of a force which, whether human or divine, has proved greater than all the rest. It has furnished the characteristic elements of Western as distinguished from Oriental civilization. It has so underlain every improvement in sociology, public policy, international law, nay, even commerce and finance, that when professedly new maxims in these departments have been promulgated, adopted, established, it is always found that they are corollaries from principles which Jesus proclaimed, and may be retranslated, and for the better, into the very words that fell from his lips. The paramount efficiency of this force is owned by its enemies no less than by its friends. No other cause enlists so devoted champions; none other awakens so intense antagonism. It is a stone of stumbling ever in the way of those who will not build upon it.

Proved, but improbable; certain, yet incredible; historical verity, still none the less an impossibility, — is this human life of Jesus taken alone. Had we this, and no more, we should have ample exterior evidence for the story, yet should be utterly unable to account for it. But the evangelists do not leave these marvels unaccounted for. According to them, Jesus bears a unique relation to the Supreme Being, — a sonship more intimate, more entirely consubstantial — if you will tolerate a word from the old theology — than belongs to any other being in the universe. He is the image, in human form, of the omnipresent and eternal God. It is his special mission, living and dying, to manifest all of the divine that can admit of manifestation. This mission is reported, not on the mere evidence of his assertions, but as attested by the exercise of such supernatural powers as put the seal of God upon him and upon his utterances. Disease flees at his touch. The maniac grows sane under his eye. He walks on the lake as by its shore. The bier and the grave yield up their dead at his summons. Chief of all, — barely to name a subject to which a Lecture of this course will be devoted, — he rises from his own sepulchre, and reappears repeatedly to those who had seen him dying, dead, and entombed.

If all this be true, there remains no difficulty in accounting for the character, the teachings, the extended and enduring influence of Jesus Christ. The divine and the human side of his person, character, and history, are in entire harmony, and cannot be severed in thought. The human presupposes the divine as its only solution; the divine could have had no inferior human manifestation. They are inseparable in the record. The life of Jesus in the Gospels is not a human life, with strange and supernatural incidents interspersed here and there. In this respect it differs entirely from numerous biographies of personages in Greek and Roman history, and of saints in the Christian calendar. Their stories contain supernatural events; but you can cut them out from the record, and there will remain a perfectly coherent and credible biography. The lives of St. Francis de Sales and St. Elisabeth of Thuringia, for instance, may, with an occasional omission, be made holy and beneficent lives, such as those saints undoubtedly led. But no such process can be performed with the life of Jesus. The divine is inextricably blended with the human. It forms part of the warp and woof of the whole story. You can no more expunge the supernatural and leave a coherent narrative, than you can cut out some of the figures of a piece of tapestry and leave a fabric that shall retain aught of comeliness and beauty. Sometimes it is the divine that forms the canvas for the manifestation of human perfections; sometimes it is in human actions, relations, and sympathies, that the divine shines forth with pre-eminent radiance and majesty. His beneficence is the most strikingly displayed in his miracles; his gentleness and condescension are brought out into the strongest relief by them. There are few of his discourses that do not refer to them. Indeed, his whole style of address betrays the consciousness of a mission far above that of the prophets who had gone before him. Some of them were men of lofty bearing ; they stood undaunted before kings and multitudes, bent not to godless power, and defied the rage and insults of the people. Yet who among them ever dared to speak in his own name? "Thus saith the Lord," is always the prefix and the refrain of their counsel, rebuke, and denunciation. Nor was it in their own names, but on the authority of the sacred books, and of honored names of rabbies of preceding generations, that the scribes of Christ's time gave their utterances. But he, the most modest and humble of the sons of men, never appeals to prescription. He speaks as one who has first-hand authority, — a right to be believed and obeyed. "Ye have heard that it hath been said by them of old time; but I say unto you." He constantly refers to his works as the credentials of his mission. Pare away his words as you may, reject the fourth Gospel, and retain the mere skeleton of the synoptics, you yet cannot eliminate the tokens of a higher than mere human self-consciousness, — of the possession of such powers as mere mortal man never wielded upon earth.

That Jesus suffered it to be believed that he possessed such powers, that his habitual speech on all occasions implied this, is an historical fact no less certain than are the universally admitted events of his earthly life. Renan, indeed, concedes this, and attempts to apologize for it, sometimes on the ground that Jesus believed pious fraud essential to his success; sometimes on the ground that his enthusiasm and the flattery of his followers, together with some remarkable, yet easily accountable instances of his power over the imagination of diseased persons in his presence, deluded him into a false belief in his own supernatural powers. We cannot hang at the same time on both the horns of this dilemma ; but they may be tested separately.

Did Jesus pretend to supernatural powers without the consciousness of possessing them ? For what purpose ? For the establishment, Renan says, of the purest, loftiest morality that man ever taught, — for the building up of a kingdom of righteousness which shall last as long as the world lasts. This may be a French mode of producing such a result, but a mode utterly inconceivable to the Anglo-Saxon mind. If, either as principal or accomplice, he lent himself to such a work, he strips himself of every title to our reverence. But if any thing is certain about him, it is that he inculcated and practised the severest virtue, and especially that he held in holy scorn and horror every kind of pretence and deception. What was the burden of his charge against the Scribes and Pharisees ? Not that they were openly and scandalously wicked : they were the farthest possible from being so ; and he always treated with peculiar gentleness and tenderness those who before the world bore the stigma of shameful depravity, if they were only honest enough to confess it. It was as hypocrites, as pretending to be what they were not, that he denounced those who sat in Moses' seat ; and in these invectives there is every mark of scathing moral indignation. It is manifest that, from the depths of his soul, he had the profoundest abhorrence for aught that was not honest, open, sincere, true.

Try we now the other alternative. "He was self-deluded." But his strength of character is no less manifest than his purity. We see him controlling both friendly and hostile multitudes by the mere power of his presence. Majesty and meekness sit together on his brow and mien and spirit. His serenity and evenness of temper show him to have been incapable of those waywardnesses and weaknesses which are wont to issue in delusive self-exaltation ; while, had his self-exaltation been imaginary, it would have tinged all the currents of thought and feeling. But his lowliness of life and spirit remained to the last as simple and genuine as when he first left his mother's home. Then, too, had any unreal fancy been possible for him, there was one which would of necessity have taken fast hold upon him so soon as he had acquired influence and a following. His people, writhing and smarting under a Gentile yoke, and encouraged by misunderstood intimations of the prophets (which, we believe, really pointed to such a Messiah as Jesus of Nazareth), were looking for the advent of a Messiah who should be warrior, king, and conqueror, and raise them from beneath the heel above the throne of the Cæsars. The popular expectation early seized upon Jesus : he was vehemently urged to assume this heroic part ; and had there been any weak place in his character, along with his extraordinary gifts, it would have been impossible for him not to yield to this pressure, borne in upon him, as it was, not only from a waiting nation, but from untold generations in the past.

We cannot, then, regard him as either deceiver or deceived. His, therefore, was a life which to those conversant with him presented a double aspect, — human excellencies and endowments which indicated a unique nearness to and union with the Supreme Being. Two of the evangelists were his apostles; we have abundant reason for believing that the other two were his disciples. I have given you what seems to me satisfactory evidence that these men really wrote the Gospels. Yet those who know all that it was ever possible for God to do, and are therefore sure that miracles can never have been wrought, and that a being superior to themselves can never have trodden the earth, set off the alleged absurdity of this unreal conception of a being both the Son of God and the Son of man, against the evidence of the early composition of the Gospels. They maintain that, however strong the grounds for believing these books to have been written by their reputed authors, the conception which they embody must have demanded more than one generation for its development from the best and noblest life that can ever have been lived upon the earth. We have, however, independent proof that this conception had reached its full dimensions long before we suppose the fourth Gospel to have been written, and as early as the earliest of the synoptic Gospels. Eusebius tells us that the authorship by St. Paul of thirteen epistles ascribed to him in our canon of Scripture had never been called in question; almost all sceptical critics admit the genuineness of ten out of the thirteen; Baur and the Tübingen critics regard four of them as having been undoubtedly written by Paul. These four are those to the Romans, the Corinthians, and the Galatians. Neither of these can have been written later than A.D. 58. The Messianic conception, as attached to Jesus, had certainly reached its full growth when they were written. Even the fourth Gospel contains no more highly colored picture of the human perfection and the divine sonship of Christ than Paul recognizes in almost every chapter of these epistles. Let me quote a few passages. "His Son Jesus Christ our Lord, which was made of the seed of David according to the flesh; and declared to be the Son of God with power, according to the spirit of holiness, by the resurrection from the dead." "The light of the knowledge of the glory of God in the face of Jesus Christ." "We must all appear before the judgment seat of Christ." "Ye know the grace of our Lord Jesus Christ, that though he was rich, yet for your sakes he became poor." "When the fulness of the time was come, God sent forth his Son, made of a woman, made under the law, to redeem them that were under the law." "If Christ be not risen, then is our preaching vain, and your faith is also vain." "Put ye on the Lord Jesus." "To this end Christ both died, and rose, and revived,* that he might be Lord both of the dead and living." In the epistle to the Galatians, St.

* "Died and lived," according to the more correct reading.

Paul describes his conferences with Peter and James, from which it appears that as to every thing appertaining directly to Christ he believed precisely what they believed, and that the only question between him and them related to the obligation of the Gentile converts to conform to the Jewish law. It is evident, beyond the shadow of a doubt, then, that thus early, and among those who had been familiarly acquainted with Christ during his lifetime on earth, there existed the very same belief concerning his person and character, which we find drawn out in detail in the Gospels. Thus, there is no reason whatever why the Gospels could not have been written at the time when they purport to have been written, and by the men whose names they bear.

With reference to the supernatural portion of the Gospel record, it is worthy of note that we see no proof of its ever having been called in question during the early centuries, even by the enemies of Christianity. Some of my hearers know what a demurrer is in legal proceedings. It is a plea in which an opposing counsel admits the facts alleged by his adversary, but denies their relevancy,—maintains that they prove nothing to the point. Now the earliest arguments against the divine authority of Christ were demurrers. Such was the statement recorded by the evangelists, "He casteth out demons through Beelzebub, the chief of the demons." Such was that of the council assembled after the raising of Lazarus, "This man doeth many miracles; if we let him thus alone, all men will believe on him." Celsus and Porphyry, it appears from the portions of their works still preserved, admitted the supernatural facts of the Gospel record, but ascribed them to necromancy. This was the favorite, and, I believe, the sole theory of Jewish teachers and writers for many centuries, vestiges of it having lingered in the synagogue as late as the epoch of the Protestant Reformation. Now this demurrer is, of course, valid only with one who can adopt the theory of the party that makes the plea. It gives very strong additional attestation to the facts admitted in common by both friends and enemies. It proves that the persuasion was early seated, and transmitted from primitive times, that Jesus Christ performed works like those which he said proceeded from the Father, and as to which none in our time who believe them to have been wrought can doubt whence they came.*

I have in this Lecture sought to present the character of Christ as portrayed in the Gospels, as the highest possible evidence of their authenticity. It is a character which, without an original, could not have been conceived by the evangelists; one for which they had neither the materials within their reach, nor the genius or culture requisite for its invention. As an actual character, it could not by any possibility have been formed by antecedent or surrounding influences. It was not a natural development; for human virtue has not yet developed up to its standard. Its human side cannot possibly be authentic, unless its divine side be equally authentic. The

* See Appendix, note E.

philosophy of our day insists on our receiving only proved facts, and the causes necessarily implied in those facts. We accede to this postulate. We claim only the unquestionable fact that, eighteen hundred and fifty years ago, there lived a man who left an indelible impress on all subsequent ages, who inaugurated a revolution in humanity, who started anew the current of the world's history, and of whose moral perfectness the best since his day have deemed themselves but far-off imitators. If our theory be disallowed, the burden of proof rests on those who reject it. Let them show the fountain of his purity in the turbid waters of Judaism or heathenism, or in the highest culture and the best philosophy of his times. Let them demonstrate the sources of his power. Let them reveal to us the secret by which the emblem of his ignominy became the symbol of all that is great, glorious, and excellent, and the crucified felon grew into the King of kings and Lord of lords. Till they can do this, we will be content with the loyal apostle's confession, "We believe and are sure that thou art that Christ, the Son of the living God."

LECTURE IV.

MUTUAL RESEMBLANCE OF THE SYNOPTIC GOSPELS. — THEIR SAMENESS OF STYLE AND LANGUAGE ACCOUNTED FOR. — GENEALOGIES IN MATTHEW'S AND LUKE'S GOSPELS. — PROOFS OF THE GENUINENESS OF JOHN'S GOSPEL. — ITS RELATION TO THE SYNOPTIC GOSPELS. — PROOF OF ITS ANTIQUITY FROM THE HISTORY OF GNOSTICISM.

I HAVE presented in previous Lectures the grounds on which we may affirm the genuineness and authenticity of our canonical Gospels. But I have confined myself to considerations common to the four. There are, however, certain special objections urged against the authorship of the first three Gospels in their present form in the Apostolic age, and against their editorship by any person of first-hand authority; and there are objections — which demand our most careful examination — to the authorship of the fourth Gospel by John or in his lifetime. We will consider, first, the questions that relate to the synoptic Gospels.

These Gospels coincide with one another in the main, not only as to their contents, but often in language. There frequently occur long passages which are the same, almost word for word, in the three, or in two of the three. There are many passages in hearing which it would be impossible for one familiar with the Scriptures to say from which of the three it was taken. A common origin or free copying from one another, it is said, alone can account for these phenomena ; and, on either supposition, these Gospels are in no sense three separate, independent, and original authorities. Even though the names of the authors be correctly given, still if two of them needed to copy from the other — Mark and Luke from Matthew — we have no ground for the assurance that those two had personal knowledge of the facts they recorded ; or if they all copied from older documents, then are they all alike unworthy of our implicit confidence.

That they did not copy from one another appears, as I have already said, from the no inconsiderable amount of material of the highest interest peculiar to each, which it is inconceivable that the others, with his record before them, should not have borrowed. This is emphatically the case as to the Gospels of Matthew and Luke ; it is also the case with Mark's Gospel as compared with Matthew's or Luke's alone, though it contains little that may not be found substantially in one of the other two.

The hypothesis more generally entertained is that these Gospels, as they now exist, did not originally proceed from individual authors ; that they were formed by successive accretions, the nucleus of all three having been a collection of the discourses and parables of Christ with some connecting thread of narrative, to which additions were made by different hands, in part from documents of which we see traces in two of the three, in part from tradition. Matthew,

Mark, and Luke may or may not have had something to do with the first crude germs of the Gospels bearing their names: but in their present form they were not written or made; they grew, and are composed of materials of different dates and sources, and of widely varying degrees of authority.

The first comment that suggests itself as to this hypothesis is, that the books themselves do not correspond to it. They have not the appearance of being made up of fragments, nor do they show the slightest traces of having been written, either of them, by more than one author. Each of them has its own peculiarities of style, its own modes of quotation from the Hebrew Scriptures, its own distinguishing words and phrases, its own marks of a specific use, purpose, or destination. Each is a complete work by itself, with no breaks or abrupt transitions, with no tokens of the intrusion of heterogeneous materials here and there. Such materials, if they existed, would be as easily recognized as are boulders from a distant locality among the native rocks on which they lie. These boulders, though borne to their present site on glaciers that were broken up before man trod the earth, still show themselves out of place, and will so show themselves till the end of time. We have no such boulder in either of the first three Gospels; but we have one lying loose in our common editions of the Gospel of John, and I regard it as of so pre-eminent value in refutation of any patchwork theory as to the composition of the synoptic Gospels, as to be worth our special consideration.

I refer to the narrative of the woman taken in adultery,* which no respectable critic supposes to belong by birthright where it stands. It not only has no connection with what precedes and follows it, and makes what follows it self-contradictory and absurd, but, when we leave it out, the preceding and following sentences run together at once, and show that they belong to the same continuous narrative. Short as it is, it contains several features of style unlike John's, and two designations — one of a place, one of persons — which John never uses, though very often speaking of the same place and persons. What is of still higher importance, it is the only story in the four Gospels that is in any degree repugnant to the moral sense which they have educated, and out of keeping with their general tone and spirit; the only passage which many who hold the highest views of inspiration would willingly and gladly see expunged from the sacred pages: for it alone gives a one-sided view of the character of Christ, representing pity for the sinner as almost lapsing into indulgence for the sin. This passage, with almost every possible mark of spuriousness on its face, is wanting in the four oldest Greek manuscripts, and in most of the oldest extant manuscripts of the early versions. Such manuscripts as contain it generally have it written in the margin, or, when inserted in the text, marked with an asterisk or an obelisk. Nor does it always occupy the same place, but is sometimes put as an appendix at the end of the fourth Gospel, and sometimes inserted,

* John vii. 53 — viii. 11. See Appendix, note F.

where it is equally out of place, near the end of Luke's Gospel. Thus there is not the slightest probability that it formed a part of John's Gospel at the outset, or was at first intended to be read as a portion of it. It was perhaps a garbled reminiscence of some story told by St. John, or perhaps a tradition, without any special authority, which some possessor of a copy of John's Gospel wrote in the margin of his copy, where he could find room to insert it. A copyist of this copy transcribed it in the same place, thinking that there was some good reason why it should be there. Thus it passed from copy to copy, till at length it was taken into the text as a passage that might have been omitted by mistake, but then not without a mark to indicate a doubt whether it belonged there or not.

I have introduced this passage as of the highest importance in the question now under discussion. It shows how utterly impossible it is so to incorporate alien materials that they shall seem of the same fabric with the work into which they are inserted. Yet, on the supposition of the gradual growth of the first three Gospels from a common original document, this process must have been performed many times over by the hands of many different authors, without leaving the slightest trace of displacements, rough edges, or awkward joinings, where new fragments were inserted, — without any tokens of diversity of style or inconsistency of representation. The existing marks of homogeneousness in diction and sentiment, of the continuous work of a single hand, in each of these

4

Gospels, could not by any possibility have been counterfeited.

Yet the coincidences of which I have spoken are so close and so peculiar a feature of these books, that those who call their genuineness in question have a right to claim an explanation of them. On examination we find, in the first place, that the coincidence, close as it is, is such as would result from common recollections rather than from the same manuscript. There are, in every instance, slight verbal variations, such as would undoubtedly be observable were any three of us to repeat from memory the parable of the talents, or that of the prodigal son. The coincidence is closer in the discourses and sayings of Jesus than in the mere narrative, as if each of the three had been at special pains to give a correct report of what the Master had said. The coincidence is most frequent and continuous between Mark and Luke, who often agree in deviating from Matthew, alike in the report of words, in the details of events, and in the order in which they occurred.

As for their agreement in reporting the discourses and parables of Jesus, it was but natural that each should have made it his prime endeavor not only to put into writing the substance of what was said, but to reproduce, so far as they could be rendered into another language, the very words that had been uttered. And is it not conceivable that Jesus purposely prepared the way for reports thus minutely literal? We have but little of what he said transmitted to us, and probably this little, embodying as it does the fundamental truths and laws of religion and ethics, was repeated more than once by Jesus in substantially the same forms, so as to penetrate by reiteration the somewhat slow and hard minds of the hearers, and to make an indelible impression on their memory. For nearly three years, at the least, after the departure of Jesus, the apostles and their most intimate friends remained together at Jerusalem. They met almost daily at one another's houses, for conference as to the great interests devolved upon them by their Master, and for such propagandism as was invited by the curiosity of the inhabitants or of strangers in the city. Their chief employment at these meetings must have been to refresh their own recollections, and to instruct those who met with them, by rehearsing what Jesus had said and done. Except as to the last scenes of his life, in which their tender and intense interest could never have waned, their discourse would have dwelt chiefly on his ministry in Galilee; for they must have always or often had those present who had seen and heard Jesus in Jerusalem, but not in Galilee, and much of what had taken place with Jesus or had been said by him at Jerusalem, prior to his last passover, may have been on visits in which he was accompanied by none or by only one of the apostles. It must have been a foremost aim with them to recall the very words that had fallen from their Master's lips, and they would have helped one another's memories toward this end, so that when they came to repeat his discourses separately, their verbal diversities would have been few and slight. Then, too, though without any special painstaking, they would have fallen into very much the same way of relating the incidents of their Master's life ; for while persons of taste and culture have each his own method of telling the same story, you must, I think, have noticed the strong tendency among comparatively uncultivated persons, in telling a story, to copy one another's precise form and style of narrative. There would thus have grown up among the disciples, before they began to be scattered, an oral Gospel common to them all, the chief staple of their preaching when they were dispersed, and to our three evangelists, especially to Mark and Luke, the germ of their written Gospels.

Mark, we know, must have been intimate with this company of disciples ; and, even were he not so, Peter, whose amanuensis Mark is believed to have been, held the first place among the authors of this oral Gospel, nor is there any thing in Mark's Gospel which we cannot easily conceive of his having learned from Peter.

Matthew, as one of the original twelve, had the best first-hand opportunities of information, so that he would have been likely to possess some materials peculiarly his own ; and as he was, so far as we know, the only one of the twelve whose business would have led him to the ready handling of writing materials, it is by no means improbable that he used memoranda taken from time to time, which would have been substantially, and often verbally, in accordance with the oral Gospel which he helped to make, yet would have covered wider ground.

Luke alone relates the mission of the seventy, and he gives a series of parables not recorded elsewhere. If he was one of the seventy, this may be accounted for; for it would appear from his narrative that the mission of the seventy took place, and that these parables were uttered after their return, while the twelve were absent on their mission. Luke's introductory chapters are peculiar to him; there is no sufficient critical ground for supposing them not to have formed a part of the Gospel as first written; and we may account for these details of the infancy and childhood of Jesus by the author's intimacy with Cleopas, a near kinsman of the mother of Jesus, — an intimacy proved by the narrative of the walk to Emmaus; for if Luke was not — as I believe he was — the actual companion of Cleopas on that occasion, it is evident that he heard the story from one who was present, and, if so, certainly from the one whom he expressly names.

We thus see that the coincidences and the differences of the first three Gospels are precisely such as may be accounted for by recorded and admitted facts with reference to their reputed authors. In our time, or in any time, three persons who had spent two or three years in daily intercourse, talking over the same portions of their common experience, would, in recording that experience, coincide with one another fully as much and as often as Matthew, Mark, and Luke coincide, while each would show somewhat of his own peculiar individuality, and each would probably have some things to tell which the others had not known or did not recollect when writing.

There is one discrepancy, striking and peculiarly open to cavil, between Matthew and Luke, which merits our special consideration. I refer to that between their genealogies of Joseph, the reputed father of Jesus. In Matthew's Gospel, Joseph is the son of Jacob; in Luke's, the son of Heli; and there are numerous other differences between the two lines by which the ancestry of Joseph is traced back to David. The first thing to be said with reference to these genealogies is that it is inconceivable that either of them should be a forgery. A genealogy is the most unlikely of all things to be forged by simple, unimaginative writers such as Matthew and Luke, if they wrote these Gospels, evidently were. Nor yet does the mythical theory or any theory of gradual elaboration account for their existence. They must both have been copied from actual documents, and from documents supposed to be genuine.

In the next place, as descent from David, at a time when the Messiah was expected from among his posterity, must have been a dearly cherished prerogative, if there were two ways in which such descent could be reckoned, tables conformed to both modes would have probably been in the possession of members of the family. That there were two such modes among the Hebrews is rendered certain by the levirate law, according to which, if an elder married brother died childless, the next brother married his widow, and the first child of the marriage was accounted as the son of the deceased brother. That this custom, if it no longer had the force of an imperative law, was not obsolete, may be inferred from the case of the seven brethren propounded to Jesus by the Sadducees. Now, if we suppose Jacob the actual father of Joseph, and Heli Jacob's elder brother by the same mother, but by a different father, we have the discrepancy fully explained. Even without pressing this explanation, we can conceive that there were among the Jews, as we know there were among both the Greeks and the Romans, other modes of legal adoption, by which a man might be in the eye of the law the son of a person other than his actual father. The phraseology of the two genealogies not only admits, but, rightly understood, necessitates the supposition of an actual descent in the one case, a legal descent in the other. Matthew evidently means to give the actual descent. Luke expressly designates his as the legal genealogy, and why should he have so designated it, unless he was aware that it diverged from the line of actual descent? The words, awkwardly rendered in our translation "being, *as was supposed*,* the son of Joseph, which was the son of Heli," literally mean "being, *as he was legally reckoned*, the son of Joseph, which was the son of Heli." Had this obvious and unquestionable meaning of the mistranslated word been taken into the account, much needless questioning and hypothesis might have been spared.

We will now give our attention to the peculiar objections urged against the genuineness of the (so-called) Gospel of John. It is alleged that the conception of Jesus in the fourth Gospel differs radically

* Ὡς ἐνομίζετο.

from that of the other evangelists; that this Gospel belongs, as regards its Messianic features, to a later age; and that it bears indubitable traces of opinions that cannot have attained shape and currency in the lifetime of the apostles.

I would remind you, in the first place, that the evidence of the antiquity of the fourth Gospel from the testimony of the early Christian writers is at least equal to that in behalf of the other three, and in one respect even superior; for the accounts which Irenæus gives of Polycarp's intercourse with John enhance very essentially the weight and authority of his full and undoubted recognition of the fourth Gospel as John's.

Here it is pertinent to ask, If John did not write this Gospel, who could have written it? Except the last two verses, — which were professedly and manifestly by another hand, probably by loving disciples, through whose agency, in his extreme old age or after his death, the book was put into circulation, — it bears throughout the tokens of a single author: the same style; the same habitual words and phrases; the same, often peculiar, designations for the same persons, places, and objects. The internal evidence on this point is so clear and strong that, among all the theories with regard to the fourth Gospel, that of its composition by two or more authors has seldom been maintained.

This Gospel is the most remarkable book in the world. Whether it be fiction or fact, there is in all human literature no narrative which so blends majesty and tenderness, sublimity and pathos, as that of the raising of Lazarus. The discourses ascribed to Jesus in controversy with his Jewish adversaries manifest as much dialectic skill as moral energy, and are on a level, both in their intellectual and their spiritual aspects, with the highest Messianic conceptions of the Christian Church. The communings and intercessions at the paschal table are an unexhausted treasury of holy thought and heavenward aspiration, the loss of which would bereave Christendom more sorely than the extinction of all that has been written in a similar vein for the last seventeen centuries, and especially would rob the dying and those who survive them in sorrow of peace, consolation, and hope, which not even the glowing words of hallowed genius and poetry to which they have given tone and spirit could begin to replace. Even in the working up of materials common to the four, there is, if you will pardon the word for the thought, an *interiorness*, a vividness of realization, not manifested by the synoptics; in fine, that closest approach of biography to autobiography, which occurs only when the biographer and his subject are associated by a spiritual twinship, in which the author of the fourth Gospel may be contrasted rather than compared with the other evangelists. As a single instance out of several that might be selected, I will refer you to the narratives of our Saviour's resurrection. Though this event can never be forgotten in the last offices of piety over the mortal form of one who has fallen asleep in Jesus, it seems more natural and appropriate to read on such an occasion from Paul's glorious chapter on the resurrection than from the account given of that event by either of the synoptics, who describe the fact as careful historiographers and devout and grateful recipients of the blessedness with which it is fraught, yet rather as those who are fully persuaded of it than as conscious partakers in it. But the spirit of the risen Jesus so throbs in every trait of the successive acts of that sublime drama as portrayed in the fourth Gospel, that the sacred volume contains no words more congenial than the very words of that narrative, with the moment when kindred are gathered for the last time around the lifeless body from which the soul has passed on to its Redeemer.

The fourth Gospel has had more influence upon the civilized world than any and all other books. Paul, indeed, by the obscurity, for the most part needless, which has been suffered to hang over his epistles, has led to a larger amount of speculation, often worthless, — of system-building, often with the "wood, hay, and stubble," of which he speaks contemptuously. But in the nurture of purity, sanctity, and loftiness of thought, soul, and life; in the unifying of the heart of Christendom through and with the heart of Christ; in the creation of the men in whom the beauty of holiness glows with a radiance which distance cannot dim or the lapse of years obscure; in the inspiration of the most beneficently influential Christian literature, and especially of those sacred lyrics which have been at once vehicle and nurse of the highest devotion of all the Christian ages, — the Gospel of John (so-called) has held the foremost place, to such a degree that its suppression, while it would still have left more of spiritual worth and power in Christ and his Gospel than in the whole world beside, would have circumscribed and attenuated the growth and working force of Christianity, and have robbed the Church of a very large proportion of its beauty, grandeur, and glory. There is, indeed, a low naturalistic view of Christ, which, not utterly rejecting him as the Sent of God, admits as little of him and in him as it can, which would find confirmation in repudiating the fourth Gospel, and which would be equally glad to expurgate the synoptics and St. Paul. But even those who occupy this sunken plane, as they have grown more spiritual, have grown into the love of the fourth Gospel; while all the saints of inmost initiation — those in and through whom the Church has shone with the purest lustre and wrought with the divinest efficacy — have found their choicest nutriment in the bread that has come down to them from heaven in this wonderful book.

Who wrote it? If it be true; if Jesus of Nazareth was all that it describes and relates, and the record was written by his nearest friend, — we can account for its authorship, and can believe that the writer, though a pure and holy man, was but a man of his time, brought into intimate communion with him who is "the same yesterday, to-day, and for ever." If, however, this is not a literal biography, but a semi-mythical narrative and a series of monologues founded on the life and sayings of a wise and virtuous, but illiterate Galilean peasant, then we have a far greater than Jesus in its author. We have in him the true founder of the Christian Church; for it is built and rests this day on no other Christ than the Christ, real or imaginary, of the fourth Gospel. Were this Gospel proved to be a fiction, the most advanced Christians of every section of the Church would exclaim, "They have taken away my Lord, and I know not where they have laid him." Who was this wonderful man, this transcendent creator, this unparalleled religious genius? As we run over the list of Christian writers for the century succeeding the apostolic age, there is not one of them whom we can pronounce equal to such an achievement,—not one of them who is above mediocrity. The few remains of the apostolic fathers fall very far below the mark. We should have to come down to Augustine or Jerome before we could find one who could even be imagined capable of such an endeavor; and they and their most gifted successors breathe more than all else the very inspiration caught from this record, and but for this would have left behind them far less illustrious names than they bear. It is impossible that such a writer should not have made his ineffaceable mark on his own time, and left a name for the admiration and reverence of all times. The apostle John is the only man of the first two centuries, the traditions of whose life and character represent him as adequate to this work; and if he was the author, we know that his record is true.

Even Renan, whose candor we have frequent reason to praise, admits a large Johannine element in the fourth Gospel, and supposes that it was compiled by John's disciples, in great part from their recollections or memoranda of his teachings. But no one who reads this book with an unbiassed mind can suppose it a composition by prentice hands; a compilation; a work of other than single authorship; an infiltration through secondary channels. Whoever wrote it had either seen and heard what he records, or else had a vividness of conception and a power of realistic description of his imaginings surpassing all that has been embodied in the literature of the ages.

But it is said that the Jesus of the fourth Gospel is an entirely different character from the Jesus of the synoptics. So far, however, is this from being the case that the most that we can say is that he is all of their Jesus, and more. The human traits are the same in the four. The narrative, so far as it is parallel, is coincident, the only difference being that the fourth Gospel bears the marks of a closer intimacy, a more realizing sympathy with its subject, as must have been the case if the author held that peculiar relation of Christ's confidential friend in which he professes to stand. But is Jesus even more or greater in the fourth Gospel than in the other three? Have we not in them intimations of all that is more fully developed in the fourth? As regards outward incident, the raising of Lazarus seems to us unique, from the intense vividness and lifelikeness of the narrative. But can it have presented a grander spectacle, or implied a more godlike sympathy or a more sovereign power in the Conqueror of death, than the scene at the gates of Nain, when Jesus meets the funeral procession, sees the widow in her desolate agony following her only son to the grave, arrests the bier, raises the lifeless form, and gives the youth to his mother's embrace, while for the wild wail of the mourners rises the glad shout, "God hath visited and redeemed his people"? Then, as to the alleged peculiarities in John's representations of the exalted personality of Jesus, are they peculiar to him? Have we not as full and emphatic, though generally less detailed, indications of them in the synoptics? Nay, one of the loftiest of these representations is drawn out by Matthew with an amplitude far transcending that of the fourth Gospel. In the latter Jesus repeatedly speaks of himself as the Judge of the world; but what are those dogmatic statements compared with the discourse recorded by Matthew, in which the Son of man sits on the throne of his glory, and all nations are gathered before him, and divided as a shepherd divides the sheep from the goats, the sheep on his right hand, the goats on his left? What higher claims does Jesus make for himself in the fourth Gospel, than when he says, "All things are delivered unto me of my Father;" "All power is given unto me in heaven and on earth;" "Hereafter shall ye see the Son of man sitting on the right hand of power, and coming in the clouds of heaven;" "Lo, I am with you alway, even to the end of the world"? Nor is the promise of the Holy Spirit, which fills so large a space in the fourth Gospel, wanting in the synoptics. "Take no thought how or what ye shall speak; for it shall be given you in the same hour what ye shall speak; for it is not ye that speak, but the spirit of your Father that speaketh in you;" and again, "Tarry ye in the city of Jerusalem until ye be endued with power from on high."

Yet it must be admitted that there are in the fourth Gospel numerous discourses of Jesus, coinciding in sentiment with his utterances in the synoptics, yet pitched, so to speak, on a higher key, more abstract, more spiritual, dwelling with greater length and with more minuteness of specification on his own personality, his relations to the Father, and his mission as the world's Redeemer. But these discourses, in the first place, contain nothing which the Jesus of the synoptics might not have said if he was what they represent him to have been. Then, the first three Gospels, confessedly in general circulation when the fourth Gospel was written, were doubtless in the possession of its author; and, whatever our theory of its composition, it was manifestly his purpose, not so much to cover the same ground as to supply their deficiencies. Accordingly, except in the events of the crucifixion and resurrection, which obviously could not have been omitted in any biography of Jesus, he hardly relates any incident which they record, unless in connection with some discourse which they had omitted. Then, too, it is perfectly manifest that the first three Gospels were written with a missionary purpose, addressed to those who were strangers to the events recorded; and they would naturally have contained only such of the discourses of Jesus as could have been readily understood by those who had not yet been initiated into the rudiments of the new religion. For such a purpose a large portion of the contents of the fourth Gospel would have been not only inappropriate, but even a hinderance to the reception of the teachings which were more nearly level with the uninstructed mind. It is equally manifest that the fourth Gospel was designed for readers who were already Christians ; who had, in St. Paul's expressive figure, been fed with milk till they were able to bear meat. Perhaps, too, many of the discourses recorded in the fourth Gospel were not heard by the apostles collectively. This Gospel gives intimations of several visits to Jerusalem not mentioned by the synoptics. On these occasions John may have been his Master's only friendly companion.

But, after all, may not a difference of receptivity among the members of the sacred college have been a prime reason and a sufficient reason for the difference between the synoptics and the fourth Gospel? We will suppose a strictly parallel case with regard to Socrates. We will leave Plato out of the account ; for his Socrates is Socrates *plus* Plato. He undoubtedly meant to be understood as often using the name of Socrates as an interlocutor, in dialogues for which his own thought furnished the whole material. But in Xenophon we undoubtedly have a faithful biographer of Socrates. He occupied toward the great philosopher the position, first of a disciple, and then of an intimate, admiring, and loving friend ; in fine, very much the relation which John is said to have sustained to Jesus. He was a man of high culture, and he gives numerous specimens of his master's discussions of philosophical subjects. Now suppose that three men of Athens, not educated men, not philosophers, had become similarly attached to Socrates, so that they followed him round from place to place, deposited the good things that fell from his lips by the wayside in faithful memory, were profoundly interested when he talked on common subjects to plain, simple people like themselves, but when he entered on a formal discussion or an elaborate argument, though they delighted to listen, yet remembered very little. If these men had written their several books of "Memo rabilia" of Socrates, their books would have borne about the same relation to Xenophon's "Memorabilia" which the synoptic Gospels bear to the fourth Gospel. They would have omitted a large part of what Xenophon has recorded, because if they heard it with the outward ear, they had not taken it in; it was above the standard of their culture, above their receptivity. If St. Paul had been among the personal followers of Christ, he would undoubtedly have written a Gospel like John's; but we may reasonably believe that such a record would have transcended the ability of Matthew, Mark, and Luke.

Here let me remind you, in passing, of what I dwelt upon more fully in a former Lecture, with regard to all the Gospels, that, though Paul gives and naturally would have given in his epistles few biographical details, his conception of Christ is not one whit less grand and lofty than that of the fourth Gospel; and his epistles were written considerably earlier than the earliest date assigned to that Gospel. The conception, therefore, was full-grown in the Church in John's lifetime; consequently there is no need, in order to leave time for its development, of fixing a later date for the Gospel.

Another ground on which the Johannine or early origin of the fourth Gospel has been denied is the alleged tendency to Gnosticism, according to some critics, at least the undoubted reference to it, in the proem to the Gospel, which, it is said, implies a date later than the close of the first century. That there are allusions to Gnostic notions in the proem seems to me certain beyond a question; but it is in antagonism, not in acquiescence. Yet these allusions do not impair the validity of the date traditionally assigned to the Gospel. Gnosticism has not, indeed, a defined place in the history of the Church till early in the second century; but it must in its essence, from the very nature of the case, have been coeval with the earliest propagation of Christianity. A mould already existed for it in the Zoroastrian dualism and the systems of æons, which prevailed throughout Asia Minor, had become largely incorporated with the Neo-Platonism of Alexandria, and had gained some measure of currency in every part of the Roman Empire. When Christianity was nominally embraced by the adherents of this philosophy, it lent its sacred names to their pre-existing notions; and thus was formed a strange compound in which an apostle could have recognized only the faintest vestiges of his own spiritual faith. It is certain that Gnostic errors are referred to in the Epistles to the Ephesians and the Colossians, the Pauline authorship of which there is no good reason for doubting,* and for which even those who deny their genuineness assign a date earlier than that which we would claim for the fourth Gospel. Cerinthus was undoubtedly a Gnostic, and ecclesiastical tradition that bears all the marks of authenticity represents him to have been contemporary with St. John, and to have been regarded by the venerable apostle as an atrocious perverter of the truth. Irenæus expressly says that John had the doctrines of the Gnostics in view in the composition of his Gospel.

The Gnostics represented the Logos, the Monogenes or Only-begotten, Life, and Light as æons distinct from the Supreme Being; they regarded the Creator of the world and Author of the Jewish dispensation as an inferior, imperfect, and — according to some of their teachers — malignant being; and maintained that Christ was sent by the Supreme God to deliver men from his tyranny and from the yoke of Judaism. Ephesus, where St. John is believed to have passed the last years of his life and to have written his Gospel, was the metropolis of Gnosticism. If the author of the fourth Gospel lived where these opinions were taking root, it was incumbent on him to show that Life, Light, and the Logos were not distinct from, but identical with, the Supreme God; that the Supreme God created the world and gave the Jewish law; and that the same God sent the Monogenes Jesus Christ not to destroy, but to complete the law; not to deliver men from its tyranny, but to consummate for and in them the blessedness of which it

* Renan admits their genuineness.

was the pledge and promise. I need not say how thoroughly this work is accomplished in the first eighteen verses of the fourth Gospel, in which the author, as with a prophet's wand, waves back to their native nothingness the chimeras of an arrogant and presumptuous philosophy.

An anti-Gnostic purpose is, then, perfectly evident in this introduction of the fourth Gospel But it deals with Gnosticism only in its first stages, in its rudiments. Had it been written, as it is said to have been, in the second century, there would have been a heavier and a more complex task devolved upon the author. The system which he opposed grew rapidly. The Valentinians, whose founder flourished about A.D. 140, numbered no less than thirty æons, in pairs, male and female. Basilides, who lived about fifteen years earlier, promulgated a system not less complicated, and even more grotesque and absurd. Still earlier in the century, there sprang up in the East the Ophitic form of Gnosticism, in which the serpent in Eden, the serpents that bit the Israelites in the wilderness, the rod which became a serpent in the hand of Moses, and the brazen serpent, all represented spiritual agencies, — the former two malignant, the latter two beneficent. Had the fourth Gospel been written after this heresy grew rife, it is impossible that the reference to the brazen serpent in the conversation with Nicodemus should have passed without comment. In fine, there are in this Gospel no traces whatever of several forms which we know that Gnosticism assumed in the second century; while there are evident references to opinions which must have been held by Cerinthus and his Gnostic contemporaries, and with which St. John must have been conversant in the latter years of his life.

I have shown you that the fourth Gospel must have been written in the first century, that John could have written it, that it is too remarkable a book to have passed into circulation anonymously, and that of all the early Christians whose names have come down to us there is none but John who could have written it. These reasons for believing in the genuineness of the fourth Gospel as the work of John, stand by their own validity and need no corroboration. Yet they are confirmed by the critical consciousness of the sincere and loving follower of Jesus, who, the more intimate his kindred with his Lord, feels only the fuller assurance that this record can have come from none other than the nearest and best beloved of the disciples.*

* For an eminently able treatment of the points at issue among critics concerning the fourth Gospel, the reader is referred to "The Fourth Gospel the Heart of Christ," by Rev. Edmund H. Sears, D.D., — a work remarkable equally for its acute reasoning and its truly Johannine spirit of devotion.

LECTURE V.

MIRACLES AN OBSTACLE TO FAITH. — PANTHEISTIC OBJECTIONS. — OBJECTIONS FROM THE SOVEREIGNTY OF LAW. — OBJECTIONS FROM EXPERIENCE. — NEED AND USE OF MIRACLES. — MIRACLES CONSONANT WITH THE PERSON AND MISSION OF CHRIST. — VERIFIED BY HUMAN HISTORY. — CONSISTENT WITH THE KNOWN METHODS OF THE DIVINE ADMINISTRATION.

THE arguments urged in the preceding Lectures would have been multiplied to waste in any other cause than that in which they are employed. The genuineness of most ancient books, and the authenticity of many universally admitted facts of earlier times, rest on much weaker evidence than sustains the genuineness and authenticity of the Gospels. Testimony as clear, strong, and manifold as we have to the leading facts in the life of Jesus would completely rehabilitate ancient history. Why is this testimony denied or doubted? There was a time when a repugnancy to Christianity on moral grounds accounted to a large extent for such unbelief as prevailed, and when that very unbelief itself had almost the weight of affirmative evidence; for such men as Rousseau, Voltaire, Paine, could hardly have been found on the right side, on the divine side, of any question involving principle and character. The objections of that school were plausible, but superficial, sneers oftener than arguments, and levelled rather at the antecedents and accessories of Christianity than at Christ and his Gospel.

Very different is the case now. Infidelity seldom appears in scurrilous forms, associated with banter and ribaldry. It is frank, honest, earnest, respectful and often even reverent toward the faith it repudiates; and among its expositors are not a few men of pure character, of high scientific attainments, and evidently sincere and zealous in the search for truth. They have no disrelish for the morality of the Gospel, no disesteem for Jesus as an exemplar and a preacher of righteousness, no hostility to Christian institutions. They reject Christianity solely on account of its miraculous element. At the same time, there are others, who with evident sincerity claim to be called Christians, profess to receive Jesus Christ as an unparalleled model of spiritual excellence, and as the wisest teacher of religion and morals that the world has yet seen, who nevertheless repudiate the record of his miracles, and maintain that he was no more or other than any man is capable of becoming. These persons profess to receive the teachings of Christ, not on his authority, but on their own, on account of the accordance of his words with their own intuitions and experience. Yet, in order to be consistent with themselves, they can receive only a limited portion of his teachings; for the paternal providence of God over individual beings and events, the spiritual help granted to aspirants after goodness, and the efficacy of prayer, — all of them prominent in the discourses of Jesus, — are liable to precisely the same objections that are urged against the miraculous narratives.

The alleged incredibility of miracles is my subject this evening.

There is one theory of the universe, very extensively maintained among both philosophers and naturalists, which would render miracles impossible, and, were they possible, worthless; namely, that which denies the existence of a personal God. Thus Renan, an atheist, or a pantheist, — if a distinction is to be made where there is no essential difference, — is entirely self-consistent in maintaining that no evidence can authenticate a miracle. He writes: "I believe that there is not in the universe an intelligence superior to that of man; there is no free existence superior to man, to whom an appreciable share may be assigned in the moral administration, any more than in the material government, of the universe." Of course, then, there exists no being who is not subordinated to the course and laws of nature.

But miracles are denied by many sincere theists, on the ground of their incompatibility with the divine order of the universe, which implies the immutableness of natural laws. This order, it is said, has been invariable so far as observation and experience — whether our own or such as it is within our power to verify — are concerned; we cannot conceive of its ever having been suspended or superseded; and our assurance of its present stability is so firm that no amount of evidence could convince us of the occurrence of a miracle now. Still less can any clearness or accumulation of testimony bearing date nearly two thousand years ago suffice to cancel this intrinsic improbability.

In approaching this subject, it concerns us to understand at the outset that the discussion cannot, by any possibility, be evaded. It is idle to say that our faith in this nineteenth century is in no need of miracles, in view of the far greater than miracle, — the moral evidence of the worth and power of Christian truth. This may be, nay, ought to be, the case with us, if we have drunk deeply of the spirit of Christ. Nay more, we can conceive that this same moral evidence might have been sufficient for those who lived for many months in his intimacy, and that the sacred flame of piety and love kindled in them might have been passed on from age to age even until now. In view of the contemptuous way in which miracles are treated by a supercilious philosophy, and are looked down upon as beggarly and obsolete elements by some who profess to believe them, we may wish that we were rid of them, and feel that we could defend Christianity all the better without them. But this is out of the question. If the Gospels are genuine, as we have seen reason to believe them to be, the miracles are inseparable from the religion and its Author. There can be no doubt that his earliest and closest followers believed in them. There can be no doubt that he professed to perform them. Christianity, the religion with which the person of Jesus Christ is indissolubly connected, is so allied with miracles that its defence without them is tantamount to its rejection.

In our investigation of this subject, it may be worth our while to inquire how far any man is authorized to deny the possibility of miracles. What created being can know all that it was ever possible for the Creator to do? Does not the denial that miracles are possible involve the assumption of a virtual co-divinity with God, of omniscience, of the capacity of searching and fathoming the depths of the Supreme Intelligence? God alone can know what God can do. If there be a God, infinite and eternal, it is at least conceivable that the cycles of his administration transcend the scrutiny and scope of a being so short-sighted and short-lived as man. If there be a God, his will is the first cause of outward nature; that will might have made it entirely other than it is, so that in the normal course of events there should not have been a single feature in common with the present course; and does not the power of constituting this entire difference include all lesser powers of the same kind and thus, of necessity, the power of modifying at will the existing order of things?

But it is said, Causation is an essential category of human thought. An uncaused effect, or a non-efficient cause, is an absurdity. Very true, and the atheist alone is chargeable with imagining this absurdity. But what are the efficient causes in nature? Has any material agent been so analyzed as to show that there is, in the structure or arrangement of its particles, an inherent reason why it should, of its

GENERAL LIBRARY University of MICHIGAN

own force, produce certain effects, and no others? The latest philosophy, as it seems to me on valid grounds, makes of the imponderable elements in the universe — heat, light, magnetism, electricity, gravitation — but one force, identical in its nature, though Protean in its modes of manifestation. Can it be pretended that the physicist has actually manipulated a substance, force, or agency, in which he detects such specific inherent properties as fully account, by physical causation, for the fire, the magnet, the thunderbolt, the gravitating planet? The same force, it is believed, sustains animal and vegetable life, sensation, muscular motion, cerebral action. But who has explored the seat of life, traced it to its source, analyzed its processes? The anatomist may demonstrate the adaptation of the various members and organs of the human body to the functions of the living man; but he cannot say why or how that man ever lived. There is no visible or tangible cause for the life of the man who does or did live, that does not equally exist for the life of the steam-engine which never did and never will live; for, according to the theory of the convertibility of force, the cause of the engine's motion and of the man's life is one and the same. A microscopic dissection of the apple-seed shows the germ from which the tree is developed; but had the man who dissected it lived on a sand waste, and never seen or heard of a tree, he would have found nothing in the structure of the seed from which he could predict the tree; nor, when he first saw a tree, would he even have connected it in thought with the seed that

U of M

he had analyzed. In fact, we know nothing of efficient causes in nature. We barely know that there are certain invariable sequences within the field of our observation and experience ; that some phenomena are always antecedent to and prophetical of others ; that is, that we live in an orderly universe. Yet efficient causation there must be. It may reside, though to us untraceable, in the antecedents which we call causes. The Creator may, as the Epicureans maintained, have lodged in the primitive rudimental atoms the power of life, growth, change, renewal, — a power which, without his interposition, can work unspent from the beginning to the end of time. But, on this hypothesis, he who, for wise and benevolent ends, endowed brute matter with this living and unwasting power, may, for equally wise and benevolent reasons, at certain epochs of the world's history have suspended or superseded its action.

But while efficient causes in nature elude our research, do not the identity and convertibility of force point to the Omnipresent God as not only the First Cause, but the sole Cause? Can his presence be inert? Can we conceive of him as eternally quiescent, watching the revolution of the machinery which in the beginning he put in motion? Is not convertible force simply God in nature, varied in manifestation, yet unchanged in power, wisdom, and love? Is there not as sound philosophy, as rich poetry, in the conception of the Hebrew seers, in whose thought "the God of glory thundereth ;" "He maketh the clouds his chariot, and walketh upon the wings of the wind ;"

"He sendeth the springs into the valleys;" "He causeth the grass to grow for the cattle, and herb for the service of man"? If this be so, it is surely within his omnipotence to perform directly, and without their usual antecedents, acts which are ordinarily preceded by signs that indicate their occurrence in the near future; to convert water into wine without its passing through the various alembics of nature and art; to cure the paralytic without the medicines which are the wonted tokens of his working; to restore life to the inanimate human form, which had drawn every breath of its previous life immediately from his all-pervading Spirit.

But it is said, While we admit the abstract possibility of miracles, they are so entirely opposed to ordinary human experience in our time and in all time, that even else strong testimony cannot make them credible. I answer that, were not this objection capable of being urged, miracles could not occur, or, occurring, would be unmeaning, futile, and worthless. The very idea of miracles presupposes their infrequency, — presupposes a general order of nature, transgressed only at the rarest intervals and for the most momentous ends. Were what we term miracles frequent, there would be no established order of nature, and consequently no miracles properly so called. The only purpose which such events could serve would be to unsettle human calculations and to baffle human expectation. Frequent, they would fail to attract attention, to elicit reverence, to put man in a waiting attitude for the voice of God. Horace's rule for dramatic composition, "Let not a god intervene unless there be a knot worth his untying" * (that is, an occasion worthy of his intervention), involves a principle which, as it applies not so much to the author as to the receptivity of the audience, we may, without irreverence, transfer to the administration of the universe. Did God intervene by miracle except for momentous ends, and at decisive epochs of human history, man is so constituted that this intervention would be of little or no avail.

Now there are objects worthy of the divine intervention. There are ends of incalculable importance to man, which, so far as we can see, can be accomplished only by miracle.

In the first place, a clear apprehension of the personality of God as distinct from nature is attained only through miracle. It is constantly and rightly maintained by the most learned non-Christian writers on the history of religion, by men as familiar with the scriptures of Brahminism and Buddhism as any of us are with the Gospel of John, that the personality of God is an element imported into religious thought solely from the Semitic religions, — that all the other old religions — alike the monotheistic, dualistic, and polytheistic — are mere pantheism, which, they maintain (and here of course I part company with them), tends with the progress of philosophy to become the dominant, and will ultimately be the sole, faith of what is now Christendom.† It is, as I have said, no part of

* Nec Deus intersit, nisi dignus vindice nodus
Inciderit. . . .

† See Appendix, note G.

my plan to detail the evidences of Judaism ; but, were there not ample reason beside to believe the Old Testament miracles authentic, I should believe them solely on account of the pure personal monotheism of the Hebrew Scriptures. Unless, in the strong figure of the psalmist, God had "bowed the heavens and come down," there is no possibility that Judaism should have differed in this respect from the other religions of the civilized or semi-civilized Eastern world. Man's inevitable tendency in the earlier stages of his culture has uniformly been to identify divine power with its manifestations, deity with force, God with nature. The gods of polytheism are separate world-forces, symbolized in the ruder, personified in the more refined, forms of idolatry. With the growth of knowledge, it is ascertained that the universe is not under a multiform administration ; that filaments of interdependence and harmony unite its various portions and departments ; that fire and air, land and ocean, are parts of the same system ; and then the many world-forces are resolved into one or two, either the Soul of the Universe (*Anima Mundi*), or Ormuzd and Ahriman. But these are not personal gods. They are the life-principle perpetually striving to develop itself in material forms, — each living being emanating from it, and ultimately reabsorbed into it. There is no manifestation of the divine, except in and through nature ; therefore God and nature are one. In the higher Greek philosophy, indeed, we have what we may term semi-detached Deity ; but the distinct and definite personality of God — the idea which pervades the whole Hebrew and Christian Scriptures, and through them the Koran — is reached in no one instance by any non-Semitic religion or philosophy. Still farther, in our own time, the inevitable tendency of the rejection of historical Christianity is toward pantheism. The rationalism of Germany, the liberalism of France, the secularism of England, the free religion of America, are all succumbing to this tendency. Greg, in his "Enigmas of Life," deems it necessary to apologize for clinging to a belief in the divine personality; admits that with his premises he cannot justify it on rational grounds; and says that it is probably due, together with his faith in individual immortality, to the lingering prejudices of a Christian education, — prejudices which have not been strong enough to hold back even the son of such a Christian educator as Thomas Arnold from rejecting a personal God along with the Christ of the Gospels. Strauss, in "The Old Faith and the New," has given the world an invaluable legacy, in his plain and logical development of the natural and inevitable tendency of rationalism to lapse into virtual atheism. At the present moment, the majority in numbers, the overwhelming majority in learning, talent, and influence, among those within the pale of Christendom who are not Christians, are pantheists or atheists.

But miracle is the demonstration of a personal God. It detaches the Creator from his works. It lays bare the Almighty arm to human vision. It shows God, not only in, but above nature, — its Controller, its Sovereign Ruler, under whose hand what seem the adamantine bonds of law are loosed, and forces that had been deemed inflexible become fluent and ductile. From this faith no believer in miracle can fall away. To this faith no religion that rests on miracle can be false. Miracle, then, is God's mode of self-revelation. Imbedded in authentic history, it need not be repeated. Its testimony is coeval in duration with its veracious record. The sublime truth which it embodies is revealed afresh to every believing soul that receives the record.

To pass to another topic, to us of hardly less momentous interest than the being of a personal God, I know not how immortality is to be made certain except by miracle. It is craved by man as he approaches his full development, and the wish naturally begets, but does not authenticate, the belief. There are in man powers and affections adapted to continuous existence, capable of indefinite growth ; and the consciousness of these inspires an apprehension — more or less clear and strong — of immortality. There are, too, analogies of nature which authorize the hope of a life beyond death. But analogy can only remove objections. It never has the force of affirmative proof or argument. It may corroborate the belief established on other grounds, but can furnish no sure ground of its own. Moreover, there are in nature fully as numerous analogies of an opposite bearing ; and whether these or those of a more hopeful character shall predominate depends on the mood of the hour. The least reassuring aspects of nature are most likely to present themselves to the thought in seasons of bereavement or under the shadow of death, when those of the happiest omen are most needed. Consciousness of immortality there cannot be; for consciousness has a present only, no past but through memory, and no future.

Accordingly, we look all through Pagan antiquity in vain for a parallel to those glorious bursts of ecstatic assurance which we find so often in St. Paul, — the desire to depart and be with Christ, the certainty that there is laid up for him a crown of righteousness, — that the corruptible shall put on incorruption, the mortal be clothed in immortality. Socrates, in dying, hopes that he is going to the society of good men, but is unwilling to make positive and confident affirmation to that effect; and, if we may believe Plato, his chief argument for the future eternity rests on the assumption of the past eternity of individual being. Cicero commences his masterly argument for immortality by showing that, if his reasoning should be found inconclusive, annihilation is no evil; and when his daughter lies dead in his house, he confesses that the proofs that had seemed to him so strong when he committed them to writing yield him no support or consolation. Seneca contradicts himself on this point, and leaves no certain utterance. Marcus Aurelius manifests earnest hope rather than strong faith. Epictetus evidently did not expect a life after death. In Plutarch, indeed, we have no token of serious doubt as to immortality; but this belief occupies with him by no means the foremost place which it holds in the faith and the motive power of every Christian, and in his eminently prosperous career it was exposed to fewer severe trials than occur in ordinary human experience.

This is a subject on which absolute certainty can come only through revelation, oral or visible, — in words that bear the stamp of divinity, or in events which shall show that death is not destruction. As immortality is not a truth of consciousness, and cannot be verified by any human experience that comes within the scope of natural laws, it can be made known to man only in modes in which natural laws are superseded or transcended.

There are yet other fundamental subjects on which the truth is objective as regards man, and, if known at all, must be known by testimony from God; that is, by miracle. To this category belong the divine Fatherhood, the pertinence and efficacy of prayer, and the relations which unrepented sin and repentance establish between man and his Creator, this last being a question coextensive in importance with immortality itself.

All these truths, indeed, have been and are to be transmitted and propagated by the speech and writing of men possessed of only ordinary endowments. But the speech or writing must emanate in the first instance from an authoritative source; else its antiquity or its wide diffusion can create for it no prestige, no claim upon belief. With regard to these subjects, no man has or can have had underived knowledge. Where the evidence of consciousness or intuition is unattainable, no degree of wisdom or goodness can fully authenticate a man's statements. If Jesus Christ was in every thing except his superior wisdom and excellence like you and me, a man with none but self-acquired knowledge and endowments, we can easily understand why he believed and taught immortality; for such a life as he was leading would have seemed to him too precious to perish, and he would have so yearned to live on that the wish by its intensity would have become prophecy to his own thought. But his belief would be no valid ground for mine. His words would have merely the authority which belongs to those of every sound thinker. But if God virtually points to him, and says of him, "This is my Messenger; receive his words as mine," — then those words become not opinion, but truth; not reasoning, but knowledge. They are attested not by the weight and worth of a human intellect and character, but by the only Being in the universe who has underived knowledge in the realm that transcends finite consciousness and experience. Now there is no conceivable way in which God can say this, except by miracle. There must be something in the antecedents, belongings, doings, or experiences of the person thus authenticated, which shall set him apart from all others as a God-marked man, and shall thus constitute his recognized commission as a divinely sent teacher. This commission may be universal and perpetual, though the teacher speak to but few, and early vanish from mortal sight. His words may be recorded with the same accuracy and transmitted with the same fidelity which characterize the record and transmission of utterances of prime importance in judicial and political affairs; and the events that constitute his credentials are as capable of becoming facts of authentic history as any other events of his time. Still farther, these events, if authentic, are a sufficient guaranty for the substantially correct transmission of the words to which they give authority; for if, by events aside from the common course of nature, God attests communications of such a kind as to be obviously designed for and adapted to all men of all ages, it is inconceivable that he should not provide for their authentic and permanent record. For this reason I regard all that is essential in the question of inspiration as involved in the authenticity of the Christian miracles. If God interposed by miracle to teach men of duty, of pardon, of heaven, and of the way to everlasting salvation, we are sure that he has given enduring validity and efficacy to his work, whatever may be our technical formula for the shape of the record or the *animus* of its writers. Thus miracle may furnish adequate and permanent evidence for the contents of a divine revelation.

It is said, however, that, from the very nature of things, physical facts, material events, cannot attest spiritual truths, which demand evidence of their own order, and can be believed only as recognized by intuition and verified by experience. This statement, which seems plausible, will not bear examination. It is not true even within the legitimate range of experience. We have an undoubting belief of very numerous spiritual facts, truths, and laws, which we are capable of testing, yet never have tested for ourselves. The psychological phenomena of drunkenness and of opium-eating are believed by those who have made no trial of them; and it is a belief, too, which has a decisive effect on conduct, on the one hand deterring not a few from those first steps down the declivity of ruin which it is so hard to retrace, and, on the other hand, sometimes exciting a morbid curiosity as to the fantastic and delirious joy of inebriation. Equally may a thoroughly bad man receive on faith the happiness that results from a virtuous course, and may be thus induced to make first experiments in that direction. It may be said, indeed, that statements of this sort need no miraculous attestation: yet it is conceivable that from a teacher thus sanctioned they might come with a stress of influence on opinion, feeling, and character, not to be otherwise attained; so that, were it only to promulgate what to the developed spiritual consciousness are mere moral truisms, there might be adequate ground for miraculous intervention, in an age of declension and depravity.

As regards such spiritual truths as are objective to our own consciousness, miracle is so far from being an inappropriate evidence, that it may be a manifestation of the very truth to which it bears witness, and so may not only verify, but be, a revelation. Thus, as I have said, an event aside from the wonted order of nature is in itself a manifestation of the fundamental truth of the spiritual universe, — the existence of God independently of nature. What, too, are the miracles of healing in the New Testament but the universal

Providence made visible? What the raising of Lazarus, but the indestructibility of the soul submitted to the evidence of eye, and ear, and hand? As regards other truths, it may be impossible to trace in miracles any specific relation to them, and they, therefore, are not directly proved by miraculous evidence; but, so far as works beyond the ordinary scope of human power authenticate a teacher, they, of necessity, attest the truths which he utters, though they be objective, and therefore not capable of verification by his hearers, or though they be such as can be verified only by the experience to which they open the way and afford the motive.

On yet another ground we may trace what might seem a necessity, or, at least, an adequate occasion for miracle. Jesus Christ professed to be more than a good man and a teacher of piety. He claimed to be the Son of God in a peculiar and pre-eminent sense, and, as Mediator and Redeemer, to stand in certain relations to God and man in which no one else has stood. It is not to our present purpose to define these relations, or rather, it is essential to our purpose to leave them undefined; for the position on which I would base my argument is, that to all Christian believers, of whatever name or creed, Jesus Christ, though man, is more than man, holds a sole place and office with reference to the human race, and thus constitutes in a certain sense and degree a class by himself. If this be so, we may maintain, first, that he could be designated to man as holding this place and office only by miracles; and, secondly, that what we call miracles, though superhuman, may be, as wrought by him, or for him, or through him, no more superhuman than he himself is, but as regards him and his office simply normal, fully as accordant with his place in the universe as the power which man ordinarily exerts over nature is with his place in the universe. These considerations are applicable not only to his own alleged miracles, but equally to those of earlier religious dispensations, typical and prophetic of his coming, and to those wrought under his immediate auspices for the establishment of his advent and mission among the indelible facts of history. If it be maintained that it was intrinsically impossible for the Almighty to put upon the earth a higher being than the normal man, then miracles may be equally impossible; for, when we once begin to limit the infinite attributes of God, we can no longer base any argument on his plenary power. But if it was possible for him to send into the world a greater than man to redeem man, then was it equally possible for him to connect with that Redeemer's advent and earthly life physical phenomena that might indicate and verify his place among men. So far then as, aside from the miraculous narratives, there is recognized in the character of Jesus, in his influence, in his position as a factor in human history, aught in which he stands alone among men, aught that worthily gives him "a name above every name," so far do those miraculous narratives become probable. Did the evangelists represent Jesus as an ordinary man, there would be a manifest incongruity between his person and his alleged miracles. If he was what they say he was, those works of power and love were no more or other than might have been expected of him and through him.

I have thus shown you that there were ends of prime importance, in the promulgation of objective truth which man needed to know, and in the authentication of a Teacher and Redeemer, which could, so far as we can discern, have been effected only by miracles, and which therefore presented occasions that seem worthy of the divine interposition. The probability thus established is confirmed by a view of the condition of mankind before and since Christ. The course of the world before Christ was a constant degeneracy and decline. His advent was at the midnight of history. There had been noble nations: there remained not one. The Greeks had lost what of manliness they once had, and their refinement had degenerated into gross sensuality. The Romans had parted with their purity and truth; while their valor had become rapacity, and their patriotism faction. The imperial city was a hospitable metropolis for the vices as for the gods of all lands, and with regard to every form of depravity the practical maxim alike of court and of populace was, "It is fitting to learn even from an enemy;" * and thence and thither, with the pulsation of a common political life to the remotest east and south, and to the confines of impenetrable Scandinavian forests, were outward and refluent currents swollen with the fetid sewage of vice and crime. Religion, such as there had been, was dead. Philoso-

* "Fas est et ab hoste doceri."

phy survived chiefly under the loosened zone of Epicureanism; for the Stoics, the only really great men that remained, were in numbers a scanty minority among those who claimed to be adepts in liberal culture. In Judæa a heartless formalism had replaced the piety of earlier ages; the harp of praise gave but the retreating echo of its wonted strains; and they who rebuilt the sepulchres of the prophets bore testimony against themselves in professing to honor those whose virtues they suffered to slumber. There was upon the earth no hopeful sign, no source of reforming influence, no fountain for renewed life. A brighter past and a darker future bounded the horizon of every thoughtful man, except so far as Hebrew prophecy had given its color to expectation.

What do we see since that age? Progress, but no decline. Dawn, sunrise, high morning, but no receding of the shadow on the sundial. Barbaric irruptions that fertilize, when they threaten to destroy. Dark ages, like those dreary spring-days whose drenching rains are the harbinger of all that is gladdening in garden, field, and orchard,—ages during which humane principles are taking root, institutions and habits of charity and mercy springing into being, slavery melting away and vanishing. There has not been since the Christian era a century than which we can say that the preceding century was better.

This advance without retrogression has been inseparably connected with Christianity, and that, the Christianity of the Gospels, resting on miraculous evidence. It is primarily in this aspect that Christianity has been received, diffused, and transmitted. We may attach a greater or less importance to individual miracles ; but we cannot be mistaken in attributing a preponderant influence to the superhuman element in Christianity, of which these miracles form a part. The Titans of our race had done their best to raise it, and had failed. The earth did not give them a strength which could "spread undivided, operate unspent." It is only the religion which claims to be heaven-born that can grow with the ages. It is only the Saviour who claims to come from the bosom of the Eternal Father, who can be so lifted up that he gives promise of drawing all men to him. When we see that belief in such a religion, in such a Saviour, though mingled with puerilities, superstitions, and absurdities, has proved the mightiest force in the moral universe, alone not yielding to the law of decline and exhaustion to which all other forces have succumbed, it becomes in the highest degree probable that mankind needed such a religion, such a Saviour ; and, if so, the miracles that attended its promulgation and his mission were in themselves antecedently probable.

I close by noticing two objections that have been often urged, and with no little plausibility. To some minds miracles are incredible because they seem an afterthought, and imply some initial imperfection in the Creator's work. What was wisely made could not have needed repair. What was fitly planned could not have demanded remedy and re-adjusting. I answer, What was made and placed at the head of this lower world was a race of free agents, with the unrestricted choice of good and evil. What was planned was a system by which, with or without help from a higher power, that race was to work out its own destiny. It may be that such a race, however nobly endowed, if less than divine, could not but try all experiments and sound all depths of moral evil; could not but lapse into a depraved and morally helpless condition from which it could be rescued only by an arm let down from heaven. It may be that in the very nature of things the kingdom of ultimate and universal righteousness, of which the Messianic prophecies give the foreshining, must needs have had its sunken foundation laid in such wrecks of humanity as the waves of time have submerged. If so, Christianity, with its apparatus of superhuman manifestations and events, was not a divine afterthought, but a divine forethought, an essential part of the initial plan of creation, — a plan by which, as the first Adam was the progenitor of a race of sinners that shall, in God's own time, run out and leave only its history, the second Adam should become the progenitor of a race, born not of the flesh, but of the Spirit, of the increase of which there shall be no end till time shall lapse into eternity.

Finally, it has been represented as incredible that in the press and throng of habitable worlds that gem our night heavens, rank beyond rank, in realms of telescopic vision which even our figures cannot overtake, still less our thought conceive, our little planet should have been specially signalized by a stupendous theophany, with its attendant pageantry of prophecy, sign, and marvel. In reply, I would ask, Who knows that our planet has been thus specially signalized? Undoubtedly its spiritual, no less than its physical, history, has its peculiar features; for Infinite Wisdom has had no need to repeat itself in the worlds. But how know we but that in some form or way a theophany has had its place in all realms and orders of spiritual being; that in methods analogous to those recorded in the Christian Scriptures God has in all parts of his creation made known his being, providence, and righteous retribution; and that if there has been, as there certainly may have been, in other portions of the universe sin, spiritual defection, soul-peril, he has interposed in mercy like that incarnate on Calvary, and has won back to loyalty and duty his children in the stars beyond Arcturus and Orion no less than among the sons of men? Enough for us that we own what he has done for our fallen race. In the eternity that lies before us, it may be that the ransomed from among men will be immeasurably outnumbered by the harps and tongues from worlds to us unknown that shall swell the self-same redemption song.

LECTURE VI.

PAUL'S TESTIMONY TO CHRIST'S RESURRECTION THE EARLIEST EXTANT. — ITS SOURCE AND VALIDITY. — ACCOUNTS OF THE RESURRECTION IN THE GOSPELS. — THE APOSTLES BELIEVED IN CHRIST'S RESURRECTION. — THE CHURCH BUILT UPON IT. — CHRIST'S SUPPOSED REAPPEARANCE NOT AN HALLUCINATION. — NOT REVIVAL FROM A SWOON. — USES OF THE RESURRECTION. — ITS PROOF GROWS WITH TIME.

THE earliest written mention of the resurrection of Jesus Christ which has come down to us is by St. Paul, in his first epistle to the Corinthians, — an epistle on whose genuineness there rests not the shadow of a doubt, and which was written some twenty-three or twenty-four years after the crucifixion. In this epistle Paul speaks of the resurrection of Christ as the fundamental fact on which repose alike his preaching and the faith of those to whom he writes. It is worthy of the most emphatic notice, also, that he does not treat this fact as needing proof, but employs it by way of argument, as of itself established and admitted beyond question. There were, it seems, among the Corinthians, some who had vague and loose notions about the life to come; denied the resurrection of the dead, or the renewal of personal identity after death; and probably, in opposition to such ultra-realistic views of the resurrection as Paul himself disclaims, maintained ultra-spiritualistic notions which refined away individual immortality, and left the disembodied spirit to be reabsorbed into the soul of the universe. To meet this error, Paul plants himself on the broken sepulchre in the garden, and takes as the basis of a masterly structure of conclusive argument the resurrection of Jesus as a universally received and unquestioned fact. He rehearses a list of witnesses, as if he had taken pains to examine the matter for himself. The risen Jesus, he says, was seen by Peter, by James, and by the apostles collectively. He certainly must have learned this directly from Peter and James, when, several years before, he went to Jerusalem to confer with them about his new faith, and was authorized by them to become its preacher; for if they had been silent about the resurrection then, and afterward professed to believe it, to a man of Paul's clear and cultivated mind the story would have seemed a fabrication unworthy of credit.

This visit of Paul to Peter and James took place not more than ten, probably not more than six, years after the crucifixion; and thus early Christ's resurrection must have been the fixed belief, real or pretended, of his disciples A myth could not have grown up in so short a time. What was professed or believed then could have been no other than a story grafted immediately upon the crucifixion, and must have been either a fact, an illusion, or an imposture.

Paul farther mentions the appearance of the risen

Jesus to more than five hundred brethren at once, and says that the greater part of them were still living, though some had died. This certainly looks as if he were acquainted with many of the five hundred, and it is hardly possible that in a matter of so grave importance he should not have examined and weighed their testimony.

Not only in this chapter, but throughout the four epistles that are admitted to be genuine by the most rationalistic critics, the resurrection of Christ is referred to as the one salient fact of the Christian history. The reader of these epistles cannot doubt that Paul believed it as firmly as he believed his own existence, and that he wrote to converts who had no thought of calling it in question.

There are not a few to whom Paul's testimony is the most weighty that can be adduced. He was a man of singular acuteness, and of large and high culture; no man of his time was his superior, if his equal; and some who are no mean judges of their fellow-men look upon him as the greatest man that God ever made. He had been a vehement opposer and persecutor of the new faith. On that route lay office, honor, influence, wealth. He chose penury, contempt, the prison, the stocks, stripes, perpetual peril of death, — and Christ; and he was not ashamed of his choice. Only the strongest conviction could have started and sustained him on this new career, and conviction with a man like him meant impregnable proof, — solid and substantial reasons. In the circle in which he moved before his conversion, Christianity was held in at least as low esteem as Mormonism is with us; and for such a man as he to become a Christian was as strange and abnormal as it would be for one of our divines, or judges, or princely merchants to join the motley community of Brigham Young. He had not a friend who was not ashamed of him, and whose respect for him was not changed into contempt. To face all this, must he not have had a belief tantamount to knowledge?

From the Acts of the Apostles, — which, whatever slurs may be cast upon it, undeniably represents the general tone, drift, and scope of the apostolic preaching, — it appears that the resurrection of Jesus was proclaimed within a few weeks after his death, in a discourse which won a multitude of converts in the city where he died; and it is hardly possible that among them there were not many who had seen him on the cross. Certainly the story was on this occasion put to the severest test possible. If there existed any means of refuting it, they were close at hand. The necessary inference is that the belief was founded either on fact, on a delusion which had a strange resemblance to reality, or on a deception planned and carried through with the most consummate dexterity. From that time onward the apostles and their associates so uniformly gave this story a foremost place in their preaching, that we might not unfittingly call theirs the Gospel of the Resurrection.

We have the most ample proof, which none can call in question, that this event was the universal belief of Christians long before either of the Gospels was written; and had neither of them ever been written, this belief would be none the less an indisputable fact in the history of the Church. But in the Gospels alone we have detailed narratives of the event. These narratives, as I said in a former Lecture, though not by any means coincident, fit into one another, each supplying details which the others omit, but for which they leave room. If all four of the evangelists were in Jerusalem at the time (as they probably were), each undoubtedly related such occurrences as came within his own cognizance; and the four harmonize as the stories of four commanders of divisions in a battle, or of four witnesses of the transactions of any eventful day would harmonize It is alleged, however, that there are some irreconcilable discrepancies. While to me, as I have said, they are not irreconcilable, yet, if they were so, they would rather confirm than shake my faith in the reality of the event described. It is to me astonishing that there should not have been such discrepancies. It is the uniform tendency of an event that strongly moves the imagination and the emotional nature to throw accessory circumstances into the background, to confuse and blur the memory with regard to them, and thus to generate narratives irreconcilable in their details. A case in point occurs to me in Roman history. The history of the Second Punic War was written by several authors, whose narratives, entire or in part, have been preserved. They all tell the story of ten prisoners of war whom Hannibal sent to Rome, bound by an oath that they would return into captivity if they failed to obtain an exchange of prisoners. One of them, at the outset, pretended to have forgotten something, returned to the Carthaginian camp as if to look for it, and then rejoined the other nine on the route to Rome. He claimed to have been absolved of his oath by this constructive return, in accordance with its letter, but in violation of its spirit. One account says that he was sent back from Rome to Hannibal in chains; another, that he remained at Rome, but was degraded for life from the rights of citizenship; and there are vestiges of still a third version of the story.* The flagrancy of the crime, in an age when good faith was held inviolably sacred at Rome, and when its infraction was regarded with intense loathing, so impressed the public mind as to throw the actual doom of the perjured man into the shadow of his own guilt. Not a few instances of the same kind, in which, in the record of momentous or startling events, accessory facts that must have been publicly known have been transmitted in different forms, might be quoted from both ancient and modern history. The principle is an important one. I see no need of applying it to the narratives of the resurrection; but, were there need, it would be to the fullest extent applicable.

That the apostles and their associates believed in their Lord's resurrection hardly needs proof. It is admitted by Renan, who expressly says that without this belief they would never have incurred the labors, hardships, persecutions, and perils, incident to the

* See Appendix, note H.

founding of the Christian Church. Strauss writes to the same purpose: "Faith in the resurrection of Jesus is a fact of prime historical importance; for without it one cannot see how a Christian community would ever have been formed;" and, again, "There can be no doubt that the apostle Paul had heard from Peter, James, and others beside, that Jesus had appeared to them, and that all these persons and the five hundred brethren were fully convinced that they had seen Jesus living, who had been dead." Baur, who has as little Christian faith as either Strauss or Renan, but whose surpassing erudition and critical acuteness cannot be denied, writes in the same vein: "History must hold fast to this fact, that for the faith of the disciples the resurrection of Jesus Christ was a certain and immovable truth, and that it is only in this faith that Christianity found a solid basis for its whole historical development." In the face of such admissions from the chief pundits of scepticism, there is no need of our doing any thing more to establish the fact that the apostles and their associates believed in the actual resurrection of Jesus Christ from the dead. Nor do these authors cast any doubt on the supposed appearances of Jesus as having been recorded in good faith by the evangelists. Indeed, it hardly needs to be said that, if they honestly believed the story, they were honest in their relation of the grounds on which they believed it. Pascal goes too far when he says, "I readily believe stories whose witnesses offer themselves to death for their truth;" but, while even such witnesses may be grossly mistaken, we must admit their truthfulness, and suppose that they think they saw all that they pretend to have seen.

The two hypotheses which divide the sceptical world on this subject are, first, that Jesus really died, and that the apostles were under an hallucination in supposing that they saw him alive; and, secondly, that he did not die, but fell into a swoon from which he recovered, and thus actually reappeared after his crucifixion.

We will first test the theory of hallucination. On this theory the body of Jesus was somewhere. Where was it? Who removed it from the sepulchre? Who could have done this? A great stone was laid on the mouth of the sepulchre, and Roman sentinels guarded its approach. But suppose that the stone was not too heavy to be easily moved, and that the Roman sentry was a mere figment, or that the soldiers slept on their watch, or suffered themselves to be bribed,—who took the body? Not the disciples; for if they had taken it, they would not have believed in the resurrection. Not the Jewish or Roman authorities; for they would have produced the body to refute the story of the resurrection. Tertullian quotes those who say that the gardener removed it, to prevent the trampling down of his lettuce-beds by those who visited the sepulchre.* But he could hardly have done this without the order of his master; he could not have removed the body far; it could have been easily

* "Hic est, quem hortulanus detraxit, ne lactucæ suæ frequentia commeantium læderentur."

found ; nay, he himself would have produced it in view of the reward which would have been readily paid to negative the growing rumor of the resurrection. Moreover, the removal of the body while the grave-clothes were left behind is inconceivable, unless it were a contrivance to substantiate the story of the resurrection : such a stratagem would have been possible only for those who were going to circulate the story, that is, for the disciples ; and we have seen that the supposition of fraud on their part is utterly untenable. Renan, with characteristic frankness, confesses himself unable to solve this mystery, yet suggests that Joseph of Arimathea may have procured the removal. But Joseph either was or was not a thoroughly sincere and steadfast disciple of Jesus. If he was a disciple, he must have taken upon himself the risks incurred by every professed believer in the resurrection, which he could not have believed, if he had surreptitiously procured the report of it. If, on the other hand, his allegiance to Christ was not genuine and stable, he would certainly have sought peace with his brethren of the Sanhedrim by aiding in the detection of the imposture. In fine, there was no party, there was no individual man, who had any thing to gain, any possible purpose to advance, by stealing the body of Jesus and keeping it concealed. This difficulty stands, then, immovable in the way of the theory of hallucination. But we will waive it, to examine the theory in other aspects.

Visual hallucinations have their laws and their limits. They occur rather by night than by day,

They are not apt to recur under altered circumstances. They affect individuals rather than groups of men. They do not run at the same moment through large bodies of men in broad daylight, so that five hundred persons falsely think that they see the same unreal man or object at the same time. They are not accompanied by imagined long conversations, by imagined serial transactions with their object, by imagined sittings at the same table, and receiving food from his hands. Had Mary Magdalene's story been the only one, it would certainly be conceivable that, in the misty dawn and with tear-dimmed eyes, she mistook the gardener for Jesus. But it is impossible to apply the same solution to the supposed separate appearances to the eleven and to different groups of disciples. It is impossible that Thomas should have been deceived as to the reality of the wound-marks; for uniform experience shows that the hand corrects the errors of the eye. There could have been no delusion in the conversations put on record, — in Christ's expounding the Scriptures, calling forth the expressions of love from the disciple who had denied him, giving his parting commands to those who were to go out into the world to preach his Gospel; nor yet when his disciples thought that he was sitting with them at their noonday meal, partaking of it himself, and dispensing the viands with his own hands. Least of all could the five hundred brethren have been deceived in mass, so that they should have imagined his presence, when where they thought he stood there was only empty air. Nor must it be forgotten that, according to this hypothesis, the only ground for the strangest series of delusions on record was the mistake of a woman whose previous insanity (for the seven demons must denote a most deplorable condition of mind, whether from natural causes or possession by evil spirits) would have rendered her the least credible witness in the whole company of the disciples. She was the only person who, unless Jesus really appeared, saw any thing out of which the phantasm could have taken shape. The apparition came to all the others when they were on the road, or assembled in the upper chamber, or fishing on the lake, — when there could have been no doubtful appearance like that which is said to have occasioned Mary Magdalene's mistake. If any one part of this theory is weaker than the rest, the misapprehension from which the story is alleged to have grown and spread is the weakest of all.

We pass now to the theory of suspended animation and apparent death, followed by resuscitation. To this we encounter at the outset what might seem to any person of sound ethical discernment a fatal objection, in the moral character of Jesus. If he had not died, he knew it, and he himself invented the figment of his resurrection. How would this story tally with the character of any of the great men with whom we so often see him named by those who admit his purity and excellence, yet deny the tokens of his divine Sonship? If Socrates had swooned and not died on drinking the hemlock, and then tried to make his friends believe that he had really died and come to life again, think you that he would stand before an admiring world on the pedestal of moral elevation which he now occupies? Was it possible for him, being the man he undoubtedly was, to lend himself to such an infamous fraud? What shall we say, then, of him in whose robe of righteousness unbelievers have striven in vain to detect rent or seam? If we are to judge of a man by his previous character, under circumstances that do not carry with them their own full interpretation, and if Jesus was but a man and no more, certainly no man ever trod the earth who in precept and example presents a more perfectly transparent honesty and truthfulness, — none whose whole aim in living and dying was so manifestly the promotion of virtue, — none who has shown so intense an abhorrence of shams and falsities.

But we will not take shelter under his character. We will try the issue as if he had been morally capable of enacting a falsehood. It is said that death by crucifixion was very slow, frequently not occurring till the second day, or even later, and that at the end of six hours there is at least a strong probability that life was not extinct. To this suggestion the first answer is that the Roman executioners were accustomed to this mode of punishment, and knew the signs of death; that they were not the men to let their victims escape from their hands with their work but half accomplished; that in this case they did not see sure signs of death in the two malefactors, though from the narrative we may infer that to an unpractised eye they seemed already dead; and that nothing but absolute certainty on the part of the soldiers would have deterred them from employing on Jesus the barbarous mode of disablement to which they had recourse in the case of the malefactors. Then, again, we have reason to believe that crucifixion inflicted fatal injury, though often not immediately fatal. It could hardly fail, in the first few hours, to produce a congestion of the vital current, of which death at no great distance of time would be the inevitable result, — a congestion, too, which would of itself render spontaneous revival from a swoon impossible.

From the nature of the case we should, indeed, have on record very few instances of the recovery of crucified persons. I remember but one — there may be others — and that is a case which, though much employed by non-believers in the reality of the resurrection, bears with great weight of argument against their hypothesis. I refer to the case described by Josephus in his autobiography. He says that he was one day sent by Titus to Thecoa, which was within sight of Jerusalem, about twelve miles distant from it; that on his return he found many captives crucified, three of them persons with whom he had been well acquainted; that he procured of Titus leave to have these persons taken down, and subjected to the most careful treatment; and that two of them died under the physician's hands, while the third recovered. From this account it would seem that the crucifixion had not begun when Josephus left the city, and the narrative would lead us to suppose that he was absent but a few hours, certainly not overnight; yet two of these men had sunk beyond recovery, and the third survived only under the most skilful treatment accessible.* The inference is that fatal lesion of the vital organs was wont to ensue even from the earlier stages of this horrible punishment. Then, too, the Roman soldiers, with characteristic barbarity, were intent, in the case of Jesus, on exploring the seat of life ; and the serous fluid that followed the spear wound indicated the puncture of the pericardium, which, if not already dead, he could not have survived. Even had not the inevitably fatal wound been given, if there had still remained intermittent flickerings of life, these must have been extinguished in the close, mephitic air of the tomb.

Moreover, if continued respiration had been possible, whence the strength that enabled him after thirty-six hours of fasting, bleeding, fainting, to raise from within the heavy stone, and so to reappear in the eyes of his friends as to seem not snatched from the jaws of the grave, but Conqueror of death ? The double walk between Jerusalem and Emmaus on that very day, and all the traces that we have of him for the ensuing forty days, indicate not slow and painful convalescence, but at least the wonted vigor of his former life. Bodily weakness would have rendered him utterly incapable of playing a part in such a drama as awaited him for its chief actor. It would have betrayed itself to the disciples. It would have thrown him upon their anxious care, instead of casting them at his feet in wondering awe. The disciples were not the fools they are commonly assumed to have been by those who account for every thing that looks strange in the

* See Appendix, note I.

Gospel narrative by their feeble credulity. They were sensible men; disciplined by a rough, hard life; familiar with the appearances and the reality of things, and amply able to know the difference between one who had barely evaded and one who had surmounted death. The latter they believed Jesus to be. They had no interest which in the former capacity could have been served by proclaiming him as their Lord. To protect him from further persecution, to nourish him in secret, and to continue their kind regard for him, was the utmost that could have been expected of them. That they should throw away all that this world had for them in the present and future, to sustain any baseless pretensions of his or of their own about him, would have been sheer madness.

The improbability of the solution which we are now considering seems still more glaring, when we remember that Jerusalem was filled with keen eyes and active brains that were implacably hostile to Jesus and his memory; that of these the Sadducees at least had neither superstition nor credulity, while the Pharisees can have had very little (hypocrites seldom have much); and that the same interests which had succeeded in bringing Jesus to the cross were still more concerned in crushing out this rumor of the resurrection. If it was merely resuscitation, there must have been numerous ways in which the real fact, if concealed by friends, would have betrayed itself to unfriendly eyes, or have got abroad in the gossip which can no more be muffled or choked in any community, than you can smother fire with linen garments.

Still farther, if Christ's was merely a case of suspended and renewed animation under ordinary physical laws, death was still before him, and friends, or enemies, or both, must have known when, where, and how he died. If he lingered on for years in retirement and obscurity, his disciples knew it; they knew that he was no longer the man he had been; and he would have been a dead weight on their faith and their zeal. If he died early, they knew it, and if he had not lived imbecile years enough to cloud the memory of his better days and to eclipse his fame, they would have recorded his final departure and done honor to his sepulchre; for, though they believed his resurrection, they yet could not have anticipated what we so clearly see, — the fitness that he should not die again: his death would have seemed to them no more strange than the second death of Lazarus or of the young man of Nain. In fine, his death could not but have been a known event and a matter of record. The very fact that he disappeared, and "no man knoweth of his sepulchre unto this day," adds a strong probability to the story of the resurrection, inasmuch as it makes the ascension probable; while, on the other hand, the ascension postulates the resurrection as its antecedent, and has its meaning, its appropriateness, its didactic power, its essential place in the Christian history, only as the sequel, crown, and consummation of the former miracle. The ascension, inconceivable as a delusion on the part of the disciples; as a figment, beyond the easy scope of their very prosaic imaginations, adding gratuitously to the heavy draft they were already making on the faith of their dupes, and contributing no one element of strength to their cause,—was yet the very mode of leaving the world which, in the retrospect, seems alone in harmony with a passage through life and the death-shadow like Christ's. It was fitting that he who, alone of all those born of woman, had "power to lay down his life and power to take it again," should not even seem to succumb to his once vanquished foe, should leave upon the earth no trophies for death to boast, but should pass on to his heavenly throne,

> "His human form dissolved on high
> In its own radiancy."

We have thus seen that the undoubted belief of the primitive disciples in their Lord's resurrection can be accounted for neither by delusion nor by imposture, but only by the actual occurrence of the event. It is worthy of emphatic remark that no alleged fact in the early history of Christianity has had so prominent a place as this, or has so constantly invited test, inquiry, cavil. The church in all time has been ready to stand or fall upon this record. The resurrection was commemorated from the beginning by the use of the first day of the week for Christian worship, at the outset supplementing, then superseding, the Jewish sabbath. Its anniversary was the earliest of the Christian festivals, and must have been so observed in the apostolic age; for in the next generation we find record of a controversy in which primitive usage was appealed to, as to the proper time for celebrating the resurrection, whether always on Sunday, or on the day succeeding the paschal full moon, whether on Sunday or not.* These commemorations might be cited, did we need them, as historical proofs; for there are no historical records so absolutely infallible as rites or festivals commemorative of single events. It is impossible that such observances should not have originated in real or supposed facts, and equally impossible that they should retain their form and change their meaning. I refer to them now, however, not for their direct evidential value, but to show that this alleged event, from the prominence thus given to it, has always presented a broad mark for attack, and has challenged the keenest weapons of the opposite camp. I have exhibited to you the most and best that these assailants have been able to effect. They have not succeeded in casting any doubt on the genuineness and sincerity of the primitive belief in the resurrection, nor have they produced any counter-hypothesis other than these which we have seen to be so baseless and flimsy. In view of the controversy, we are entitled to say that no fact in history rests on more solid and substantial evidence than this.

But we may be held to the Horatian rule, "Let not a God intervene, unless there be an occasion worthy of his intervention." The uses of the resurrection may be called in question; and though God is not bound to account to man for what he does, still we may reasonably expect that man shall understand in part what he does for man, and those who deny the

* See Appendix, note J.

resurrection may justly claim that we should show how and why it was needed. It may be said, The resurrection does not prove immortality, and it is this which we want to have proved. I answer that it demonstrates all that we need to know, in order to be sure of immortality. Death is the only obstacle in the way of our belief of eternal life. Could we follow with our apprehensive faculties those who die, and see them living on, we should have no doubt that they would live for ever. The gulf once safely passed, the heavenly shore once reached, we should have no farther fear of the suspension of being. Now the resurrection of Jesus proves that death is not destruction ; that if a man die, he may live again. Jesus did not return to life ; but he resumed his dead body to show that he had not ceased to live, and that no soul born of God can ever die ; and we know not how this could have been so clearly shown in any other way.

The resurrection was also needed to put the seal upon Christ's example, and to demonstrate the safety and the wisdom of following it. Whatever purposes in the divine counsels his death may have served, his earthly life, without the resurrection, was an utter failure. If we may in our thought listen to the conversation of the two disciples on their way to Emmaus, it might have run in this wise, " To what purpose is this life, wasted, thrown away ? A little yielding would have been to him an infinite gain. Let him at the outset have had a wise reference to his own interest ; let him have made a few harmless concessions to popular tastes and prejudices; let him have stepped aside now and then instead of marching straight on in the face and eyes of what he deemed wrong and evil: he might have gained a name and influence; he might have been efficient as a reformer; he might have raised up a strong sect among the very rulers and Pharisees; he might have lived to see his cause triumphant, and have passed away in old age with universal reverence and honor. But now all that has come of his uncompromising rigidness of principle has been a scanty, lessening and discouraged following, the general hatred and scorn, a hard lot, a barbarous doom, a felon's death." This was sound reasoning on the day when he slept the death-slumber in Joseph's garden; and, had he not awoke from that slumber, it would be sound reasoning now, and the best morality of our race would still be comprehended in that incomparable maxim of worldly wisdom, "Be not righteous overmuch; for why shouldest thou destroy thyself?" When the powers of evil have hunted Jesus to his destruction, and laid him low in the dust, they certainly have for the time the upper hand. But how is all this changed when, like the midsummer sun on the verge of the Arctic circle, Jesus just dips beneath the horizon, and lo! from the very twilight of his setting bursts the glorious dawn of his resurrection day! It now appears that the power of life and death is not in the hands of moral evil or its abettors; that they cannot kill; that virtue, integrity, piety, live on unharmed through death, as asbestos in fire; and that it makes no manner of difference whether the right seem to succeed in this world or not, while it has the eternal years of God for its ascendancy and triumph. The resurrection has thus made Christ's example availing for all who pursue the right with earthly and human influence on the adverse side. His path, had it stopped short at the sepulchre, would have won no follower; but now that it stretches on in a line of living light through the valley of the death-shadow, it has drawn a multitude that no man can number of elect and loyal souls to follow him in his death to sin, that they may follow him in heaven and for ever.

But it may be asked, Why should the revelation of the eternal life have been given in this dramatic form? Why might not a verbal assurance of immortality, with unmistakable tokens that it came from God, have met the needs of human faith and virtue equally with this scenic transaction, which has given rise to so much doubt and cavil? Why should a physical testimony have been borne to a spiritual truth? I reply that immortality, and especially resurrection, that is, the essential identity of the being that lives for ever with that which lived and died on earth, is primarily a physical truth, and may therefore admit, or even demand external, visible proof. If eternal life be the destiny of man, it is because God has made the vital organism in man indestructible by material forces. Had it been made destructible by those forces, there might have been re-creation, not immortality. Now, God has shown us in the resurrection of Christ that human life is not destructible by the agencies that destroy the body, and has thus literally made the eternal life manifest in the flesh, and more clearly manifest than mere words could have made it.

Still further, verbal revelation addresses the reason alone; but in the matter under discussion the imagination and the emotional nature are profoundly concerned. They are concerned, are influential, and often dominant on all subjects of religious belief and evidence. Moreover, they are apprehensive faculties no less than reason. They have their own tests of truth, no less authentic and trustworthy than those employed by the reason. The dogmas which they, in their legitimate exercise, repudiate are not true, though logically proved; the dogmas which they postulate have in their favor a strong prestige prior to proof. The naturalism which excludes the Christ-element from religion, and reduces it to abstract propositions and principles, finds no point of attachment to humanity except through the intellect. The imagination spurns it. The affections shiver in the face of it.

Now these portions of our nature have their special needs and cravings with reference to death, and what may lie or may not lie beyond it. There is in many minds a shrinking, even to horror, from the physical phenomena and accessories of death,—the ebbing pulse, the shortening breath, the sad surroundings, the conscious nearness of the plunge into an untried state of being, the solitary passage through the death-shadow. It is a feeling which, entirely independent of belief, cannot be allayed by mere belief. This condition of the imaginative or emotional nature can be soothed and transformed only by influences of its own order, and such are those flowing from a scenic display of the conquest over Death on the very stage where he is wont to move in kingly guise. All these accessories of the dissolution of the body — in their mildest forms so appalling — were clustered in their direst aspects about the cross and burial of our Lord ; and they are all transfigured in the light of the resurrection morning, — symbols no longer of death, but of undying life, — no longer of the soul unclothed, but clothed upon, — no longer of the dismantling of the earthly tabernacle, but of the opening portals of the house not made with hands, eternal in the heavens. Who that has watched by the Christian deathbed has not felt moved to dwell in converse and in prayer on the place where the Lord lay, and witnessed the sweet peace and the hope surmounting fear, as the dying believer has thought of that far-off sepulchre in Judæa while he was sinking into his own grave?

The sensibilities which crave this support are not confined to weaker minds, though, if they were, we should expect to find them only the more tenderly cared for by Infinite Love. They are often keenest and most craving in the very minds that might seem most capable of satisfying themselves by abstract truth. I know of no more explicit and touching confession of them than in the words of Dr. Arnold, whose firm faith and clear reason might have seemed sufficient, if they ever are sufficient. He says, in writing about the death of one of his children: "Nothing afforded us so much comfort, when shrinking from the outward accompaniments of death, —

the grave, the grave-clothes, the loneliness,—as the thought that all these had been around our Lord himself, round him who died and is alive for evermore."

These needs become solid arguments, when we are reasoning about Him who knoweth our frame, and who, as a Father, pitieth his children. If from the resurrection of Christ spring a consolation, peace, and hope which even his words could not give, we have added confirmation of no little force for that crowning miracle of power and mercy on which the Church is built, on which the faith of these Christian ages has rested with a unanimity of consent that can be affirmed of no other truth or fact appertaining to our religion or its history.

One closing thought, which impresses me with great force. The evidence of our Lord's resurrection, so far from being impaired by time, has gained strength with the lapse of ages. I think that even with regard to a common man such proof as we possess would constrain our belief in his resurrection, yet not without a vague reluctance, a rebellion of reason against reason, of strong opposing probabilities against overwhelmingly strong testimony. But suppose that the man whose resurrection was thus attested were not a common, but a unique man; one in whom had been witnessed from infancy to death an unequalled purity and loveliness; one whose words had seemed to those who heard them as utterances from heaven, and with an authority to which men had instinctively yielded as divine; one who had not his like in the whole antecedent history of the world,—then, that death should not have had the same power over him as over other men would not seem so very improbable. Suppose, still further, that, as the centuries roll on, this man, said to have risen from the dead, proves to be the author of a new epoch for humanity; that his influence broadens and deepens from age to age; that the very tokens of his ignominy become more glorious than the badges of royalty, and the effigy of his death as a felon-slave is made the most precious ornament of crowns and sceptres; in fine, that not only God in his revealed purpose, but men—his opposers no less than his adherents—give him a name above every name,—then does his culminating career on the way to universal empire add perpetually new attestation to the record of his resurrection from the tomb and his ascension on high.

LECTURE VII.

ALLEGED DEFICIENCIES OF CHRISTIANITY. — ITS COMPLETENESS AS TO INDIVIDUAL NEEDS. — REASONS FOR ITS SILENCE. — ITS SILENCE A PROOF OF ITS DIVINITY. — ITS TREATMENT OF COURAGE. — OF PATRIOTISM. — OF FRIENDSHIP. — SUMMARY OF THE EVIDENCE FROM TESTIMONY.

IN my Lectures thus far I have given you an outline of the grounds on which the testimony of the evangelists as to the life and character of Jesus is worthy of confidence. I have shown you also that this testimony is greatly confirmed by the contents of the record, especially by the consistency of the marvellous and else incredible portions of the narrative with the facts which no one ventures to call in question. But were these contents defective, — did they, while they profess to transmit the life and words of an all-sufficient and divinely appointed teacher in morals and religion, omit many things which might properly be expected of such a teacher, — did they present, on the magnificent substructure of a miraculous theophany, only a paltry, fragmentary, and unfinished work, — these defects would reflect back doubts upon the testimony, and, if they could not annul its evidential weight, they would at least impair its value; for a religious record which fails to satisfy our needs is not worth our investigation or defence. Accordingly the omissions, the blanks, the *lacunæ* in Christianity and its records, have been strongly urged in abatement of its claims. I propose to present them in the opposite light, and to draw added proof of the genuineness and authenticity of the Gospel record from what it does not contain.

As to the range and quantity of its professed revelations, the Gospels certainly contain less than any other sacred books with which we are acquainted. They do less to satisfy the curiosity of those who would extend their knowledge beyond the normal scope of human research. They are silent on many subjects on which the Koran and the Mormon scriptures enter into minute detail. They do not approach the brink of the depths sounded in the sacred books of India and Persia. They have not satisfied many Christian sects, which have built outside of them cumbrous systems, bodies of divinity, — often fitly so called for their lack of soul. These have, indeed, derived their materials from the Christian Scriptures, but less from Christ's own teachings than from the Pauline epistles, including that to the Hebrews, whether it be Paul's or not. It cannot be denied that the Christianity of Christ, as recorded in the Gospels from his lips and life, is exceedingly simple, — even meagre, if estimated by the number and diversity of its topics. I believe the Christianity of the Pauline epistles to be equally simple. It is merely the application of the plain doctrines and precepts of Christ to the exigencies, questionings, and controversies of converts who had a great deal of Judaism or heathenism still clinging to them ; and many of the technical terms, which from these epistles have been imported into the religious phraseology of modern Protestant churches, and have given rise to minute dogmatic subtilties without number, were, as used by the writer, in no sense Christian terms ; that is, they were not occasioned or demanded by Christianity, but had their sole necessity and use in the refutation of now obsolete opinions, through which Christianity had to cut its way in the apostolic age.

But let us look for one moment at the actual fulness of this meagreness, the real wealth of this poverty. I, as an individual man, conscious of a nature containing more than flesh and blood, and of wants that remain when the bodily wants are satisfied, go to Christ and his Gospel, and what do I find there? Ostensibly all that I personally need. Whether it be really so, will be our inquiry in the next two Lectures, which will be devoted to the test of experiment as applied to Christianity. But on the face it offers me what, if genuine, ought fully to satisfy me. As for belief, it presents to my faith a paternal Providence, a full and righteous retribution, an equally full and complete redemption from the penalty of repented sin, an eternal life, a passage through death to endless happiness on conditions which I cannot misinterpret. As to my conduct, it tells me just what I ought to be and do toward God and man, how I am to discipline my thoughts, how to pray, how to demean myself in the various relations of life ; and there is not a single occasion or exigency on which it does not furnish the principle from which I may, without danger of error, construct the appropriate rule, and determine the course of action which it demands. As for motives, they are supplied by the love and fatherhood of God, by the dying, ever-living love of Christ, and by the powers of the world to come, — motives which, if authentic, are of unsurpassable and inexhaustible force. I cannot say that I need any thing more. With this spiritual apparatus, if genuine, I can live in peace and die in hope.

But there are a thousand inquiries growing out of my nature and position in this world, and not a few suggested or intensified by my faith in what Christ has revealed, on which he does not begin to satisfy my curiosity. I would fain get some rounded and complete view of the divine nature, while clouds and darkness rest on many of its aspects. I would gladly account for evil, physical and moral. I should like to know more clearly the precise relation of Christ to the Eternal Father. I should rejoice to look behind the veil of death, and to form some conception of the mode of being in the future life. But in none of these particulars does Jesus or his Gospel give us the light we crave. Let us draw, if we can, speech from this silence.

Such silence would not have characterized a pseudo-revelation, the result whether of imposture or of delusion ; yet it is precisely what we should expect to find in a divine revelation. The first of these propositions is almost self-evident. An impostor would, of course, have adapted himself to the prevailing appetency for a knowledge of things beyond and above the sphere of human life. In no other way could disciples have been so easily enlisted or so strongly attached. Add to this advantage the consideration that fraud cannot be detected in a region outside of human experience. No one comes back from the unseen world to confront the celestial topography of the Koran with his own observation. Equally would the imagined revelations from the brain of a fanatic have been ultra-mundane; for religious delusion always has the realm beyond mortal vision for its field, and, so far as it affects one's views of things seen, it does so wholly by the lurid light cast upon them from things imagined, but invisible. In fine, delusion would have expatiated, and fraud have sought its best hunting-ground, in the very regions of thought where Christianity gives us only faint and vague glimpses, often such as rather stimulate than appease our desire to know. Let us now see why Christianity, if divine, should have remained silent on these themes.

We should have expected a divine revelation to remain silent where fanaticism and imposture will not hold their peace, because restless curiosity is thus reduced to a minimum. All knowledge raises more questions than it answers. The broader the visible horizon, the broader is the invisible circle that bounds it. Every truth attained abuts upon other truths still unattained. Had the teachings of Christ answered the questions which we most desire to have answered, the answers would have prompted still more numerous and difficult questions. Truth is infinite, and, were its entire realm made ours, "even the world itself could not contain the books that should be written;" while nowhere short of this complete conquest would the mind of man pause and say, "It is enough." Had every inquiry that we could now raise been fully satisfied, the region of the unknown would only seem more vast than it now does, and from longing souls would go forth only the intenser demand for more light.

It may also be maintained that the imperfection of our knowledge where we want to know more is essential to our best spiritual nurture. Faith has a transcendent value, not so much for its contents as for the filial spirit of which it is equally nurse and nursling; and we can imagine a fulness of vision, an accuracy of proved and tested knowledge as to the great truths and facts of the spiritual life, which should come to us as the knowledge of terrestrial facts and of daily events reaches us, but by means of which the soul would forfeit that most wholesome discipline which consists in trusting where it cannot see, in taking on authority what it cannot know, in holding fast the clew for its guidance through cloud and mist and dense darkness. Certainly this trait has been most conspicuous in the greatest souls that we have known, and it has seemed one of the chief elements of their greatness. It has strengthened the fibre of character, and at the same time has given to the inward life a repose and equipoise which cannot come from mere knowledge, but are born of that faith which rests on a wisdom beyond its own. Who shall say that the faith thus nurtured may not be as essential in the future life as now, — that even there our ignorance may not grow faster than our knowledge, — that at every stage of our eternal progress faith may not precede clear vision, in the face of mysteries still unrevealed, of heights and depths of the Infinite Providence not yet scaled or sounded?

Hope, too, needs a certain degree of vagueness, no less than of assurance, to give it full working force. Were its objects too distinctly defined, they might make us impatient of the toil and pain through which they are to be won; while their very dimness urges the aspiring soul ever on toward those serener heights where they may be more fully apprehended. The Mohammedan paradise is described in minute detail, and the result is indifference to life, — a fatalism which has indeed made the Moslem armies desperately brave, but has at the same time checked industrial activity, arrested progress, given despotism its holding ground, and paralyzed all the energies which underlie a healthy social and political condition.

There are some directions in which, no doubt, the silence of Jesus tends to cherish devout thought and reverent imagination. It may be of untold benefit to think where we cannot know, to exercise our discursive powers where our highest conceptions are entirely inadequate. Fruitless contemplation on the mysteries of the Divine Being may yet feed adoration, and deepen the fountain of loving piety. Though mysticism has brought no new truths to light, it has nourished the purest, loftiest devotion; its subtilties have been cleansing and elevating; its vague terminology has been the chariot of fire on which many an earth-dwelling spirit has been wafted to heaven. The discussions as to the modal union of the Father and the Son, though they have established nought to enlarge the bounds of that knowledge which, Jesus says, resides in the bosom of the Father alone, and though they have often been only a fierce and bitter logomachy, sometimes giving aim and sweep to more material warfare, have yet oftener cherished a loving intimacy with Christ, and have been by none more earnestly pursued than by souls at peace with God and man, and more intent on following Christ than even on knowing him. Above all, we have reason to own the unspeakable blessedness of Christ's silence as to the future life. Other founders of religions, as I have said, have not been thus silent. They have constructed paradise of what they deemed the choicest earthly materials; and their heavenly societies have been such as would compel every pure and devout man to say, "O my soul, come not thou into their secret; unto their assembly, mine honor, be not thou united." But here Jesus tells us nothing; nor yet do we have any intimations from his apostles, except that in the glorious epic of the Apocalypse — a poem, though not in numbers — heaven is indicated by heaping together — designedly, as seems to me, without coherence or mutual compatibility — the most magnificent figures which human language can furnish, not to describe it, but to pronounce it undescribable, — to reiterate in the rapt utterance of the seer what St. Paul says in simple prose, " Eye hath not seen, nor ear heard, neither have entered into the heart of man the things which God hath prepared for them that love him." In this absence of definite knowledge, imagination has free range and unrestricted scope. She has the plumb-line and the measuring-rod in her own hands, can lay out her own plot in the garden of the Lord, erect her own mansion within the golden gates, — transferring thither all that she has worthily loved, pursued, desired on earth, yet all the while assured that her highest conceptions are but faint types and dim foreshadowings of the far more exceeding glory, when for fancy there shall be open vision. Thus, undoubtedly, heaven is kept more constantly, glowingly, lovingly before the thought than by any detailed description, were such description possible. What is of still more worth in this silence of revelation, the heaven of our thought grows as we grow, becomes loftier as we rise, richer as we increase in soul-wealth, always in advance of our clear conception, hovering on its outermost verge, yet in so near contact with what is best, purest, noblest in our consciousness and experience, as to give vividness to our hope and a felt reality to its objects. Moreover, the ideal of heaven, which we thus project from our own souls and fill with the best that is in us, in its turn reacts on the soul that gives it shape, attracts us more and more to its own higher sphere, and, as it grows richer and more beautiful, endows with its wealth and clothes with its beauty the whole life and character.

Yet another reason presents itself for the silence of Jesus, where religious teachers in general have been by no means sparing in their utterances. On many subjects on which we would gladly know more, Jesus may have told us little or nothing, because of the poverty of human language and its inadequacy to the interpretation of the mysteries whose solution we crave. The teaching power of words is limited by our own consciousness and experience. On subjects that transcend this limit, language assumes one of two types. It either runs into anthropomorphism, and belittles and degrades divine things to human measure and level; or else, in soaring into the empyrean, it is arrested midway in impenetrable clouds and mists that never part. Of the latter tendency we find no trace in the simple, transparent words of Jesus; and I am equally impressed by the reverent care which he evidently takes to shun the former, of which the examples in the Old Testament are very numerous, — in part, no doubt, on account of the meagreness of the Hebrew vocabulary. Christ's method of teaching by parables, with all its other excellencies, is specially adapted to man's condition with reference to the subjects of religious curiosity. He thus suggests conceptions of the divine nature and providence which transcend the scope of literal language, and therefore of clear and definite thought, yet which may none the less move the affections, inspire the will, and shape the conduct. For instance, the parable of the Prodigal Son gives us views of the divine character, tender, familiar, loving, which we could not put into literal language without irreverence, like that which we sometimes detect in the hymns sung by persons who have more piety than taste, but which we can feel with the profoundest gratitude, and recognize in those upliftings of the soul in fervent praise when we "mean the thanks we cannot speak."

Let us look for a moment at some of these subjects on which Jesus says so little. Let us see if they are not obviously and intrinsically beyond the range of any teaching of which we are susceptible, so that any definite utterance with regard to them must be of necessity unauthentic and spurious. I will specify but two or three of these subjects, though I might present several other themes of curious inquiry and speculation as belonging to the same category.

The origin and ministry of evil must manifestly be classed under this head. There are analogies that enable us to see how our inevitable ignorance as to this whole subject exists, but not to remove it. Were you to explain to a very young child, in the best words at your command, the entire scope and bearing of those provisions and customs of civilized society by which individuals are constrained to do, forego, resign, and endure unnumbered things, against their own will and private interest, for the general good, and sometimes even to the loss and detriment of the present and of more than one generation for the benefit of remote posterity, you would find your exposition clogged by words and phrases which had never come into the child's vocabulary, and could have no meaning for his ear: the view in space and time would be broader and deeper than his four or five years' life would enable him to take; and the only result would be that, if he were docile and trustful, he would receive an impression that the hard things of which he often heard complaint would somehow and at some time issue in good. Still less can we, with our narrow range of vision and our brief earthly life, take in or be enabled to take in the entire problem of evil, which comprehends the universe and twin eternities, or to trace the vestiges, which undoubtedly exist thick-sown around us, of that all-wise and all-merciful optimism, which subsidizes suffering, wrong, and sin to its own culmination and triumph. Jesus could have revealed all this only to a mind broad and profound as his own, and to such a mind probably not in the tongue of Greek or Jew.

Another subject on which for a like reason, no doubt, Jesus kept silence, is the nature of God. He defines his relativity to man, opens the door of access to his mercy, and manifests to us as much of him as can be incarnated in perfect humanity; but that is all. And must it not of necessity have been all? Have the metaphysical subtilties of the Christian fathers, the schoolmen, or modern theologians, upon the essence of God, ever expressed or conveyed an intelligible idea? Undoubtedly God is immeasurably more than man has seen or imagined; but our conceptions of him are limited by the capacity, the receptivity of our own natures. He may have attributes as little within the range of our possible conceptions as fancy or metaphysics is within the comprehension of a zoöphyte. Or, on the other hand, this partition of his being in our thought into separate attributes may have a meaning to us, only because our own inward being at best so lacks coherency and unity. Who knows that in the speech of heaven there are separate names for divine perfections? It may be that what seem to us distinguishable attributes are mutually equivalent and convertible, as are the imponderable forces of the material universe. But we are already beginning to "darken counsel by words without knowledge;" nor can we ever glance a searching thought into that infinite depth of being, without admiring the wisdom of Him who taught us to say merely Our Father, and has inbreathed into our hearts the child-spirit which gives that title its restful and beatific meaning.

In this connection we cannot but recur to the silence of Jesus about the future life. For the reasons already given, I doubt whether he would have told us more, if he could. But could he? What life is; how the body and soul interact; what portion of their joint existence and functions belongs to each; how far finite being is dependent on material conditions,—these are questions which we not only cannot begin to answer, but the very terms of which have no definite meaning for us. How, then, could any language of ours be made the vehicle for instruction as to the philosophy of the life to come, its mode of being, the nature of the passage to it, the relation of our present bodily existence to the resurrection-life? Had Jesus entered upon these questions, so far from throwing upon them for us the light of his own clear understanding, he would only have involved the whole realm of the future in deeper obscurity. We may, then, regard the bald simplicity of his words of eternal life, the entire absence of descriptive detail, and the confirmation of those words, not by reasoning, but by the cardinal and fully attested fact of his own resurrection, as among the strong tokens of his mission as a teacher sent from God.

We have seen, I trust, that, so far as Jesus has failed to satisfy the curiosity of men as to matters beyond their scope and sphere, he has given us only added reason for accepting the testimony in behalf of the records of his life as authentic, and thus for regarding his religion as divine.*

But omissions on the plane of human duty also have been alleged. It has, I think, never been denied by unbelievers or misbelievers that the morality of the New Testament tends to make men true, pure, kind, generous, modest, humble ; but it has been said that it fails to fit men for the daily life of the world, that it cherishes gloom, asceticism, and indifference to the worthy objects of endeavor and emulation, and that it ignores such virtues as courage, patriotism, and loyalty to friends. While, as to the defects which we have already considered, we confess the impeachment, and glory in it, in the particulars just now enumerated we deny the charge of omission or deficiency in the teachings of Jesus.

As regards the alleged tendency of Christianity to

* See Appendix, note K.

asceticism, we repudiate it, and challenge proof. There is not a trace of this tendency in the Gospels, except in John the Baptist, who was not a disciple of Christ, and whom Christ pronounced, in point of spiritual illumination, less than the least of his disciples. Jesus instituted no fast, nor is there the slightest proof that he ever observed any. He was reproached for neglecting the fasts which formed a part, not indeed of the Mosaic religion, — for that has no fast, — but of the Rabbinical refinements upon it. On the other hand, there is not on record a single instance of his declining any of the few festive occasions on which he was an invited guest; and asceticism in the bosom of the Christian Church has found no stumbling-block so difficult to evade or surmount as the story of the marriage at Cana.

Jesus indeed enjoins certain forms of self-denial; but self-denial is not so much a duty as a universal human necessity. There is not a child of five years of age who has not learned this; who does not know that he cannot have all that he wants, but can supply his foremost wants only by denying himself those which he holds as of secondary importance. Now the problem that Christ solves — and he alone solves it — is how so to deny one's self inferior benefits as to secure the largest measure of superior gifts, by yielding up bodily for spiritual goods, selfish pleasures for the higher and more enduring pleasures of beneficence, temporal happiness for eternal happiness. Where there is no conflict between body and soul, self-indulgence and charity, the life that now is and that which is to come, Jesus enjoins no gratuitous self-denial, no sacrifice for the sake of sacrifice. Whatever of bodily, self-centred, and earthly good can be ours without detriment to the soul or to our fellow-beings, he would have us utilize and enjoy to the full; and he best fulfils the law and most truly breathes the spirit of Christ, who drinks freely and with full draughts at every pure fountain of joy that springs by his life-path, — who, with every power and faculty of body, mind, and soul, takes in the most that he can of this rich and beautiful world, in which there are many things obviously made for no other purpose than that we should enjoy them and thank God for them.

There was, indeed, a great deal of asceticism in the early Church. But it was imported from the dualism of the Oriental philosophy, according to which, as the outward world and the human body were created by the Evil Principle, his reign was to be abjured and defied by the mortification of the flesh and abstinence from the good things of this world.

As regards indifference to the worthy objects of endeavor and emulation, there is not a precept of Jesus that has any bearing in this direction. He encourages and seconds the modest industry and humble enterprise of the apostles. He does not, as our translators have it, pronounce an indiscriminate ban upon the rich; but, with reference to the stress of the times and the impending persecution of the infant Church, he speaks of it as hard for one to enter the kingdom of heaven, or his visible Church, rich, because enforced poverty was then the price at which alone one could become a disciple. There was, indeed, something like community of goods for a little while among the disciples at Jerusalem; but there is not the slightest intimation that this was by the command of Christ, or as a matter of absolute duty. It was merely a temporary arrangement, which, as may be amply proved from St. Paul's epistles, was never extended beyond Jerusalem; and it probably had but a very brief existence there.

As to courage, there is not, indeed, a word of Jesus that can sanction the aggressive courage which is ready to incur hazard for whatever cause, — that which arms the man-slayer, the duellist, the prompt and stern avenger of his own or another's wrongs; that which glories in war, delights in carnage, and loves the garment rolled in blood. This courage has been the greatest of curses to humanity, and, if the world shall ever be thoroughly Christianized, it will be looked back upon with very much the same horror with which we now regard cannibalism. Not that I believe the time will ever come when the brave men who have laid down their lives in defence of their country, of freedom, or of human rights, will be held in diminished honor; but it will be seen that the vast majority of wars have not had a particle of right on either side, and that those in which men have been on one side urged by sacred duty have none the less had their origin in atrocious wrong. But the courage which dares death rather than disloyalty to one's convictions of truth and right has in Christ both its most emphatic command and its most illustrious example.

What can be stronger than "Be not afraid of them that kill the body, and after that have no more that they can do"? Or what spectacle of courage has the world seen that can bear a momentary comparison with that of Him who, "travelling in the greatness of his strength," had the cross perpetually in view, went up to Jerusalem to die, and by his own words and deeds, at every stage of his ministry, stimulated the powers of darkness and hastened the fatal hour?

As regards patriotism, there is in the Gospel no justification of that blind and reckless love of country professed in a much-lauded sentiment of one of our naval heroes: "Our country, may she always be right; but, right or wrong, may she always be victorious!" Yet we find in Jesus a love of country intense and tender. One of the only two occasions on which he is said to have been moved to tears was in view of the impending devastation of his native land, and the levelling of her glory with the dust. Oh, had we abounding among us patriotism like this, — to weep over our national sins, to deprecate the righteous judgment of outraged Heaven upon our time-serving and corruption, our intemperance and our greed of gain, our profligacy and infidelity, — there would be hope that in this our day we might give heed to the things belonging to our peace, before they be hidden from our eyes.

As to friendship, even if we can appeal to no precepts of Jesus with reference to the mutual duties of those bound by the closest intimacy, we can at least cite his example. What more sacred tie can there be than that indicated by his words to the apostles, "I have called you friends; for all things that I have heard of my Father I have made known unto you"? In that little circle, too, let us not forget that there was still an inmost company of three; and, of these three, one who will hold to the end of time the spiritual primacy of the sacred college as pre-eminently "the disciple whom Jesus loved." Christ's friendship, in each degree of intimacy, was manifested by tokens of fellowship and affection which would have been inappropriate to a union less close and confidential. But the expression of friendship never scanted thoughts or labors of love for the outside world. On the other hand, we may learn from him that love generates love, not only in him who receives, but in him who bestows it. There is no such laboratory of diffusive benevolence and efficient philanthropy as a home whose atmosphere is love; and precisely the same office is performed by intimate friendships; for love grows by spending,—the more is given, the more remains. But while all this is implied in the teachings and manifested in the life of Jesus, there was no need, and there never is need, of special precepts for the cultivation of friendship. It cannot grow to order, or be formed by rule. It springs up of necessity where there are warm hearts, with common proclivities, tastes, and interests, and especially where there are hearts united by the love of God and in the work which he has given them to do. There was in Christ's time no lack of friendship, whether between good men or bad men; nor can there ever be. If Christ had given any rules for friendship, they would probably have been limitations, in the spirit in which Cicero writes, "If all things which friends desire are to be done, such alliances should be deemed conspiracies, not friendships." * But these limitations are included in the paramount law of love and service, first of all to God, and to the dearest among kindred and friends, only in, and to, and through him.

I have thus enumerated, I believe, all the deficiencies with which the morality of Christ and his Gospel has been charged, and have shown you that in these its actual deficiency consists in shunning excesses and abuses.†

I must here close the first division of my proposed plan. My endeavor has been to demonstrate that, as regards the evidence of testimony, Christianity occupies at least as high a position as the truths of science. I have shown you that our four Gospels can be traced by quotations, references, descriptions, and coincidences as far back as the first century of our era; that they have borne from the beginning the names of their now reputed authors, without the vestige of a doubt as to their authorship; that those writers had the means of knowing the truth as to the materials of their record; and that they had no conceivable motive for false testimony in those matters, but every conceivable earthly motive for suppressing what they report as facts. I have shown you that, as St. Paul evidently believed all

* "Si omnia facienda sunt, quæ amici velint, non amicitiæ tales, sed conjurationes putandæ sunt."

† See Appendix, note L.

that the evangelists recorded about Jesus, we get rid of no difficulties by resorting — even would documentary evidence permit this — to the hypothesis of the gradual and slow growth of the Messianic idea, and its full development in a later than the apostolic age. I have adduced Jesus as his own witness, maintaining that his actual existence alone can account for the Gospels. I have given an adequate explanation of the peculiar phenomena of the first three Gospels, and have exhibited the special grounds that we have for maintaining the genuineness of the fourth Gospel. I have attempted to prove that the miraculous element in the history of Christ is in entire harmony with the rest of the narrative, and therefore not to be rejected or doubted, if that narrative as a whole be fully authenticated. I have shown that the actual resurrection of Jesus Christ is the only method of accounting for the record of that event as it stands, for the undoubted belief in it on the part of the primitive disciples, and for the influence of that belief in the early history of the Christian Church. Finally, in the present Lecture I have sought confirmation for this testimony in behalf of the Gospels, from the alleged omissions and defects in the teachings of Jesus.

Now what I would maintain is that the facts recorded in the Gospels are established on at least as trustworthy testimony as are the facts remote in time and space to whose testimony scientific men are constantly giving credence, and on which the science of the present day is based. This last-named testimony I am by no means disposed to deny, doubt, or undervalue. I rejoice that it is so rich, so clear, so various in its sources, yet so harmonious in its utterances. I bless God that he has thus made numberless men who had no conception of scientific truth tributary to its establishment and verification, — that the stones of the temple of knowledge have been quarried, squared, and polished by so many simple, honest men, who knew not what a great work they were doing. But there is no principle on which their testimony can be pronounced valid, and that of the early Christian witnesses untrustworthy. We must accept both, or else reject both, and include science and Christianity in indiscriminate scepticism or denial. God has joined the two in the witness for their authenticity; what he hath joined man may not put asunder.

LECTURE VIII.

II. EXPERIMENT. — EXPERIMENT AS A TEST OF SCIENTIFIC TRUTH. — CLAIMED AS A TEST BY THE AUTHOR OF CHRISTIANITY. — CHRISTIANITY AS A FACTOR IN THE FORMATION OF CHARACTER. — AS A SOURCE OF ENERGY. — AS A SUPPORT IN TRIAL. — AS SUSTAINING HOPE IN DEATH. — CUMULATIVE ARGUMENT FROM EXPERIMENT.

I SAID in my first Lecture that science and Christianity alike depend for their evidence on testimony, experiment, and intuition. I have compared them as regards testimony. We will pass now to experiment. This bears a most important part in the ascertainment and verification of scientific truth. In some of the sciences, as in chemistry, for instance, it is at once guide, discoverer, and test. The ultimate reason why such and such results take place no mortal can know; yet no one hesitates to infer from these results universal laws of nature, and in many instances a single experiment has been sufficient to establish a principle of large scope and profound significance. It is by experiment alone that the sciences of heat, light, electricity, and magnetism have been created, and what are called their principles or laws are but the outcome of individual experiments generalized. A large part of the science of human and animal physiology has been built solely on experiment.

Christianity claims to be tested by experiment. Its Founder repeatedly proposed this test to his disciples, and gave them clearly to understand that the growth and honor of his religion would be contingent on the manifestation of its efficacy in their lives and characters. Experiment of Christianity has been made for more than eighteen centuries. Its claims have been put to the test. Men have resorted to it for the fulfilment of its promises. The correspondence of its working with its professions has been tried at every point. Has it succeeded? Or has it failed? This is a fundamental question, even if the evidence of testimony be unimpeached. Testimony might, indeed, establish the authenticity of the Gospels, and thus prove that Christianity was of divine origin. But so, we believe, was Judaism. So, the Mohammedans say, were both Judaism and Christianity, no less than the doctrine of their own prophet. What we Christians would fain prove, if we can, is not merely that Christianity is a divinely given religion, but that it holds the foremost place among all religions; and that place it can make good only by what it does. Its paramount worth can be tested by experiment alone. The experimental test of Christianity may be considered, first, as regards the influence of this religion on individual character; and, secondly, in its action on society, civilization, government, and the collective character and history of nations. The former of these divisions will suffice for the present, the latter will be the subject of the next Lecture.

Christianity purports to be a guide to virtue, a

fountain of inward strength, an unfailing support and solace in trial and grief, a beatific influence under the shadow of death; and in these particulars it claims pre-eminence over all other forms of belief and culture. Its Founder urges in his own behalf these paramount claims in such terms as their truth alone can justify. "I am the light of the world: he that followeth me shall not walk in darkness, but shall have the light of life." "I will give you a mouth and wisdom, which all your adversaries shall not be able to gainsay nor resist." "Peace I leave with you, my peace I give unto you: not as the world giveth, give I unto you." "Come unto me, all ye that labor and are heavy laden, and I will give you rest." "I give unto them [my sheep, or followers] eternal life; and they shall never perish, neither shall any pluck them out of my hand." "He that heareth my word . . . hath everlasting life, and shall not come into condemnation; but is passed from death unto life."

It is of no small evidential value that these words have for so many centuries been familiarly read by wise and discreet men; that they are read to-day by thousands upon thousands of sensible men and women all over the civilized world, without surprise or repugnancy, without their being regarded as misplaced or extravagant, — as indicating audacity or insane self-exaltation. I doubt whether there has lived any other man, in whose saying these things persons of superior intelligence and culture would acquiesce. I do not find that the founders of other religions — not even Mohammed — have ever professed in their own persons to stand in such direct beneficent relations to their disciples. Certainly we read nothing like this in Moses or the prophets, nor yet in the words of comfort and strength addressed by the Christian apostles to their converts. Had Socrates talked in this way about himself, the hemlock would have been brewed for him when he first began to teach, and his best friends would have forced the cup upon him, unless they had given him hellebore instead, as to a madman. Even the sages of our own time, whose oracular utterances profess to comprehend and exceed the wisdom of all antecedent centuries, have never yet said such great things about themselves as Christ said; and were they to say them, it would completely disenchant their disciples. We are not surprised that Jesus Christ should have spoken thus, simply because many know, or think they know, that he uttered no more than they have themselves experienced in their relation to him, and many more think that they have witnessed in their friends and neighbors phenomena corresponding with such experience. Let us look at these claims in detail.

There can be no doubt that Christ claims the ability to form the very highest style of moral character, the most symmetrical grouping of virtues and graces, the most consummate spiritual beauty of which the soul of man is capable. This claim certainly seems to justify itself on a superficial view of the moral history of our race. If we compare good men before Christ with good men in and through Christ, there can be no possible doubt that the latter are by far the better. Of patriarchs and prophets under the Mosaic dispensation, those whose lives are described with any degree of fulness have, indeed, single traits of devotion, fidelity, or patriotism, which make their memory illustrious ; yet they manifest decidedly sub-Christian characters, and even of Abraham, Jacob, Samuel, David, Nehemiah, it might be said, "The least really in and thoroughly of the kingdom of heaven (or Christ) is greater than he." Still more can we say the same of nearly all the best men of classic antiquity ; for in them we generally see splendid merits allied with equally conspicuous faults. Thus, above all the ancients outside of Judæa who preceded Christ, Cicero makes himself the object of sincere, almost affectionate admiration to his diligent reader ; yet his portrait is sadly defaced by a vanity of which a single sitting at the feet of Jesus would have cured him, and by a lack of sincerity and consistency which showed how sadly he needed the tonic power of the Gospel. It is worthy of notice that the two illustrious men of classic fame who seem most Christianlike, Plutarch and Epictetus, both flourished after the Gospel had been extensively diffused. I do not imagine that they knew any thing definite about Christianity : if they had, they would have been Christians. But the spirit was in the air ; the tone of Christian sentiment had penetrated farther than any fact or dogma of the new religion ; and there were receptive souls that caught it, without knowing whence or how. To return from this digression, if digression it be : John and Paul not only represent higher types of character than we find in the entire Jewish and Gentile world before Christ, — types, too, which had no antetype except the Master whom they called divine; but they stand before us still as unsurpassed, if equalled. The only account that they could give of themselves was that through contemplation of the image of God in Christ they had grown into the same image; and, if they were and still are pre-eminent, we have no way of accounting for it but that they were proof-impressions of that image before it had become dimmed by time, or had suffered the partial obscuration inevitable on its being transferred from a living form to an uttered story,* and then from an uttered story to a written book.

The post-Christian history of human virtue presents precisely the same contrast between Christian and extra-Christian excellence, which we have already traced. Let any impartial person draw up a list of the eminently good men and women who have left their enduring record within the last eighteen centuries, or are writing it now, and then divide the names on the list into Christian and non-Christian, — the muster-roll of the latter would be exceedingly meagre, and would probably include none of the pre-eminent; and I doubt whether, even in this lesser catalogue, we should find any whose characters had not been formed under Christian influences. Among

* The peculiar circumstances of St. Paul's conversion, and the facts in his own psychological experience to which he makes repeated reference, placed him virtually in the position with reference to Jesus occupied by none else but his immediate disciples.

those who in our own time and land are understood to be non-believers in historical Christianity, there are not a few whose characters cannot but win abounding reverence and love; but of these I know not one who had not his nurture in a Christian family, and some of the more distinguished among them were in early life members of the Christian Church, and were then certainly as pure, amiable, and philanthropic as they are now. I doubt whether you can point to a single person that has grown up under the discipline of a sceptical philosophy, whom you would designate as a fit example for those whose characters are now in the process of formation.

Christian virtue is a peculiar type, and peculiar for its comprehensiveness. The title over the cross was written in Hebrew, Greek, and Latin; and it is an index of the broad spiritual culture of those who have become what they were or are under the nurture of Him who was then termed in derision the King of the Jews. The Hebrew spirit was distinctively religious; but, because divorced from refining influences and from large opportunities for secular activity, it had been narrowed and etiolated into a stupid and superstitious ritualism. The Grecian mind was in the closest sympathy with material beauty, art, poetry, and song; it bore the imprint of the most thorough æsthetic discipline; but, destitute of religious ideas on which faith and reverence could repose, and at the same time feeble and capricious, it had degenerated into gross sensualism. The early Roman state was pervaded by the spirit of law, and thence of force;

but, for lack of religious discipline and elegant culture, it had become rapacious, despotic, sanguinary. It is the glory of Christianity to have restored these effete elements of character, and blended them in its nurture. The developed Christian character has the intense religiousness of the Hebrew psalmists and seers; however destitute of the wonted means of culture, it takes on, or rather in, a culture of its own, sweet, gentle, kind, spiritual; and it submits itself to law, not, indeed, as to a hard yoke, but as to a loving service, while law gives it a forceful energy, which pervades the whole life-work, and makes it constant, loyal, noble. These elements are blended, unified in the Christian, because they were, each and all, perfect in the Master whom he owns and follows, who was "King of the Jews,"—the love and worship of God, his purple robe and diadem; more than Grecian in the grace and amenity of his spirit and his walk among men; more than Roman in the entireness with which he made himself the incarnate law of God, and alone, among those born of woman, finished the whole work which God gave him to do. You can trace these elements in all the exemplars of Christian excellence, —not only in those who fill high places and wield an extended influence, but equally in the most lowly and unprivileged spheres. Wherever in humble and obscure life you find one of untaught grace in speech and mien, and rigidly faithful in the least requirements of duty,—when you look farther, you trace also the Hebrew religiousness, only of the Zion rather than the Sinai type, and you may "take knowledge" of such a one that he has been with Jesus.

In experimental philosophy there are various ways of testing the properties of a substance under trial. One question is, Does it show its identity and hold its own, when combined with various substances, in different proportions, and under altered conditions? Thus the presence of iron is detected by infallible tokens alike in unnumbered compound mineral substances, in the sap of various plants, in the human blood, in the rays of the spectrum, — in all unchanged in its essential characteristics. In like manner Christian culture has been associated with every other conceivable element of culture, and in all these combinations it preserves the same essential properties of piety, sweetness, and strength, — not, indeed, in the perfect equipoise which we behold in the one great Exemplar, but in a sufficient measure to indicate their source, and to discriminate them from traits elsewhere derived and otherwise nourished.

The experimental philosopher, again, simplifies his experiments, — tests the substance in hand with a single other substance, carefully eliminating all foreign elements. We have had abundant opportunity to subject Christianity to this test also. It has been applied to the human *rasa tabula*, the unpreoccupied mind, the moral nature that has had no previous culture, the little child, the ignorant adult, the untutored savage: it has been, in such cases, the only training, subduing, intenerating, energizing force; and in unnumbered instances it has shown its adequacy to mould the spirit in sanctity, beauty, and power.

Moreover, the Christian consciousness not only

betrays, but acknowledges its source. While an infinitesimal proportion who have at some time seemed the disciples of Jesus, retaining much that they derived from him, have disclaimed him and "walk no more with him," the overwhelming majority of those who have manifested the type of character of which I have spoken hesitate not to ascribe all that they have and are to Christ. They will tell you: "This virtue I have cherished, because I see it in my Master. That sinful propensity I have subdued, because his word and spirit rebuke it. I have been uplifted in prayer on the wings of his devotion. I have been furnished for duty by the instructions that fell from his lips. I have been armed against temptation by the panoply with which he girded me. The life which I now live in the flesh I live by the faith of the Son of God, who loved me, and gave himself for me."

I am fully aware of the objection which may be urged against this argument, on the ground of the very imperfect moral development to be witnessed in the vast majority of those who profess to have learned of Jesus how to live. The argument is not, indeed, so strong as it might be,— not so strong as it will be in the better time to come. Were Christians in general all that they profess to be and ought to be, I doubt whether there would be need of offering any other evidence for Christianity than the lives of its disciples. But we are willing, as the case stands, to base our argument on the following statement. The best men that the world has seen have been Christians, and have professed to derive their virtues from Christ. Among men of a less excellent type of character, yet belonging, on the whole, to the class of virtuous men, we have reason to believe that the greater part have derived whatever of goodness they possess from Christ; while we find that immorality and vice are never to be traced to the presence, but are, in unnumbered instances, obviously due to the absence or deficiency of Christian training and influence. Were Christ and his religion to be eliminated from among the factors that constitute the moral character of modern Christendom, all the highest forms of excellence would be eliminated also; the next highest would be nearly extinguished, and all lower grades sadly depleted. Nor have we within our experimental knowledge any moral force, agency, or influence, which could begin to do for human character what Christ and his religion have done. As much as this has been proved, and is at the same time so patent and manifest as hardly to need proof; and up to this point Christianity sustains the test of experiment, by having done what it promises and purports to do for the formation of character.

Christianity claims, in the next place, to be regarded as pre-eminently a source of strength, a motive power for whatever man is bound to do or needs to have done. There are, indeed, many Christians who are not distinguished as workers. Yet you will find that the two characters coincide much more frequently than they exist apart, and that it is under the undoubted impulse of expressly Christian motives that the most and best work has been done and is doing throughout the civilized world.

The working force of Jesus himself has been kept too much in the background, in the glowing admiration called forth by the peculiarly lovable traits of his character. But we have reason to place as transcendent an estimate on his energy as on his gentleness. His public ministry was but from a year and a half to three years in duration ;* and in that period what a wide diversity and frequent change of scene, — in Judæa, Galilee, Samaria, Peræa ! What successions and varieties of stubborn soil to be broken up, and made penetrable by the seeds of evangelic teaching ! What constant and urgent appeals for his services to the suffering and afflicted ! Some of his days, of which we can trace the record, are so crowded with ever-changing claims upon his energy, that they might seem to have required the sun to linger on his course to make them adequate to their work. Then after those weary days he seeks new strength for the morrow, not in sleep, but more effectively in prayer ; for as the touch of his mother earth renovates the vigor of the fabled demigod, so from communion with his own mother-land flows fresh might into the soul of the heaven-born.

Closest among his standard-bearers, St. Paul exemplifies the energizing efficacy of Christianity. How intense his activity ! How broadly comprehensive his plans of labor ! A pastorate embracing all the habitable regions of the earth would now be scarcely greater, considering the present facilities for locomo-

* The chronological data in the Gospels certainly render the shorter period not improbable. See Appendix, note M.

tion, than was for him the care of all the churches in the diocese erected by his toil. No navigator could tell more than he of the perils of the deep; nor was it without the utmost hardship and hazard that he made his way, often where there was no thoroughfare for ordinary intercourse, in the rugged interior of Asia Minor, or on the inhospitable coast of Macedonia. Ubiquitous in his oversight and presence, where he has once been, he makes himself felt ever onward as an efficient force. And it is with his whole being that he labors, — with mind, and heart, and soul, — so that the imprint of his massive spirit and his burning zeal has still remained on the life of the Christian Church, and is renewed with pristine vividness whenever there is a fresh impulse toward spiritual growth, or an access of earnest endeavor in behalf of the unevangelized. Moreover, we have from him the clear exhibition of the convictions and motives under which he wrought his life-work, — a profound sense of the love and sacrifice of Christ, of the claims of his brother-men on him for the sake of the common Father, and of his own instrumentality as an agent for the accomplishment of God's purposes of love.

It is in these exclusively Christian elements that the great workers of the last eighteen centuries have been of one mind and heart. No matter what their sphere of labor, — whether it is Ambrose, with his own unaided prowess keeping at bay the forces of the empire; or Luther, with the "words that shook the world;" or Oberlin, gathering in the Lord's lost sheep among the mountains; or Howard, sounding the lowest depths of misery in prisons and pest-houses all over Europe; or Wesley, pouring fresh life-blood from Calvary into the desiccated veins of ecclesiastical formalism and indifferentism; or Judson, sacrificing the aims of a towering ambition for toil amidst a thousand deaths, with no forecast glimmering of earthly fame; or Arnold, inaugurating a new era for liberal Christian culture wherever his life-record shall be read; or Florence Nightingale, restoring the order of nobility founded when Jesus washed the feet of his disciples, and carrying off, with her sisterhood of mercy, all the laurels of the last great wars, — wherever we see pre-eminent ability and success in a life-work worth performing, we find but the reproduction of the specifically Christian elements of St. Paul's energy, — a spirit profoundly moved in grateful sympathy with a loving, suffering Redeemer, a strong emotional recognition of human brotherhood, and a merging of self in the sense of a mission and a charge from God. The absence of either of these injures the work, mars its staple, or scants its quantity, and without the first of the three the others are wanting or deficient; for Christ by his sufferings, so far as they are laid hold on with loving faith, reconciles man to man no less than man to God, while it is only in view of his transcendent excellence and his paramount claims upon us that our own selfhood is humbled, our suit for wages cancelled, and we are endowed with the true spirit of service. Accordingly you will find that, when divorced from Christ, even philanthropy grows sour or bitter, or narrow and exclusive, runs in veins, makes distinctions of persons, or else becomes feeble and inane, the heart-work lapsing into mere handwork or tongue-work.

We could ask for no more decisive experimental test of Christianity than this. We would apply it chiefly to such labors as inure to the benefit of humanity. Of reforms which have marked stages of actual and irreversible progress; of institutions for the promotion of human health, comfort, happiness, intelligence, virtue; of propagandisms that have had a single view to the improvement of mankind; of new forms of charity such as spring up with the fresh needs of every age; of lives devoted, in the whole or in great part, to specific labors of love, — how many can you find in the world's history anterior to Christianity? How many can you find since, or now, that may not be placed, without controversy, to the credit of Christianity; that is, of Christians who would disclaim the praise for themselves, and demand it for the Master whom they serve and follow?

I cannot see that infidelity, so far as it has prevailed, has even profited by the example of the magicians of Egypt in the time of Moses, who endeavored to copy the works which they could not rival. It has had its fair opportunity. When it had free scope in France, it left, I think, no vestiges of philanthropy, or even of humanity. Nor in Protestant countries are they who reject Christianity distinguishing themselves by any services that will have their witness on earth and their enduring record in heaven. You have in this city an infidel organization that has its own press, its festivals, its saints' days. There are names which its members love to keep ever green, however remote their fragrance may be from the odor of sanctity. They observe the birthday of Thomas Paine, as you do Christmas. Are they doing any great works in his name? Are they beginning to show, or do they promise to show even in the remote future when they shall have crushed out Christianity, that Antichrist can do more for man than Christ has ever done?

In fine, Christianity has so far manifested its superiority in beneficent action to all the other working forces of the world combined, that the experimental evidence for it under this head is oppressive and unmanageable from its multiplicity and fulness. If you were to take away Christian work and workers from the world, and destroy the vestiges of what has been wrought in Christ's name, I doubt whether those who now reject or despise the Gospel would think the world any longer worth living in.

Christianity claims, also, to afford such support, solace, and peace under trial and grief as can be derived from no other religion or philosophy. We cannot, indeed, ignore the fact that there has been no little brave endurance in which Christianity has borne no part. We cannot forget that Stoicism professed to account calamity, loss, and pain as not in any sense evils, and that among its disciples were illustrious men whose lofty serenity no misfortune could cloud, whose stern courage no suffering could daunt. I will yield to no one in my admiration of the Stoics. Were I parted from Christ, I certainly should fall back into their ranks; for the man-born philosophy of life and duty has not advanced a single step since the era signalized by their most illustrious names. Yet there was in their resignation something grim, fierce, defiant. They yielded to Fate, not to Providence. They had not the alchemy by which to extract good from seeming evil, which, therefore, was only endured by them, not transfigured for and in them. For them, too, there was a limit of endurance, and from evils beyond earthly remedy or hope their philosophy opened for them a lawful escape through suicide. They were, indeed, calm, self-possessed, strong, but not happy, under severe affliction. There is, therefore, in the Christian's joy in tribulation, in the peace clear to his consciousness, yet passing all understanding, during seasons of straitness, grief, and suffering, an element peculiarly his own. The happiest person I ever knew was a widow, who had survived all of a large family of children of beautiful promise, had sunk from an easy competence into utter penury, and had been through declining years of growing infirmity sustained solely by the loving ministry of friends, not one of them of her own kindred. Her last audible words were of gratitude to God for the thick-sown mercies of that widowed, desolate life; and our funeral service for her was one of thanksgiving to God, not that he had taken her out of a world of trial, but that in it he had made her so radiantly happy. This is not a solitary case; were it so, it would have no place here. Every Christian minister has been conversant with like experiences, and we have traced them to their source. It is through the felt sympathy and fellowship of a suffering Saviour, by entering into the spirit of his cross, by making his prayer of resignation their own, and by taking into their hearts the power of his resurrection, that his disciples attain this perfect peace, this consummate gladness of soul. An aged mother once met me with a smile when I went to condole with her on the death of her only son, and her first words were, "I have been like the women at the sepulchre, who said, Who will roll the stone away for us? but when they came to the spot, an angel had removed it for them." Was there not an angel, nay, the Lord of angels, at her side, to strengthen her?

Another contrast presents itself between Stoicism and Christianity. Stoicism was a philosophy in the highest import of the word, attainable only by prolonged mental culture and self-discipline; and it was one of its fundamental tenets that the virtues of ordinary life were only an imperfect semblance of virtue. On the other hand, Christianity proffers its support where there is no other culture than its own mere rudiments, where there is not sufficient grasp of mind to take in its more recondite dogmas, to interpret its more obscure texts, or to comprehend any thing whatever "save Jesus Christ and him crucified." We have witnessed, times without number, the experiment in the simplest form, — the contact of the dying, risen Saviour with the mind that had no other resource; and we have seen that this alone was sufficient for the child, for the slave, for the unlettered and unprivileged, for those who, but for their faith in Christ, would have been among the refuse of society. Such souls it has transformed into kingly spirits that can encounter penury, bereavement, suffering, a life with no sunny side or hopeful aspect, and rise more than conquerors over all. If there be any other religion, philosophy, or culture that can show such trophies, we will then take our stand with those who term Christianity one of the great religions, and name Christ in the same category with the sages of Greece and Rome, Europe and America.

Finally, Christianity claims as its prerogative the victory over death. This, however, it may seem to share; for there have been many calm and brave deaths on which the light of Christian faith has not shone. Yet here there is not so much a resemblance as a contrast. The closing hours of Socrates present, perhaps, the most Christianlike instance of a conscious approach to the margin of the separating stream. Far be it from me to say a word in depreciation of the solemn grandeur of those last communings of the venerable sage with the friends that stood with him on the brink of eternity. Rather let us believe that there were about his soul foregleamings of the Light that was coming into the world, — yet but the dim day-dawn, not the risen or rising sun. Compare his doubtful utterances, as quoted in a former Lecture, his express disclaiming of certainty in a matter necessarily so obscure, with the words of the Christian apostle, "I am now ready to be offered; the time of my departure is at hand; . . . there is laid up for me a crown of righteousness, which the Lord, the righteous Judge, shall give me;" "I know whom I have believed, and am persuaded that he is able to keep that which I have committed unto him."

Then, too, the assurance of Socrates, such as it was, was the result of a life devoted to thought and reasoning, and to daily offices of philosophical teaching. The immeasurably fuller and more elastic assurance of Paul has belonged to multitudes, in every age, of the illiterate, of imperfectly developed minds, of persons who, but for their Christian faith, would have been confessedly among the feeblest members of society. We all know that in death Christ gives the victory to spirits else frail and timid, — that they pass out of the world in the undoubting confidence that they are going but from room to room in their Father's house, — that their only consciousness is that of an eternal life already begun, over which death has no power. In these cases we have again the experiment in its simplest form, — Christ and the soul of man, with no other possible ground of support, source of strength, or object of hope, — with no hoarded resources of philosophical reflection, with no capacity of reasoning on immortality, of throwing out a bridge of speculation and theory over the abyss that yawns before them.

Let us now sum up our argument. Christianity has nurtured every type of goodness, — the tender, the heroic, the philanthropy that has ministered to all forms of social wrong and evil, the compassion that has relieved all descriptions of want and misery, the intrepid courage which has counted life of no worth in comparison with loyalty to the true and the right It has given peace and gladness to unnumbered souls in every form of distress, suffering, bereavement, and desolation. It has inspired an elastic and immortal hope in those who have watched by the death-bed of their best beloved. Its notes of triumph have been rehearsed and echoed by believing souls over the open grave. It has filled the hearts of the dying with solemn joy, and merged the agony of dissolution in the clear vision of an open heaven. These are the highest, the most benignant ministries that have ever been or ever can be rendered to humanity. Christianity has rendered them and is rendering them to thousands upon thousands. It stands alone. No other (so-called) religion, no other type of belief or unbelief, can be brought into momentary comparison with it. Those who have made these experiments testify with one heart and voice to the source of their virtue, their peace, their joy. The greatly good, if crowned, will cast down their crowns before Christ, saying, "Thou alone art worthy." The heavily afflicted have found consolation, because they have trodden the wine-press, not alone, but leaning on the sufferer of Calvary. The dying have looked so steadfastly with the inward eye on the countenance of their risen Lord, that the vision has not infrequently seemed phototyped on the fleshly orb. Are all these successful experiments to pass for nothing, while the commingling of an acid and an alkali shall be vaunted as proclaiming a fundamental law of nature? I believe in the teaching of the acid and the alkali, even though the experiment be but once performed. Shall I, can I, doubt the thousand upon thousand-fold experiment of the commingling — with gracious and glorious issues, indicating eternal laws of the spiritual world — of the life and soul of Jesus Christ with the life and soul of his disciple?

LECTURE IX.

CHRISTIANITY AS A RENOVATING POWER IN HUMAN SOCIETY. — WHAT IT PROMISES TO ACCOMPLISH. — ITS RAPID PROGRESS IN THE FIRST CHRISTIAN CENTURIES. — INFLUENCES OPPOSED TO IT. — ITS POWER OVER PUBLIC SENTIMENT. — ITS AGENCY IN DOMESTIC LIFE. — AS REGARDS SLAVERY. — IN THE THEORY AND PRACTICE OF GOVERNMENT. — IN THE RELIEF OF HUMAN WANT AND SUFFERING. — NO OTHER RELIGION TO BE COMPARED WITH IT.

IN my last Lecture I exhibited the results of individual experiment or experience with regard to Christianity. These might be decisive as to the pre-eminent worth of the religion, even were the instances in which it has done its full work very few. Indeed, the argument from experiment was never felt with more force than in the apostolic age, when the Christian type of character had very few specimens, yet was both attractive from its novelty, and peculiarly Christlike from the personal intimacy of those who bore it with Jesus. But the efficacy of Christianity can be thoroughly tested only by ascertaining what it has done for society, communities, nations, the human race. It is not, however, incumbent upon us to show that it has effected all that we might antecedently have expected from a divinely promulgated religion. This is a matter in which we have no data or precedents by which to graduate our expectations. Our short lives may make the cycles of the Divine Providence seem slow and long. The two questions which we need to answer with regard to Christianity are: 1. Has it done for man all that its Founder promised? and 2. Has any other religion done as much for man, or even placed itself in this respect in favorable comparison with Christianity?

We will first inquire, Has Christianity done for man all that its Founder promised? He predicted that it would be early preached throughout the then known world; that its growth at the outset would be rapid; that it would encounter the severest persecution and the most strenuous antagonism; that its immediate effect would be to send not peace, but a sword upon the earth; that it would not lead to the establishment of a theocracy, or to the separation of his disciples from the rest of mankind, but that Christians and non-Christians would remain side by side, as wheat and tares in a field; that, however, his religion would gradually modify existing institutions and habits, without external show, by a quiet interior working, like that of the leaven in the mass of moistened meal, thus making all things new, not by sudden revolution, but by slow and often insensible stages of progress. Let us see how far these predictions have been fulfilled.

The early growth of Christianity is without precedent or parallel in human history. Within a century after its Founder's death it had been received by multitudes in every region of the then civilized world, and had made numerous disciples in those great eastern empires that lay wholly beyond the reach of Grecian and Roman culture. Within two centuries there was more of learning and philosophy in the Church than outside of it; in Alexandria, which had supplanted Athens as the world's centre of erudition, almost all the distinguished scholars were Christians; and the Platonic philosophy, especially, had scarcely any but Christians among its eminent disciples, while it had furnished not a few of the Christian martyrs. Within three centuries, Christianity had mounted the throne of the Cæsars; the cross had become the proudest ensign of power and state; and the idolatry whose shattered temples and statues in Athens and Rome modern art may copy, but can never equal, had become literally Paganism, and — though at uncertain intervals stimulated into a brief revival in the Italian cities — had for the most part only obscure *pagans* or villagers for its votaries. Of the ten successive persecutions enumerated by ecclesiastical historians of the old school, the greater part were wars of extermination, waged with the whole force of the empire against the new faith; yet the agents of the imperial power had such success in extinguishing Christianity as a little group of emigrants might hope to have in trampling out the fire in a burning prairie.

Christianity in its progress had to contend with religions which had their roots in immemorial antiquity, were intertwined with the whole fabric of society, were intimately associated with domestic and civic life, and were made beautiful and glorious by the highest art and the most finished literature to which human genius has given birth.

Still more hopeless seemed the conflict of Christianity with the grossest moral corruption. Art and poetry, music and song, had become the satellites of vice. Philosophy — with exceptions, illustrious, indeed, but few — had relaxed her stern features, and under the broad charter of Epicureanism smiled on excess and licentiousness, and employed all her acumen in seeking paths to happiness that might not trespass on the confines of virtue. Gross sensuality was less the recreation than the business, aim, and end, of large numbers who occupied the highest places in station, wealth, and culture. The only public amusements were such as ministered to the coarsest and vilest passions, — the contests of wild beasts, the deadly combats of gladiators, the tearing of criminals limb from limb in the amphitheatre, the representation of all that was most foul and obscene in comedy. Vices that have no longer a name among men were glorified in ode and epigram, and sanctioned by the example of the so-called guardians of the public virtue.

Under all these unprop'tious influences, Christianity seemed placed at the greater disadvantage by the obscurity of its Founder and his associates. He, born in a manger, reared in a despised village, bearing the reproachful name of a Galilean, often houseless and destitute, the companion of humble fishermen;

the eleven who took up the standard of the infant faith when it dropped from his hands, illiterate, inexperienced, unhonored men, re-enforced in the early stages of their work by but one associate of large attainments and masterly ability, and that one bearing the stigma — degrading everywhere out of Palestine — of Jewish parentage,— these are the destined creators of a new era, and founders of a spiritual sovereignty to which supreme earthly power shall own allegiance. These disciples, ignorant of every language but their own native *patois* of Hebrew alloyed with Chaldee, and a rude Greek bristling with strange Hebrew idioms, are to proclaim the Gospel throughout and beyond the Roman empire. Unskilled in rhetorical arts, they are to persuade those familiar with the traditions and successors of Cicero and Hortensius. Unpractised in logic, they are to dispute in the schools of philosophers. They are to go, not to corners and by-places, but to the radiating centres of civilization and culture, interpreting the Unknown God among the monuments of Athenian genius, preaching the self-denying and hardy virtues in luxurious and effeminate Corinth, teaching the empress city of the world to bow to the sceptre of the King of kings.

With all these opposing influences and unfavorable circumstances, the progress, nay, the continued existence of Christianity is the miracle of the ages. If the religion was man-devised and earth-born, its surviving the crucifixion of its Founder was intrinsically less probable and credible than the rising of

Lazarus from his four days' death slumber. The early history of Christianity, however, accords in this respect with the predictions of Christ; and — what is more to our present purpose — it furnishes an experimental evidence of its capacity for extended propagation, that is, of its fitness to meet the varying demands, conditions, and needs of universal humanity, — a fitness of which it is now giving proof, as in primitive times, by the revival in our own century of the missionary spirit, and by the eminent success of Christian propagandism among races debased by centuries of barbarous or savage life, and in their obdurate stupidity presenting a far less inviting soil for spiritual tilth than the fields so promptly made white for the harvest in the time of the apostles.

But what has Christianity done for the world? Wherein is modern Christian civilization in advance of the old Greek and Roman civilization which it superseded? It must be admitted that the outward transformation of society has been far less radical and thorough than a Christian optimist of the first century would have anticipated. The vision of the seer of the Apocalypse, to whose prophetic eye the ages seem to have been foreshortened, and the far-off future to have looked very near, is immeasurably more remote now than it was in his view. Yet there are many aspects in which old things have passed away, and all things have become new.

In the first place, the greatest of all transformations may be marked in the relation borne by vice and sin to public opinion. There are many respects in which portions of Christendom are hardly less corrupt than was the Gentile world in the time of Christ. But moral evil is now nowhere beheld with complacency and approval. Undoubtedly there is in circulation now as vile literature as the foulest passages in Horace, Ovid, Catullus, or Martial; but, if so, it is to be found only in the slums and sewers of society, while their poems were dedicated to emperors and courtiers, were in the hands of the most refined and cultivated persons, and were in harmony with the purest taste of their times. Naples is believed by those conversant with its lowest depths to be hardly less depraved than when it was the second Corinth, only coarser, but not less dissolute than its antetype. But the excavations in Pompeii show that what is now secret and under the ban of the Church and the law, was then paraded everywhere; so that homes, places of public concourse, and even temples, must have been nurseries of the vilest licentiousness, and Sodom can hardly have invited her doom by a more utter destitution of the semblance of virtue than did the cities — suburbs and imitators of Naples — that were buried under the ashes of Vesuvius. In our own country, venality, bribery, peculation, defalcation, and corruption, on the part of men in office, trust, power, and high position, could hardly find more than their parallel in the worst days of Rome; Verres might seem to have been the patron saint of large numbers of our commissaries, Indian agents, and revenue detectives; and no pro-consul can have been more rapacious than some of our public men who exercised proconsular jurisdiction in our southern cities during the late rebellion. But before Christ there was no sensitiveness of the public conscience on these matters. Thus it was long the recognized usage in Rome for an edile to incur enormous debts in furnishing public shows and entertainments, with the understanding that he was to reimburse himself by the spoils of the province which in due course of time would fall to his administration ; and it is reckoned as among Cicero's special titles to honor and admiration — a solitary distinction — that, when he had the government of a province, he committed neither theft nor robbery. Cicero, who, so far as I can remember, does not in his ethical treatises pass in a single instance a favorable judgment on an immoral act, tells the story of the two foremost citizens of Rome, men of high reputation, openly receiving legacies by a will which every one knew to be forged, as retaining-fees for their declining to advocate the cause of the rightful heir. He cites, as a case in which even Stoic moralists were divided in opinion, the question, whether if a wise man — that is, a truly virtuous man — had ignorantly received counterfeit money, he may knowingly use it in the payment of his debts. You cannot now find the man who approves theft or fraud of any kind, or will dare to defend or excuse it. The men who are false to their trusts may cover up or deny their offences, and may, by corrupt means, retain and extend the power they abuse ; but they could not stand a single day in face of the clear proof of their guilt. The Crédit Mobilier would not have been out of keeping with the best usage in Rome. Here it has driven its detected accomplices, in spite of undoubted public services and high religious pretensions, into the grave, or a living death of enduring ignominy. The case is the same throughout Christendom with every form of vice or crime. No one ventures to approve it. No one is bold enough to apologize for it. However it may abound and run riot, its actors and abettors are ashamed of it. Were they, in conclave, to construct a code of morals from their own sincere conviction and belief, it would be a Christian code. We have here, assuredly, an immense gain, in the conversion of the public conscience, in the establishing of a Nemesis in the individual consciences of evil-doers. Jesus has, at least, produced a conviction of sin, a pervading sense of right, and a rectitude of moral judgment, of which, before his time, we have but few traces.

We will next consider the agency of Christianity in domestic life. At the Christian era, the conjugal relation, whose stability is the sole safeguard for the peace and well-being of the family, was held in reverence nowhere in the civilized world. Divorce, in theory justifiable on the slightest grounds, was facilitated by law, sanctioned by custom, and held blameless in the best public opinion. In Judæa, the Mosaic law, which, in the ages when writing was a rare accomplishment, interposed serious difficulties by requiring the malecontent husband to furnish the wife with a legal document, had ceased to operate as a check. In Athens, there was not only liberty of divorce without cause, but the husband had a legal right to sell his wife into second nuptials to which she was not a consenting party; and, in case a father died, leaving no children except a married daughter, the nearest kinsman of his name could legally dissolve her marriage and make her his own wife. In Rome, men and women alike exercised the legal right of divorce, with a sole view to new marriages; and there were women of illustrious rank who, as Seneca says, reckoned the years not by consuls, but by husbands, divorced to marry, married to divorce. The malign associations connected with the term *noverca* (stepmother) of which the literature of the Augustan age furnishes numerous instances, grew not from that office legitimately assumed, but from the frequency with which an artful and intriguing woman contrived to supplant the mother of the family, and of course could hardly have any other relations with that mother's children than those of mutual distrust, suspicion, and hatred.* Under such a domestic regime, there was, of necessity, no home-culture for the children; nor was even home-love able to survive the wrenches and outrages to which it was perpetually doomed. The mother was liable to be separated for ever from her children before they could know the preciousness of her love, and it was the prime endeavor of her rival and successor to supersede them in their father's affection for the benefit of her own children. We have abundant evidence that in the richer families children were left till adult years

* See Appendix, note N.

almost entirely to the care and training of slaves, without even the pretence of parental supervision.

The primitive power of life and death over the child, though not legally repealed, had fallen into disuse, in consequence, less of growing refinement, than of the massing of powers that had been distributed into the more and more autocratic sway of the emperor: yet still there seems to have been not a little of tolerated, nay, legalized infanticide in the case of feeble or sickly children, and of those whom it was inconvenient to bring up; a license claimed by Plato, sanctioned by Aristotle, and, so far as I know, accepted without contradiction in all classic antiquity. St. Paul, in his Epistle to the Romans, speaks of the Gentile world in general as "without natural affection." How far this applied to the Roman people of his time we may learn from the frequency with which the property of fathers was wholly diverted from their children, through the devices of stepmothers, the intrigues of legacy-hunters, and the adoption of children from motives of interest or ambition that have no parallel in modern society. Nor yet could the son acquire any thing of his own, or dispose of the earnings of his own industry, with the single exception that under Augustus the wages of sons that served in the army were decreed to be their own property; this, however, not on the score of right and justice, but to facilitate the recruiting of the military service with native citizens.*

This cursory sketch of the condition of home-life under

* See Appendix, note O.

the ancient civilization may account for the absence of any word corresponding to *home* in the classic languages, and for the plural form, *ædes*, in which a house is commonly designated in the Latin ; for the house consisted of a quadrangle of apartments, with separate entrances from the central court common to all, and there was no sentiment of family union to unify in thought and speech the several portions of the domicile.

We have seen what the family was when Christ came into the world. He re-established the family by pronouncing the marriage covenant sacred and inviolable. Under his auspices it at once became a religious bond, sanctioned by prayer and by the emblems of the redemption-sacrifice. Tertullian, the earliest of the Latin fathers, writes: "The Church prescribes the contract; holy rites confirm it ; the benediction seals it ; God ratifies it. The believing husband and wife bear the same yoke: they are of one mind; they pray together; they fast together; they are together in worship, at the Lord's table, in adversity and in prosperity. Divorce is now prohibited ; for what God has joined man shall not separate, lest he sin against God. He who has joined alone shall separate." Thus, so fast as Christianity was diffused, chaste and permanent homes, with their shelter, nurture, and love, everywhere grew into being. Constantine, though himself probably not very profoundly penetrated with the spirit of Christianity, was, nevertheless, greatly under the influence of the clergy; and, in every feature of his reformatory legislation, we trace their hand and the hand of the Master whom they served. He, by his imperial edict, brought the liberty of divorce within restrictions almost as narrow as those of the Gospel rule, extending the license beyond that limit only to cases in which the accused party had been guilty of homicide, sorcery, or the violation of sepulchres. In this direction legislation rapidly grew more and more rigid, until the one crime which is in itself divorce became the only recognized ground for it.*

In behalf of children legislation equally followed the leading of Christian sentiment, and gave form and body to its spirit. Constantine, in one of his earliest edicts after his so-called conversion, for the purpose, as he said, of preventing infanticide, provided for the feeding and clothing of the children of destitute parents from the public treasury. At nearly the same time, he secured for the benefit of adult children the income of various offices and professions in both Church and State, equally with the wages of military service. The succeeding Christian emperors vindicated still farther the rights of children, though the very religion which inspired their edicts made them no longer necessary;† for the hearts of the fathers were now turned to the children, and of the children to the fathers, so that from that age onward the cases of parental oppression and injustice, whether in life or by will, before normal, have been so rare and exceptional as to arrest general attention and to call forth emphatic condemnation.

* See Appendix, note P. † See Appendix, note Q.

From these beginnings sprang the domestic life of modern Christendom, — indissoluble marriage the corner-stone of the edifice, the basis of all the institutions and customs, amenities and endearments, that make ordinary homes peaceful and loving, truly Christian homes types of the family unions in heaven. It is worthy of remark that the marriage institution has been assailed in our own time by the very men, women, and classes of people who profess to have outgrown Christianity; that among these the more advanced, as they term themselves, would retrograde to the condition of things in the most licentious days of Athens and of Rome; and that such modifications of the gospel law of divorce — till of late universal in Christendom — as have been made in this country and in Europe have been resolutely opposed at every stage by the Church, and carried through under the disapproval and protest of its loyal ministers and members.

I am aware that it is sometimes said that civilized Europe owes the purity and sacredness of home relations to the irruption of the Northern tribes into Gaul and Italy, and that the rudiments of the Christian home are to be found in the *Germania* of Tacitus. I would reply, first, that the Roman home-life in the best days of the republic was equally pure with that of the Germans at the Christian era, and this, because, in either case, idleness and luxury had not engendered vice; secondly, that the domestic revolution had become co-extensive with Christianity before the German element had modified the institutions of southern Europe; thirdly, that the description of Tacitus was very far from being applicable to the Goths, Huns, and Vandals, who were among the chief agents in the destruction of the Western Empire; and, fourthly, that the influence of Christianity on men's home relations may be traced as clearly in those of the southern nations that never had any considerable northern admixture, as in those stocks which became transformed by northern grafts.

Homes worthy of the name are, then, among the gifts of Christianity, and the contrast of modern with ancient civilization in this regard is of itself sufficient to place Christianity foremost among the beneficent forces that have acted on human society.

The work which Christianity has done in the amelioration and abolition of slavery constitutes another of the experimental proofs of its efficacy. In all antiquity, so far as we know, domestic slavery existed as if by a necessity or law of human nature, without rebuke or question even from the severest moralists. The lapse of a free man into slavery, in consequence of debt, captivity, or conquest, was very easy; and as the slave was often of the same or an equal race with his master, or even his superior, as in the case of the numerous Greek slaves in Rome, the social wrong, though not one whit more utterly unjustifiable, must have been more galling and depressing than when the enslaved are of an inferior race. In Rome, by a law of the Twelve Tables, a debtor who remained insolvent after an imprisonment of sixty days, might either be sold into slavery, or killed and his body divided among his creditors. In many communities the slaves largely outnumbered the free population. In Athens there were at one time twenty-one thousand citizens and four hundred thousand slaves. In the little island of Ægina there were four hundred and seventy thousand slaves. Single citizens of Rome sometimes owned from ten to twenty thousand.

Slaves in the Roman Empire had no legal rights, not even the right to life, and no mode of redress for injury. Their evidence was never taken except by torture. If a master was murdered by an unknown person, it was not unusual to put to death all his slaves, even to the number of several thousands ; and slaves were not infrequently set up as targets for the fatal archery of the master and his guests, or thrown into the fish-pond to improve the flavor of the lampreys, or put to death to test some novel weapon or mode of slaying, or killed in the wantonness of drunken sport, or crucified for breaking a vase, or dropping a turbot on its way to the table, or mistaking an order of the most trivial import.

Christ and his apostles made no violent onslaught on slavery : if they had, it would have been of no avail. But they recognized the slave's equal humanity with his master, his equal position before God, his equal privileges under the Gospel. Paul sends the fugitive Onesimus home to Philemon, no longer as a slave, but as a brother beloved, and enjoins it upon Philemon in the name of all that is sacred thus to receive him. Masters are reminded that with their Master in heaven there is no respect of persons, and, as in his sight, are bidden to render justice and equity to their slaves.

Accordingly, from the Epistle to Philemon all through the early Christian centuries, among the many historical references — direct and incidental — to slavery, there is not one in which the Church does not show herself the friend of the slave. The Church never admitted the distinction between bond and free as creating any difference under her jurisdiction. Quite a considerable number of the martyrs, held from the first in the highest reverence, and among the earliest canonized, were slaves. Slaves and their children were trained and ordained for offices in the Church, and not a few of the bishops came from the servile rank. The emancipation of slaves was represented as among the most Christian works that could be performed ; the business was conducted and registered in the church or through its officials ; and, after Sunday began to be observed by the suspension of secular labor, this alone, of all kinds of business, was deemed fit to be done on Sunday. Slaves that anyhow became the property of particular churches were almost invariably set free, and it was early regarded as damaging to the character of an ecclesiastic that he should remain a slaveholder.

With and after Constantine, the law kept even pace with this growth of Christian opinion and feeling. An edict of Constantine first made the killing of a slave criminal homicide ; and this edict has a painful historical value in enumerating, as punishable, various most horrible ways of putting slaves to death ; which, of course, would not have been named had they not been practised. Thenceonward there was an unbroken series of enactments, relieving slaves from disabilities, augmenting their rights, and encouraging their emancipation ; till at length, in the twelfth century, at the very climax of the power of the Church, there remained not a vestige of domestic slavery in Christendom.*

To the shame of modern Christianity, slavery reappeared in our western world ; but it would never have survived the initial enterprise, had the arm of the Church been long enough to reach it across the intervening ocean. It had grown with amazing rapidity into a giant wrong and sin before Christian sentiment could be organized and combined in opposition to it. On its own soil it contrived to bribe or awe into silence the feebler and less loyal officials of the Church, and to drive away or keep away those who would have declared their Lord's whole counsel. Yet there never was a time when large numbers and large bodies of Christians did not in the name of Christ denounce slavery and disclaim all fellowship with its abettors ; and, from all Christian organizations that remained quiescent, there were numerous secessions of earnest and devout men and women, who raised a revolt against the Church in the name of its Lord and Master. At length the burden of guilt which Christian Europe had thrown off long before she knew America has been lifted from this western world by the overmastering might of Christian sentiment, with the entire force of interest, policy, inveterate prejudice, and political time-serving

* See Appendix, note Q.

arrayed against it. We cannot believe that the work will ever need to be done again; and, in this final abolition of slavery, Christianity has been nothing less than revolutionary, annulling a class distinction between human owners and human chattels which had existed from the very earliest stages of society that have left any vestiges of their history.

An equally entire revolution has taken place in the theory, and to a large degree in the practice, of government. Said Jesus, "Among the nations the princes exercise dominion over them, and they that are great exercise authority upon them. But among you, whosoever will be great, let him be your minister; and whosoever will be chief among you, let him be your servant; even as the Son of Man came not to be ministered unto, but to minister." The idea of government implied in these words does not seem to have entered into the thought of the ancient world. There were, indeed, humane and beneficent rulers; but they were not so *ex officio*, if I may use the phrase, — by virtue of their position, and as fulfilling the only condition on which they could rightfully hold their places. Power, in the single or multiform head of a nation, had its rights, but not its commensurate obligations. There was, indeed, an excess of tyranny which a people of spirit would not endure; but that within certain limits the ruler should accumulate treasures for his own sole benefit, wage war for his own sole glory, and conduct his administration for ends in the main self-centred, was precisely what was expected, and deemed entirely legitimate. Now it must be admitted that there are in ancient history few more atrocious specimens of unprincipled, selfish, and brutal despotism than have been exhibited in modern Europe, and, in the kingdom of the Two Sicilies at least, almost to the present day. Yet you will at this moment find it to be the universal opinion in Christendom, that government has a right to exist only for the sake of the governed; that the selfish exercise of power is an abuse of power; that hereditary rights, where they are recognized, are justified only by the necessities of civic and social order, and that they impose charges and services for the body-politic fully equal to the privileges which they confer. At the present time it is the most absolute governments that are the most paternal; it is the most highly privileged aristocracies that are doing the most for their fellow-countrymen and for humanity; many of those who hold chief places in the state acting under the immediate influence of the evangelic principle, that rank and authority can be rightfully held only for purposes of service; and others fully aware that this sentiment is so widely diffused that they can ignore it only to their own ruin. Strange to say, there is more of the old heathen notion of irresponsible right, and less of the spirit of service, in the officials of our own country than in those of any other country in Christendom; but, because we have retroceded from the days when our great men were our chief servants, we should not blind ourselves to the approach of the whole sisterhood of nations to the ground which it is our honor to have been the first to occupy, our burning shame to have yielded.

I have not time to enter fully into the various other aspects in which Christianity has shown itself a transforming and renovating power. But there is one of its benign ministries, so manifest that only he who was blind at noonday could overlook it, and so familiarly known as to need no long or labored exposition. I refer to the various forms of public, social, collective, institutional charity. These are all of Christian origin. There was, undoubtedly, almsgiving, kindness, generosity, among the ancients of classic history, still more among the Hebrews, whose poor-laws — at the Christian era obsolete — are redolent of a more than human wisdom and love; but when Christ came, there was no organized provision for wants, needs, or infirmities of any description; no plan by which the benefactions or services of the rich or the able could be combined and systematized for the benefit of the poor or the suffering. The nearest approach to such charities was the distribution of wheat among the Roman populace at the charge of the public treasury, and the largesses given to the people by aspirants for their favor. These, however, were not regarded as charitable donatives; but the former as the means of keeping the mob quiet, the latter as an outlay to be remunerated ten times over when the votes thus purchased should place the plunder of a province at the candidate's disposal. But no sooner was the Christian Church gathered than the poor became its care. The primitive deacons were the first official guardians of the poor of whom history gives us knowledge. The earliest systematic contribution for the relief of the needy was that taken up in the churches out of Palestine for the sufferers by famine in and about Jerusalem. We cannot go back to a time when almsgiving was not so essential a part of the service of the eucharist, that, with the reserved portions of the sacred elements carried by the deacons to all who were necessarily absent, substantial supplies from the offertory were bestowed upon the needy. Particular types of calamity and suffering had appropriate provision made for them. The sick, especially the lepers, were sedulously cared for; large sums were raised for the redemption of captives; orphan children became everywhere the children of the Church; strangers, for whom and enemies there had been one and the same name, were now honored guests for the sake of him who owns, as rendered to himself, every generous service and kind office in the name of a common humanity. Even in what are called the dark ages, though many lesser lights were veiled, the lamp of charity suffered no eclipse; and Christendom emerged from those misnamed centuries, with an apparatus of relief for want and misery, considered with reference to the condition and habits of those times, hardly less efficient than our present modes of philanthropic ministration.

To come down to our own day, when we consider the endless diversity and vast multitude of institutions and appliances for charitable ends of every description; the immense number of liberal givers and self-devoting workers; the still greater number of those who, like the widow at the temple, contribute from their poverty to the Lord's treasury; and the uniform proportion borne by the sincerity and fervor of Christian faith and piety to the promptness and fulness of offerings and services, — we have but a repetition, magnified and multiplied a thousandfold, of the answer of Jesus to John's question, "Art thou he that should come, or look we for another"?

I named a second question as belonging to the subject of this Lecture, — Has any other religion done as much for man as Christianity has, or even placed itself in this respect in favorable comparison with Christianity? I do not believe that there is any need of adding a word to the monosyllabic answer, No. Certainly there is no one of the particulars that have been named, in which Mohammedanism or Buddhism can be even alleged to have had an equally or similarly renovating and benignant influence; and we know of no other religions which it would not be irrelevant to name in such a connection.

Christianity, then, has done for man what it promised to do through the lips and pens of its Author and his apostles, and it has performed for man such services as no other religion has begun or pretended to render. It has thus, on an extended scale, as in its action on individual character, sustained the test of experiment. It has shown itself as from God by doing the works of God. It has attested its divinity by the very marks and tokens which on *à priori* grounds we should expect a divine religion to exhibit. It has proved its heavenly birth by its heavenly gifts and ministries to man.

Experiment thus confirms testimony, and gives us added assurance that we are not following cunningly devised fables when we own in Jesus Christ the Son of God and the Saviour of the world.

LECTURE X.

III. INTUITION. — SCIENTIFIC INTUITION. — CHRISTIAN INTUITION. — INTUITION DEFINED. — OBJECTIVE INTUITION. — SUBJECTIVE INTUITION OF CHRISTIAN ETHICS. — OF TRUTHS APPERTAINING TO GOD. — OF TRUTHS APPERTAINING TO CHRIST. — EVIDENTIAL VALUE OF INTUITION. — SUMMARY.

I PROPOSE this evening to compare the evidence of intuition for the ultimate and fundamental truths of science with the evidence for the alleged truths of Christianity derived from the same source.

Intuition is the last test of science. When facts and phenomena have been duly collated, when experiments have been fully made, when partial inductions have been generalized, and a law or principle of extended application has been reached, it seems to the scientific man a necessary truth. He sees, not only that it is, but that it must be. It becomes self-evident, and forms thenceforward a part of his scientific consciousness. No universal scientific truth is fully established, until it is thus intuitively recognized as, of *a priori* necessity, appertaining to the department of science which it defines and comprehends.

A like intuition the Christian possesses as the result of his experience. He may at the outset rest for his belief mainly on testimony; he may enter on a series of experiments in Christian living with faith rather than with knowledge: but, if he is true to his own soul, the time comes when he sees and knows from his own spiritual intuitions the verities of his religion; the excellence of its precepts; the beauty, holiness, loveliness, power of its Author. There is a stage at which argument or cavil may impair or overthrow his belief. There is a stage at which the truths of Christianity and the divine attributes of its Founder have so become a part of his own consciousness, that no force of reasoning can by any possibility dislodge them. Here, for instance, is a lone widow, who has been a mark for all the shafts of adverse fortune. Poor, infirm, lowly in estate, she has no treasure but her Bible, no hope but in its promises, no fountain of joy but that which flows "fast by the oracles of God." Yet she has a peace more profound, a joy more intense, than worlds could give. Her soul is a living transcript of the evangelic record. Her prayer is not the groping after an unknown God, but, as it were, a face-to-face communion. Her heaven is not in the far-off future, but in her own beatific experience. She has realized the promises. She has entered into the rest that remaineth for the people of God. Ply her with all the infidel arguments that have been started from the days of Celsus to the present moment, you cannot ruffle for an instant the serenity of her faith and trust. She knows whom she has believed. His life throbs in her veins. His words are strung in the living fibres of her whole being. She feels herself transformed into his image, — a member of his body ; and who shall separate her from the love of Christ? Now this intuitive knowledge of Christianity has been possessed by thousands for every one who has intuitive knowledge of scientific truths.

It is, moreover, the prerogative of Christianity over all other religions that its alleged truths can thus become intuitions. There could have been no intuition of the ceremonial law, which forms an essential part of Judaism. There can be no intuition of the vagaries of the Koran, of the avatars of the Hindoo mythology, of the chimæras of Buddhism. But there is not a (so-called) truth of Christianity, which, if true, is not of such a nature that it may, in some form or measure, enter into the consciousness, and thus rest on the same evidence on which we believe in our own existence. This statement cannot indeed be made as to the individual facts of the biography of Christ, nor yet as to the objective side of certain Christian doctrines: but the facts of Christ's life are mere tokens of and pointers to the spiritual relations in which he professes to stand to the individual soul, as a sure guide, as a safe exemplar, as an infallible teacher, as an all-sufficient Saviour, and these relations, if real, may all become subjects of consciousness; while of the doctrines of Christianity there is not one which is simply and solely objective.

Let us not, however, content ourselves with general statements. Let us see what intuition comprehends, and how far, or under what conditions, it is availing as a source of evidence.

Intuition is inlooking. It is intellectual perception.

It is that apprehension of the truth which comes not from reasoning or proof, but from the nature of the case, from the nature of our own minds, or both. What we perceive intuitively shines either in its own light, or in light which we ourselves cast upon it. It either is self-evident, or it has the attestation of our own consciousness, and needs no other proof.

Intuition may thus be either objective or subjective. We may either so look into the object-matter of our thought or inquiry as to see in it that which could not but have been, — that which, once apprehended, is its own sufficient evidence; or we may so look in upon our remembered and current experience as to recognize in it truths so manifest as to need no other proof than that of consciousness. Objective intuition has its chief scope in the mathematical and physical sciences; subjective, in mental and moral philosophy. Both objective and subjective are claimed in behalf of Christianity.

I will first speak of objective intuition. Christianity alone gives us a tenable theory of the universe. Independently of revelation, there are in the universe unmistakable and innumerable tokens of design, and thus of an intelligent Creator; of beneficent design, and thus of a merciful Creator. There are, in every department of nature, not chance coincidences, but organisms, processes, and products, which are manifestly adapted to the enjoyment of man and of other sentient beings, and which can have no other destination, can serve no other purpose. There are, on the other hand, no organisms, processes, or products, of which the necessary and inevitable tendency is the creation of pain, grief, or misery; but in the course of events physical evil is incidental, or subsidiary to greater good; its agencies, such as may be evaded, controlled, neutralized, often transformed and utilized, so that in proportion to the growth of man's intelligence they become subject to his command, and constantly tend to disappear. Man's own native powers of mind and soul, in their normal exercise, in the only exercise of them which the developed intellect can approve, tend to his self-respect, his growth in intelligence and capacity, and his enduring happiness. There is, however, in human society, and there has been in all past ages, an overwhelming amount of degradation and misery, almost all of which is visibly due to the depraved will of man. To this are chargeable, not only the immediate consequences of vice and sin, but as surely, though less directly, by far the larger part of the poverty, hardship, and physical infirmity and suffering in the world; for in a community of saints there would be no abject want, no social oppression or depression, and probably an ever-diminishing heritage of bodily disease and pain.

That a beneficent Creator should suffer this deteriorated condition of what is in potential capacity his noblest work upon earth to remain uncared for, is inconceivable. That he should provide in man and around him all possible powers of and materials for happiness, and yet leave him to make himself vile, and to bequeath from generation to generation, to the end of time, an accumulating burden of depravity and misery, would imply either a lack of power, which cannot be in him whose Omnipotence has its record in the vastness, order, and harmony of creation; or a lack of love, which cannot be in him whose tender mercy is manifested in every realm, nay, in every nook, cranny, and crevice of the universe, which is not perverted or made unfruitful by human guilt. Free agency, which is essential to man's highest dignity and happiness, may, indeed, in the nature of things have rendered his fall and guilt inevitable, notwithstanding the infinite goodness of God; and it may be of inestimable benefit to the race as a whole that man should have been left in the earlier stages of his history to solve all great moral problems by a sad experience, which, we believe, is to have immeasurably more than its counterpart in the ultimate reign of righteousness. But we should antecedently expect to find in the divine economy the antidote and remedy for moral evil. This antidote, this remedy, can consist only in God's revelation of his being and will; in the establishing on the earth of a regenerating agency; in the forgiveness of sins repented and forsaken; in help for those who seek to be delivered from inherited or acquired proclivity to evil; in a power of amelioration and progress for the race in this world; and in a state of being in which human virtue, at best imperfect and inchoate here, yet capable of indefinite growth, may have its full consummation. In Christianity, and nowhere else, we have precisely what might have been thus anticipated. We have a revelation of God in the person of Christ, of the law of God in his precepts and his life; a regenerating power in his whole earthly ministry; the forgiveness of sins in his cross and sacrifice; help for our infirmities in the Holy Spirit, proceeding from the Father and the Son in accordance with his promise; a power of progress in his everlasting Gospel; eternal life made manifest in his resurrection. Moreover, by his emphatic recognition of the Hebrew Scriptures as authentic, we learn that God had never "left himself without witness" in the world; that primeval revelation preceded even man's first transgression; that the knowledge of divine things, given to man, was lost by man; that this knowledge was at intervals renewed, only to be circumscribed and obscured by the depraved wills of those on whom it was bestowed; and thus that Christ came, not after ages in which God had abandoned men wholly to their own evil devices, but as the supreme term of a culminating series of interpositions on his part for the relief, reformation, and spiritual training of his human family.

We thus, and thus only, can reconcile the history of man with the being, omnipotence, and infinite love of God. We thus, and thus only, have a rational and consistent theory of the universe, — a God who has never forsaken his own work; a free agency whose proclivity to evil has never been left without check or remedy; a redemption and everlasting salvation for all who, under whatever culture, are faithful to such light as they have received and such law as they know; a provision by which, without annulling human freedom, sin is to be purged away, the right to culminate, and the reign of God to be ultimately established in the realm of living souls no less than in outward nature. The system is coherent and complete. It satisfies, if I may so speak, the scientific consciousness. To the Christian it not only seems to be true, but he cannot conceive of its not being true. It comes to him through what he receives as the record of divine revelation; but it justifies itself,—it is its own evidence. Still more, it adds confirmation to the very record from which it is derived. We are certain, from such evidence as has been presented in former Lectures, that the Gospels are genuine and authentic; but evidence of a different and even higher type is furnished by the coherence of their contents among themselves, and with what beside is known of God and man. I say, evidence of a higher, not a surer type: for testimony may be—and is, as I have attempted to show you in this matter—sufficiently multiform, explicit, and strong, to produce absolute certainty of conviction; yet there is a more vivid and realizing sense of the veracity of the sacred records, when their contents thus present intrinsic tokens of their truth. While testimony prepares the way for intuition, intuition calls forth the testimony of our own apprehensive powers to supplement the witnesses from without,—indeed, transfers us from the number of those who depend on testimony to the list of those who themselves bear testimony.

We pass now to subjective intuition, or the evidence of Christian consciousness. As I have said, there is no alleged truth of Christianity which may not be tried by this test, and in behalf of which this evidence is not claimed. Such is the case, in the first place, with the ethics of the Gospel. There were in the Sermon on the Mount and in various other portions of the teachings of Christ not a few things so entirely opposed to the mind, voice, and practice of antiquity, as to have made a hard strain upon the faith even of the most docile hearers. It is worthy of remark that it was not any dogmatic statement, but the command to forgive an offending brother seven times in a day, that called forth the exclamation from the disciples, "Lord, increase our faith," — forbearance that could not be wearied out by pertinacity in wrong-doing seemed to them so utterly unreasonable and impossible. Indeed, had not their Master embodied his precept in his life, and reenacted it on the cross in the prayer for his murderers, it may be doubted whether his followers would ever have had faith enough to make experiment of it. But no one has made trial of it, and persevered in so doing, who has not been profoundly conscious of its divine excellence; for it has been as proof-armor to the soul against all assaults from without; it has blunted the keenest weapons of calumny and malevolence; it has kept the spirit in sweet serenity under insult, provocation, and violence, and has made it more than conqueror in its conflicts with evil.

Similar has been uniform Christian experience as to the seeming paradox that "it is more blessed to give than to receive." The imperial glutton craved a hundred palates, that he might multiply indefinitely the coarse indulgence of the table. His brutal wish is the type of what has been enjoyed by those who have followed their Master as he went about doing good. They have inwardly fed at every table that they have spread for the needy. They have drunk living waters from every fountain and rivulet of charity that has flowed from their fulness, or trickled from the scanty, yet glad munificence of their penury. They have had as many sources of pure felicity as there are hearts and lives that they have made happy. Above all, when by example, influence, and active effort, they have healed men's spiritual infirmities, shed light upon their darkened souls, led their wandering steps into the path of eternal salvation, they have literally entered into the joy of their Lord, have received immeasurably more than they gave, have drawn a revenue beyond all proportion to their expenditure, have had in their own beatific consciousness the foregleamings of the heaven to which they have pointed and led the way.

Thus, also, have those who have made trial of humility found in it exaltation. It has raised them above the world. It has given them an unassailable position among their brethren. It has in unnumbered instances brought them much larger honor and profounder deference than they disclaimed; and even when this has not been the case, it has fortified them against disesteem and misappreciation by the consciousness of the honor that comes from God, and by the realizing foresight of the chief places that shall be theirs, when the Lord shall find them in the lowest room, and shall say to them, "My friends, go up higher."

A like consciousness attests the truths concerning God in his relations to man, promulgated through Christ. The divine Providence is a truth of consciousness. That "all things work together for good to those who love God," the mature Christian needs no longer to learn from the record of the apostle; for the apostle's experience is repeated in his own soul. As he looks back on the way in which God has led him, he sees that it was for him the safe and the best way. He has had trials, but they have strengthened his faith and deepened his joy. He has had sorrows; but the bread of affliction has been to him the bread of life, — in the valley of weeping he has drunk of fountains that flow from the river before the throne of God. He has parted from those with whom half his own life seemed to go; but they have opened for him new avenues to the upper rooms in his Father's house. He has had experiences that have loosened his roots in his native soil; but the vine, unearthed, has struck out tendrils that have clung closer and climbed higher around the tree of eternal life. Thus in the faithful soul is God's loving providence so fully verified, that no words of holy writ can bear to it more explicit testimony than is borne by the inner consciousness of the believer.

The efficacy of prayer is verified in like manner. The Christian knows that he has never prayed in vain. True, there have been specific petitions that have not had their specific answers; but even these have been more than answered. So was it with Jesus himself, and it is enough for the disciple that he be as his Master. He prayed that the cup might pass from him, — it passed not; but there appeared an angel from heaven, strengthening him. So the great apostle prayed that "the thorn in the flesh" — some bodily infirmity which he feared would prove disabling — might be removed, — it was not removed; but it was said to him, "My grace is sufficient for thee; for my strength is made perfect in weakness," and he thenceforth gloried in his infirmities, through and above which the power of Christ rested upon him. The Christian finds that prayer and sin, prayer and hopeless sorrow, cannot coexist; that prayer disarms temptation, renders prosperity safe and adversity sweet, makes work worship and joy gratitude, his home a sanctuary, the house of merchandise his Father's house. It more than keeps the soul; for it gives over its guardianship to him of whom it is written, "He that keepeth thee will not slumber." Thus does the consciousness of the praying soul bear perpetual testimony to the words of Jesus, "Ask, and it shall be given you; seek, and ye shall find; knock, and it shall be opened unto you."

Christian consciousness equally attests the truths appertaining to Christ in his relation to the human soul. Do you ask, How is it that in this field of thought there have been so many diverse, nay, opposite theories, while a common consciousness ought to make some approach to a common expression of itself? I answer, that the dogmatic differences among Christians relate to those aspects of Christ's nature and work which cannot be subjects of consciousness; while as to the part which he bears in Christian experience there is a substantial agreement. Who Christ is, cannot be determined by my consciousness; but I can know what he does, what he is, for me, to me, and in me. There is a divine side of Christ's work of redemption of which I cannot be conscious; but if he has wrought that work for and in me, I can know from my own consciousness the blessedness of having received the atonement, — the inward assurance of forgiveness and reconciliation with God, — the peace, not as the world gives, which flows from the heart of Christ into the heart of his disciple. In fine, the Christian is inwardly conscious of influences at work in his heart and upon his life, which precisely correspond to the power of Christ's death and the power of his resurrection, — influences of which he had no experience till he came within the sphere of Christ's attraction, of which he cannot conceive as flowing from any other source, and through which he feels that he is brought into a vital union with Christ, corresponding to that of the branch with the parent-vine. The physiology, if I may so term it, of Christian regeneration is described with no little diversity of nomenclature; but the phenomena of consciousness which attend it — the death to sin, the consecrated will, the affections set on things above, the fruits of the Divine Spirit in the heart and life — are the same in those whose formal theories vary however widely; and they are such phenomena as are not alleged to be produced by any other than Christian belief, culture, or influence.

To the individual soul this consciousness of Christian verities is, of course, the most convincing of all proofs, surpassing even objective intuition. What one feels he cannot but believe; and when there has been for him a source from which he knows that he has derived peculiar inward experiences, it is impossible that he should not associate the source and the experiences as cause and effect. He, the better part of whose being and life has taken shape consciously through the instrumentality of the Gospel of Christ, so far as outward means are concerned, and, inwardly, through an influence upon the soul corresponding in all its characteristics to the influence which Jesus promised should rest upon his followers, cannot but believe in Christ and his Gospel with a positiveness and strength of conviction such as experience alone can produce.

We now arrive at the question, What is the evidential value of intuition to those outside of the Christian circle? Can the scientific or spiritual consciousness of one man be made availing to another, and, if so, how? I answer, first, that the attitude in which intuitive conviction places the Christian believer, inspires, extends, deepens such faith as falls short of intuition. When those who call themselves Christians have a faith like Penelope's web, daily unravelled and rewoven, yielding to every show of cavil or scepticism, bending before every adverse blast, Christianity receives ghastly wounds in the house of its professed friends, is tolerated rather than honored by those outside of its household, and, so far from making new converts, drops from time to time those who hang loosely on its skirts. Equally, when the faith that exists, though firm and unyielding, is traditional and not vital, when the Church clings to its belief without being penetrated by its spirit and its power, unbelief prevails. The epochs when infidelity has been most rampant have been those at which externality rather than inwardness has been the prevailing type of the religious life; and, whenever that life has been so rekindled as to present the spectacle of intense and glowing vitality, unbelief has been arrested in its progress, and new confidence in Christian verities has taken possession of the collective mind of the community. Such faith — sincere, no doubt, of its kind, but *dead-sure* — as existed in the licentious court and the time-serving clergy of the age of Louis XIV., was among the chief causes of the French infidelity of the eighteenth century. The eminent champions of infidelity in England and Scotland, during the same century, were nurtured in the bosom of the easy-going Erastianism and lukewarmness of the national churches. Its tide was turned, not by the masterly and unanswerable defences of Christianity which it called forth, but by the infusion of spiritual life, alike into the establishments and the dissenting churches, under the auspices of Whitefield, Wesley, and their coadjutors. Men

 U of M

ceased to doubt and cavil when they witnessed a faith which indicated a profound, active, and influential consciousness of its contents.

Similar views would present themselves throughout Christendom, and in every period of its history. At the present moment, you might go from place to place, and in each community, in and around every congregation, you would find that the amount and strength of belief on the part of those not within the circle of professed Christian experience bear a very close proportion to the inwardness and energy of the faith of Christian men and women: the quiescent, worldly, and formalistic church being surrounded by people who either avow their scepticism, or do not think the subject of sufficient importance for them to take any cognizance of it; the living church, surrounded by those who give religion their assent, respect, and honor, and lie open to influences that may win them to sincere discipleship. This principle underlies all successful revivalism. Nothing can be done outside of the Church, till its inward life is renewed. The sole error of revivalism is that it seeks to make occasional and paroxysmal that which ought to be constant and perennial; for did the light shine as it ought and might always in the heart of the Church, it would be seen all the time, and there would be no pause in the accession of those who, seeing it, would give glory to their Father in heaven.

Nor is the conviction thus produced mere feeling. It has a logical basis. Intuition is a valid argument

MOU

to those who have not attained to it. Even objective intuition is so. It is constantly admitted in other departments than religion. Of those who learn and implicitly believe the truths of science, of astronomy for instance, by far the greater number do not occupy a position in which they can have a clear scientific consciousness of them. Were these truths in the minds of their representative men mere hypotheses, they would be no more than hypotheses to other intelligent persons. But we take them on trust and believe them without a question, because we are assured by those who have given their lives to their investigation that they are so related to one another and to the phenomena of the universe, that they cannot but be true. Now it seems to me that we are similarly impressed by the clear vision of religious truth, which has been a characteristic of the greatest minds of these Christian ages. It is of no small worth to an intellect of feebler grasp that to such men as Milton, Newton, Boyle, Locke, Pascal, and a host beside that might be named, Christianity has seemed self-evident, shining in its own unborrowed light, incapable of being obscured by doubt or cavil. These men, indeed, believed with the heart no less than with the intellect; but their mere intellectual intuition is of itself an independent ground of argument. They were men in whom feeling could not have preceded or produced belief, as in many lesser minds. The eyes of their understanding were wide open. They had before them the grounds of unbelief; they could see round and through the objects of their faith; and that their faith was clear as sight and impregnable to doubt, may well give reassurance to intellects of less keen and comprehensive vision.

But, above all, subjective intuition furnishes valid ground for belief. The Christian camp presents, indeed, not a homogeneous aspect, but unnumbered rival hosts, often turning their arms against one another rather than against the common enemy. Yet there are points of view from which their differences are merged, their enmities harmonized. There are certain traits which are common to the best men of all sects. The definition of the Christian spirit and life given by one would be accepted by all. The same manuals of practical piety are in the hands of all. The same Christian lyrics are sung with equal fervor in sanctuaries that stand over against each other like Zion and Gerizim. To the prayers of each all would add a hearty amen. Were they brought together, forbidden the use of technical phraseology, and induced to utter in the simplest language their several modes of consciousness as to what Christ had done for them, their duty to God, to Christ, to man, their abnegation of self-dependence, their trust in a divine redemption, their hope full of immortality, there would be no Babel-like confusion of tongues, as when they parade their distinctive dogmas, but a sweet concent and heavenly harmony. Now those who would thus with one heart and voice reveal a common consciousness are the foremost men in the esteem of their fellow-men, the leaders in all good works, — those whose lives are confessedly pure, true, faithful, generous, holy. Is there not in the united testimony of such men of all ages, nations, and sects, evidence of no mean worth to that which they all affirm ; namely, that Jesus Christ is the Sent of God, the Saviour of men, the Source of all excellence, the Inspirer of all virtue, the Way to the Father, the incarnate Truth, the eternal Life made manifest ?

As in thought I take my stand outside of the Church, of any church, I am profoundly moved by the unanimity of this cloud of witnesses. Supposing myself not even in the humblest measure a partaker of their consciousness, I see evidently that it is in them not mere belief, but consciousness; that they are in their inmost souls so identified with Christ that you cannot separate them from him, with his Gospel that you cannot wrest it from their hearts ; that to them, literally, "to live is Christ." I must believe that which is so interwoven with their whole being a reality, even though it have not become a reality to me. I must give my assent, though I be not yet ready to give my consent. The elect spirits of my race cannot be the slaves of a puerile superstition. Falsity and delusion cannot bear the noblest fruits that have ever ripened on earthly ground. Their lives give to their testimony a confirmation which I cannot disallow. Their manifest consciousness must constrain my faith. The Gospel which they profess not to believe, but to know as the truth, has proved itself to and in them "the power of God unto salvation" from folly and sin ; and can I doubt that the salvation is divine and everlasting, as they believe it to be ?

We thus see that as to intuition science and Christianity occupy the same ground, with this advantage on the side of Christianity, that the intuition is more intimate and vital, permeating the whole being, moulding the character, and manifesting its reality and intensity in the life to which it gives aim, direction, and end. How then, from the outer circle, can I accept the intuitions of scientific men, and reject those of Christian men? Or if I can with my own inward vision gain some clear and self-evidencing views of scientific truth, and at the same time trust that I have some measure of insight, independent of and above external proof, into Christian verities, how can I yield credence, as I must, to the former, and yet suffer aught of incredulity or doubt to obscure the latter?

I have now completed the plan which I announced in my first Lecture. There is in our time no scepticism as to science, but only too willing assent to whatever purports or claims to be science, though only in the form of postulates or hypotheses. The established truths of science no one is so bold as to call in question. Scientific truth rests on the joint evidence of testimony, experiment, and intuition. I have shown you that Christianity has in its behalf testimony unequalled in its clearness, fulness, and validity; experiment, in a vast diversity of forms, in numberless individual instances, and in the history of the civilized world for these eighteen centuries; and professed and manifest intuition, on the part of the greatest and best of our race through these same centuries,—I trust, also, in the minds of not a few who have listened to me, and have borne witness in their own consciousness to the divine worth and power of the everlasting Gospel, and of him who is the believer's hope. Science and Christianity rest on the same foundations. Let no one, then, suppose that he does honor to Christianity by jealousy of science. Let no one imagine that he serves science by discrediting Christianity. They are equally divine, equally from the inspiration of God, and each has essential ministries for the other. Science illustrates the very attributes of the Supreme Being which Christianity proclaims; while Christianity prepares only the more generous receptivity for the truth which God has written on all things that he has made. May we not, then, join in the prayer of the great instaurator of the inductive philosophy? "This also we humbly and earnestly beg,—that human things may not prejudice such as are divine; neither that from the unlocking of the gates of sense, and the kindling of a greater natural light, any thing may arise of incredulity or intellectual night towards divine mysteries; but rather that by our minds thoroughly purged and cleansed from fancy and vanity, and yet subject and perfectly given up to the divine oracles, there may be given unto faith the things that are faith's."

APPENDIX.

I.

THE apostles were, of necessity, the most authentic witnesses as to what Jesus was, said, and did. An express and formal analysis of their testimony would have been given in the foregoing Lectures, had not the author delivered and published a Lecture on this subject in the third course of Boston Lectures on Christianity and Scepticism. Leave has been obtained to reprint that Lecture in the present volume, as an essential part of the argument from testimony. It is reprinted without omission or alteration · for, though a small portion of it is parallel in thought, and one or two sentences nearly identical in language, with portions of the preceding volume, these passages could not have been omitted or changed without mutilating the argument of which they form a part.

THE TESTIMONY OF THE APOSTLES.

RENAN'S Life of Jesus, which before the Franco-Prussian war had reached in the original its thirteenth edition, besides not a few in its English dress, is now the gospel of the doubting and unbelieving on both sides of the Atlantic, and will remain so till some one bolder or more subtle than he shall displace him, as he displaced Strauss. His book is a charming one in its delineations of everybody and everything but Christ. In his chapter on the original disciples, he gives a very vivid sketch of their respective individualities; and both in his "Life of Jesus" and in his work on the Apostles, he acknowledges the authenticity of the accounts we have of them, the miraculous narratives alone excepted. There is in the Introduction to his "Life of Jesus," one very extraordinary testimony to the truth of the evangelic history, which I cannot forbear quoting.

"I have traversed in every direction the district where the scenes of the Gospel are laid. I have visited Jerusalem, Hebron, and Samaria. Almost no site named in the story of Jesus has escaped me. All this narrative, which at a distance seems to float in the clouds of an unreal world, thus assumed a body, a substantial existence, which astonished me

The striking coincidence of texts and places, the wonderful harmony of the ideal of the Gospels with the country which served as its frame, was for me a revelation. I had before my eyes a fifth Gospel, and thenceforth through the stories of Matthew and Mark, instead of an abstract being who one might say had never existed, I saw in life and movement a human form that challenged admiration."

In fine, Renan treats the entire New-Testament history as an unquestionable record of actual historical personages and events, except where the supernatural element crops out in the narrative; thus far, at least, showing himself both a clear-sighted and an honest critic. In point of fact, the historical books of the New Testament have at once so many external proofs and internal tokens of their authenticity, as to leave no question concerning the substantial truth of their narrative of ordinary events, however we may dispose of the abnormal incidents they record.

Resting, then, on the admitted authenticity of this narrative, I propose to draw from the apostles who bear in it so prominent a part such testimony as they offer in behalf of their Lord and Master.

In the first place, there is not the slightest doubt that of eleven of these apostles, most or all incurred hardships, losses, perils, persecutions, and sufferings of the severest character, in attestation of their belief in the Divine mission and authority of Jesus; that several of them, as itinerant preachers, devoted themselves for the residue of their lives to the promulgation of this belief, their zeal carrying them into distant lands, and enabling them to overcome natural, social, and national barriers, insurmountable except to the most ardent and self-forgetting enthusiasm; and that several of them, in the same cause, encountered and bravely endured beheading, crucifixion, and other agonizing and ignominious forms of death. These things attest, at least, the sincerity and the intensity of their belief. Sacrifice and martyrdom always prove as much as this. But they do not prove the truth of a belief, — if they did, there would be no end to the shams, contradictions, and absurdities, which, as sealed by the blood of their believers, we should be compelled to recognize as true.

There is, however, this peculiarity which distinguishes the apostles from all other martyrs, even from other early Christian martyrs. The declarations which they maintained at the peril and cost of their lives were not dogmatic articles of faith, but statements of alleged facts, of which they professed to have been eye and ear witnesses. Foremost among these facts was the resurrection of Jesus from the dead. That they believed themselves witnesses of the reality of his death and of his reappearance among the living, there cannot be the slightest doubt. This Renan admits. He maintains that Jesus really died; that the apostles caught eagerly at the first rumor of his resurrection, which grew from the stealing of his body (it is hard to say by whom, but more probably by Joseph of Arimathea than by any one else), and from Mary Magdalene's mistaking the gardener for him in the dim dawn and through the mist of her tears ; that they so firmly believed this story as to imagine that they saw him repeatedly, by day as well as by night, at Jerusalem and in Galilee, the whole eleven of them at a time ; and that this hallucination lasted many days, and, on one occasion, extended to the more than five hundred brethren mentioned by St. Paul. He says emphatically that had the apostles possessed less than the strongest assurance of their Master's resurrection, they could not by any possibility have been the earnest propagandists and heroic sufferers that they undoubtedly were. We thank him for this admission ; and indeed no champion of the Christian faith can ask for a firmer basis for his superstructure of argument and evidence than the concessions made all along by this pre-eminently fair and frank, yet for all this only the more captivating and dangerous, Corypheus of the anti-Christian host.

But the undoubting belief of professed eye and ear witnesses is not in itself sufficient to inspire confidence in their story. If these men were fools or fanatics, their testimony, though blood-sealed, is of no value. The question for us then is, whether they were persons of sufficiently acute perceptions, clear mind, and sound judgment, to be relied on.

To answer this question, let us look first at their writings. Five of them, Matthew, John, James, Peter, and Jude, are among the reputed authors of the New Testament. As to these writers, we have as good reason for believing in the genuineness of Matthew's and John's Gospels, of John's First Epistle, and of Peter's First Epistle, as we have for believing in the genuineness of Virgil's Georgics, or of Cicero *de Officiis*. We find them, from the earliest mention made of them, named and quoted as written by their now reputed authors, without any record or intimation of a doubt or question as to their authorship.

I am aware, indeed, that rationalistic criticism does not admit that the Gospels came into being as other books do. The development theory is applied to them, as to the whole realm of living nature. Their genesis is like Topsy's, in Mrs. Stowe's tale, — "I 'spect I grow'd, don't think nobody never made me." But Renan admits that memoranda of our Saviour's discourses written out by Matthew were the nucleus of the Gospel which bears his name. He thinks, too, that the narrative portions of John's Gospel, which he regards as singularly truthlike and accurate, were derived from that apostle, and that the whole book was written by his immediate disciples.

Here let me offer some considerations with special reference to the authorship of the fourth Gospel. As I have said, the testimony of antiquity that it was written by John is unanimous and full. As to his having written the Apocalypse, that testimony is less clear and conclusive. Yet the critics of the Tübingen school maintain that this last book was undoubtedly written by the Apostle John. But it is very certain that the same man wrote the Gospel of John (so-called), the first Epistle bearing his name, and the Apocalypse ; for there are several very striking characteristic conceptions and figures, which are both peculiar and common to these three writings, or to the Gospel and the Apocalypse. For instance, the term *Logos* (the Word) is applied to Jesus in all three of them, and nowhere else ; and again, Jesus is introduced in the Gospel under the figure of a *lamb;* the same figure reappears in the Apocalypse, in almost every vision of the glorified Redeemer, and he is called by this name nowhere else. These are but two instances, to which several others might be added, of peculiarities common to the Gospel and the Apocalypse, and rendering it very certain that, if the Tübingen critics do not err in ascribing the latter to John, he must have written the former.

Yet another consideration strikes me very forcibly in favor of the authorship of the fourth Gospel by John. True or false, this is the most remarkable book ever written, and has had more power over the human mind and heart than any other, both in determining belief, and in awakening tender, profound, and fervent devotion. The sublimest narrative ever written is that of the raising of Lazarus. The words put into the mouth of Jesus in that scene, "I am the resurrection and the life ; he that believeth in me, though he were dead, yet shall he live, and whosoever liveth, and believeth in me, shall never die," are the grandest utterance ever heard on earth, and must and will be rehearsed in hope and triumph, by the grave-side, till the last of the dying shall have put on immortality. The recorded communings and intercessions of the night of the betrayal surpass in every element of pathos all human literature beside, and there are at this and at every moment, all the world over, thousands upon thousands of the weary and grief-stricken, who, oft as they read these blessed words, feel pillowed on the bosom of Infinite Love.

Now, there are but two hypotheses possible. One is, that we have the faithful narrative of what was said and done by the Truth and Life incarnate, transmitted to us by the hand of one who saw and heard what he wrote. If this be so, while it makes no manner of difference which of the apostles wrote the book, no one would venture to doubt its having been written by John. The other supposition is, that the author of this Gospel, by his own genius, without a copy, shaped and filled out in those transcendently glorious and beautiful proportions and tints the figure of Jesus Christ, and from his own fertile brain, spun those discourses into whose depth none can enter without seeming to listen to the very voice of God. If this be true, then the author of that book deserves the place in human gratitude, reverence, nay, adoration, which the Christian Church has assigned to Jesus. He towers up above all other writers, all other men of his age; nay, more, as the greatest mind, the greatest soul of his race. The book is, indeed, superhuman, if he whom it portrays was not so. How then could the name of such a writer have been lost, and his fame transferred to another? It was a name too great to perish, a fame too exalted not to have its enduring record. We are then compelled to accept as our only alternative, our first supposition, — the belief resting on unbroken tradition from the earliest times, that this book, great and glorious as it is, was written by an illiterate Galilean fisherman, and that it owes its superiority to all other books, not to any surpassing ability of the author, but to the Divine life in human form, as to which he only related what had been uttered in his presence, or done under his personal knowledge.

As for the Epistle bearing the name of James, we have evidence that it was generally received as genuine, and was from a very early period read in the churches. As of the two apostles bearing that name, the brother of John died early, this letter must be ascribed to James, the son of Alphæus. We have about the same kind and nearly the same degree of evidence, for the genuineness of the epistle called that of Jude, or Judas, — evidence which would be deemed amply sufficient for any book outside of the sacred canon. The epistles of James and Jude have also characteristics of style and sentiment which ally them to the undoubtedly genuine epistles of John and Peter, and show that they belong to the earliest time and the apostolic school, and not to the next succeeding Christian age, whose few extant writings are of quite a different type.

We have then, undoubtedly, in our hands the writings of some of those men, who, at the risk of every thing earthly, professed to have been eye-witnesses of what Jesus said and did. How do they write? Like intelligent, sober, credible men? Or do they in their writings show themselves so stupid and foolish, or so wild and fanatical, that they could easily have been the dupes of pretension or imposture? This question would seem to be answered by the regard which has been paid to their writings in every subsequent age by the foremost men in point of intelligence, good sense, and culture. These writers have generally been supposed, in Christendom, to have been specially enlightened and inspired by God. Whether this be so or not, it is aside from our present purpose to inquire; but the fact that such an opinion concerning them has been held by a large proportion of the first minds of our race is a sufficient proof that their writings are at least free from the tokens of weakness, folly, or infatuation.

This view of their character is certainly confirmed on examination. The books present all the marks of truth, when tried by the usual tests. The Gospels of Matthew and John contain a great many names, dates, local and historical references; it was a period of very frequent change in the political relations of Palestine, — a period as to which later writers would inevitably have committed gross anachronisms; yet we find in these books only the closest accordance, in geography, chronology, and history, with all the authorities of the time, especially with the minute and circumstantial history of Josephus. Then, too, we have between the Epistles and the Gospels, just the kind of coincidences which we should expect to trace in genuine works. Thus we find in the Epistles not any formal statement of facts, or set rehearsal of the words of Jesus; but we detect in them unmistakable tokens of firm belief in the contents of the Gospels, and what is more, of precisely the condition of mind and character which these contents were adapted to produce. The coincidences between the Epistles and the Gospels are closely analogous to those which we should expect to find between the domestic or friendly letters of statesmen or generals concerned in either war of our independence and authentic histories of the same war.

Then, again, there are no books in the world that show greater serenity and clearness of mind than these manifest. Their style is simple, artless, free from exaggeration, hyperbole, apostrophe, declamation, ambitious rhetoric, outbursts of impetuous feeling. Matthew and John, in describing the marvellous life and works of Jesus Christ, write as quietly and dispassionately as if they were narrating ordinary events. They show no fear that they shall not be believed. They use no forms of strong asseveration. In fine, they write as if they had become so accustomed to experiences on a higher plane than that of common humanity, as to be unconscious of their position,—just as natives of Switzerland might talk and write calmly and unexcitedly about glaciers, and avalanches, and scenes of which the mere thought thrills us with profound emotion.

The Epistle of James is a very remarkable composition. Had it come down to us, with such slight verbal changes as might have been necessary, as a treatise of Plutarch, or Epictetus, or Marcus Antoninus, it would now be regarded as the finest ethical monument of antiquity, and would hold an unrivalled place as a school and college classic. For common sense, shrewd observation of men and things, deep insight, and practical wisdom of the highest order, it may resign all vantage-ground on the score of any sacred associations, and still retain its prestige unimpaired; while it is no less remarkable for the sharp edge and keen point and brilliant sheen of many of its single maxims and apophthegms.

I have said enough about these writings for my present argument, — enough to show you that at least those of the apostles whom we know as authors were not feeble, silly, credulous men, who could have been easily deceived by an impostor, or drawn by a self-deluded pretender into the vortex of his fanaticism; but that they were clear-headed, sober-minded, intelligent, and in every way competent witnesses of the events which some of them record as from their own personal knowledge, and the others recognize as undoubted facts.

Let us now take note of the professions of the apostles, so far as they are specified in the New Testament. Six of them, perhaps more, were fishermen on the little lake of Galilee, — not sailors in any large sense of the word (for they were probably never out of sight of land, or in their boats for more than a day at a time), so that there was nothing in their simple, prosaic life to nurture the imaginative element, or to cherish credulity and superstition, but much that was adapted to educate their perceptive faculties, their powers of observation, and their plain, practical common sense. Hardy, straightforward, honest men, jostled and jostling on the rough paths of daily life, the weaker sinews of character broken down, the hardier developed by incessant toil, they would have been firm adherents to one who could give them unmistakable credentials of his claims, but not such persons as could be enlisted in the cause of a fanatic, or become the easy dupes of a plausible deceiver. We have in the first chapter of John's Gospel, in a series of conversations whose life-likeness Renan (in an Appendix to his last edition) adduces as a token of their authenticity, a very vivid picture of what these men were before they became the disciples of Jesus; and the picture is that of self-respecting, intelligent, thoughtful men, — such men as the Hebrew theology and the institutions of Moses were adapted to produce among the laboring classes, but such as were developed under no other type of ancient civilization, nor have yet been formed, except in comparatively small numbers, under the half-Pagan auspices of what I fear we miscall Christian civilization.

Of these fishermen, one indeed, Peter, appears to have been ardent and impulsive in his nature. But it is equally manifest that he was testy, petulant, captious, easily offended, and ready sometimes even to find fault with his Master. Such a man as he would have been disgusted with sham and pretension. Had there been aught in the works, words, or daily life of Jesus that was not genuine, honest, pure, noble, he was the very man to take umbrage at it, and to transmute his allegiance into implacable enmity. But his attachment flickers only for a few moments under the natural reaction from a foolhardy courage; a single look from his Master drowns his denial in a passion of tears; and thenceforward none is more prompt and earnest than he to bear testimony, at whatever cost and risk, to the power and love of God as incarnate in Jesus Christ.

Another of the twelve, Matthew, was a tax-gatherer in the service of the Roman government, probably a collector of the imposts on the brisk though petty inland traffic on the Lake of Galilee,—gathering tribute from a people that scorned to pay it, and sought every possible subterfuge to evade it. His office could have been borne only by one who was all eye and ear. He was a detective by the necessity of his profession,—the last man to be duped either by fanaticism or by imposture. He, too, had more to lose than the fishermen. The hands of all the fiscal agents of Rome, great and small, had viscous palms; and we have intimation of his substantial worldly estate in his making a great feast for the Saviour,—an occasion important enough for the Pharisees to know who the guests were, and to carp at them as below the standard of Jewish gentility and purism. His testimony, then, has a peculiar value, both on the ground of his profession, and on account of the heavy sacrifice which his discipleship made inevitably necessary. As for his Gospel, its entire character accords closely with what we know of him. There is something journal-like in its narrative portions, as if it were written by a man of business. It contains more about the Saviour's sayings and doings at Capernaum — Matthew's post of duty — than either of the other Gospels. Moreover, when he speaks of his own house, he calls it *the* house, as a man generally does when he has a place of business separate from his home. The uniform tradition of the early Church represents his sacrifice for the cause of Christ as life-long, his service as a missionary of the cross having been first, for fifteen years, in Judæa, and afterward in remote regions of the East, and perhaps of the South; for there is some reason to believe that his Christian enterprise carried him as far as Ethiopia.

Another of the sacred college was Simon, the *Canaanite*, as he is called by Matthew and Mark, *Zelotes* (or the Zealot), as Luke styles him, — the former being the Syro-Chaldaic, the latter the Greek designation of a sect of Jewish fanatics, who pushed their loyalty to the Mosaic ritual and economy to absolute frenzy, regarded the Roman power with the intensest hatred, deemed murder and even stealthy assassination justifiable in defence of the national integrity and faith, and were the foremost agents in producing the condition of things which led to the destruction of Jerusalem and the exile of the Hebrew people, — enormities opposed to the ordinary and else invariable Roman policy, but forced upon Titus by the unparalleled obstinacy of these very ultraists of whom we so strangely find one among the followers of Jesus Christ. The Zealots were literal interpreters of the prophecies that seemed to promise extended temporal dominion to the Messiah, and were in constant expectation of his advent. We know nothing very definite about this man's subsequent life; but the tradition is, that he was an indefatigable propagandist of the new faith, and that he finally suffered death on the cross.

That a man of this sort should have been among the apostles indicates, as it seems to me, the reality of the coincidence, claimed by the Evangelists, between the Messiah of the prophets and Jesus of Nazareth. This man was one of those who were all the time watching the Eastern sky for the dawn of the Messianic day, and that a day, as they imagined, of vengeance and of victory. There was not a prophetic sign with which he was not familiar; but only a convergence of these signs, too patent and too full to admit of doubt, could have made a Zealot acknowledge a Messiah in every feature so utterly unlike the mailed and harnessed chieftain of his day-dreams.

This is a point which seems to me deserving of more than a passing notice. The evangelists relate numerous circumstances of birthplace, birth, parentage, condition, and experience, in which prophecy concerning the Messiah was said to be fulfilled in Jesus. Rationalistic critics represent these coincidences as in part factitious, and in part fictitious. They allege that Jesus did some things, in order to simulate the Messiah of the prophets; and that, as to the greater number of those particulars in which he could have had no agency, as about his birth in

Bethlehem and his descent from David, the evangelists coined facts in accordance with predictions. It might seem sufficient to say that, as the coiners of these coincidences risked their lives by coining them, they must, before undertaking thus to deceive the world, have accomplished the more difficult task of deceiving themselves. But here we have a specially strong case. A man pledged at once to the most literal interpretation of prophecy and to a line of conduct utterly opposed to the spirit and character of Jesus is so impressed with the Messianic tokens that meet in Jesus, as to throw aside his old sectarian convictions, to renounce his former self, to become a new man, and to adhere in life and death to a Teacher and Leader with whom at the outset he could have had nothing in common except reverence for the Word of God in the Hebrew Scriptures.

We come next to the case of Thomas. He was evidently sceptical by nature, — I would even say, by the grace and gift of God, who evidently made use of this trait in his mental character for the strengthening of his own faith, and of that of multitudes who should come after him. The other ten have seen the risen Lord, and have no doubt of his identity. He very naturally thinks it more probable that they have been deceived by some family likeness or casual resemblance in another person than that the Crucified is really alive. He demands to examine the wound-marks, to trace the prints of the nails, the incision made by the spear. He was in the right. His was an honest and reasonable doubt, and we are thankful for it. His name should never be spoken with less than the highest honor, and had he been the type of a larger proportion of those ministers of religion who have been successors of the apostles, there would be much less of infidelity than there now is. Credulity generates unbelief; and infidelity has no weapons of its own forging that have half the efficacy of those which it picks up among the crazy outworks, built by a faith both blind and timid, around the impregnable citadel of everlasting truth.

There are two kinds of scepticism, — that of the heart and that of the intellect. The former is adapted to make unbelievers; the latter, to make Christians. The former will not look at the hands and the side, because it is determined not to be moved morally and spiritually as they would move the honest soul; the latter insists on seeing the wound-marks, because it wants to know the precise truth, and therefore avails itself of whatever evidence God has given. The scepticism of the heart hates the light, and will not come to the light, lest its deeds be reproved. The scepticism of the mind is that which cannot believe without sufficient evidence. It proves all things, and holds fast that which will stand the test. It examines both sides of a question, and adheres to that which imposes the least strain on its belief. Such a mind needs only to have the evidences of Christianity fairly presented, to yield to it entire and cordial faith. Many of the firmest believers, many of the ablest defenders of the truth as it is in Jesus, belong to this class of minds. In this sense, Lardner, Paley, and Butler, whose contributions to the Christian evidences are invaluable, and will be so for generations to come, were pre-eminently sceptics. They would not believe, without examining the hands and the side, trying all the witnesses, testing the objections against Christianity with the opposing arguments, weighing coolly and impartially the evidence, real or pretended, on either side; and the result was a faith in Christ, which sight could hardly have rendered clearer or stronger.

God has made many such minds, and they are among the noblest and best of his creation. I have known, you probably have, some extreme specimens of this kind among the most loyal and exemplary Christians. Take a case like this, — I paint from life, an individual as the type of a class. He whom I describe wants for every item of his belief a solid basis of fact, and a superstructure of unanswerable reasoning built upon it; and he will let his faith reach no higher than he can lay this superstructure, as it were, stone upon stone in insoluble cement. He has no relish (and I think him wrong there) for those speculations about spiritual and heavenly things, in which, from a mere hint of holy writ, fancy takes her flight in those higher regions of thought, which, I believe, God has purposely left undescribed, that we may have our free range in them. In the house built on Christ as the foundation, he prefers to live in the lower story, where he can test the strength of the floor and the walls. But so firmly has he by careful examination convinced himself of the Saviour's redeeming mission, sacrificial death, miracles, resurrection and ascension, that he speaks of them as he would of sunrise, or the phases of the moon, or any of the well-known phenomena of the outward world, as matters long since placed by him beyond question. He conforms his life to these great spiritual facts, as he does to the laws of nature. And when he comes to die, he passes away, not with any glow of ecstasy, but with the quiet confidence of one who knows just where he is going, and has just as firm a belief in the many mansions in the Father's house as in the several apartments in his own house. This is the style of faith that grows from the honest scepticism which insists on always having sufficient reasons for its belief. It often has less unction than might seem edifying ; but if you want valiant soldiers of the cross for times when unbelief is rampant, boastful, and aggressive, these are the men to bear the shock of arms, and come off more than conquerors.

We care not, then, how many there are of the same order of mind with Thomas. The condition of the Christian evidences is specially adapted to their natures. The infidel has much harder things to believe than the Christian, severer difficulties to encounter, contradictions, inconsistencies and absurdities which only a credulous mind could entertain, -- from which a natively sceptical intellect is inevitably drawn into the Christian faith. For, if Christianity be not true, we have to believe in numerous well-known effects without any adequate cause ; in extensive conditions of mind and of conviction for which there was no basis whatever; in the growing up of confessedly the most perfect system of morality the world has ever seen, in the brain of an illiterate Galilean peasant, in a degenerate nation and a corrupt age, and not only so, but in the brain of one who was either weak enough to imagine, or wicked enough to feign, himself possessed of supernatural powers; in the simultaneous illusion of the senses of multitudes and bodies of men for many successive days, when it was the interest and the wish of those very men to find that false which they were constrained to recognize as true; in the imposition of pretended or imagined miracles upon a hostile people, so successfully that they were compelled to admit their actual occurrence, and (as we have abundant Jewish evidence) imputed them to the aid of Beelzebub, the imagined prince of demons; and in many other things equally incredible and opposed to all recognized laws of belief. The fact is, that not a few of the most noted infidels of modern times have been equally noted for their credulity; and that at the present moment the superstitions hardly less gross than fetichism, which are connected with pseudo-spiritualism, are most rife in the very quarters where the miracles and the resurrection of Jesus are thrown aside as unworthy of credence.

One word more about the eleven, before I pass to the twelfth. These eleven, it must be remembered, were not only witnesses of leading events in the life of Jesus, but were for many months his constant companions, on the road, in the house, on the lake. They knew his whole manner of life, — his modes of intercourse with all sorts and conditions of men, — the degree to which he embodied his precepts of piety, purity, justice, forbearance, and kindness in his daily walk and conversation. They staked their lives on a body of statements, prominent among which was the alleged fact of his faultless and absolutely godlike sanctity and excellence. They must have known whether this was true or not; and that they suffered and died to attest it, proves that they knew it to be true.

I have spoken of eleven only. There remains Judas, by far the most important of all, for whom the Church has been slow to own her debt of everlasting gratitude to the God who makes the wrath and guilt of man to praise him. Judas had the same opportunities with the other eleven for knowing every thing about his Master that could be known. He was employed in a confidential relation, as custodian of the scanty funds of the apostolic family. He was probably from the first a selfish, greedy, deceitful man; our Saviour early and repeatedly intimates his recognition of these traits; and he probably chose him on account of them, that, if malice itself could find aught against him, it might have free scope and full swing.

Judas entered into negotiations with the chief priests and their associates for the ruin of his Master, and, mercenary as he was, he would certainly have effected that ruin in the way most profitable to himself. Now it was only as a last resort that the leading Jews wanted to get possession of the body of Jesus. They felt by no means certain that they could persuade Pilate to kill him, and they dared not kill him themselves. They would have immeasurably preferred to destroy his influence, to detect some imposture in his alleged miracles, or to find some weak point in his character, some damning incident in his life. They were so doubtful how they could dispose of their prisoner, that they offered a very low price for him. But they had large means at their command, and would have given a much greater reward for a surer service. Could Judas have gone to those men with evidence of jugglery, pretence, or exaggeration in the wonderful works reported to have been wrought by Jesus, or could he have proved a single deed or utterance that would impair the reputation of perfect sanctity which Jesus held among a large portion of the people; in fine, could he have borne the slightest testimony against his Master's character, he might as easily as not have made his thirty pieces of silver three thousand, — he might have named his own price, and if there had not been money enough in hand, they would have taken up contributions in all the synagogues to pay it. But there was absolutely nothing secret which could injure Jesus and his cause by being made known. There was nothing for this bad man to betray except the place in the environs of the crowded city where Jesus was going to pass the night, — it being necessary to arrest him by night on account of the large number of friendly Galileans who would have resisted any attempt to apprehend him by daylight. For this mean and paltry service he had a commensurately pitiful compensation.

But even he repents of what he has done. The power and beauty of that blessed spirit, the majesty, meekness, and love of that holy countenance come over him, but too late to recall his deed. He seeks, as so many do in all times, in our time, to escape the contamination of ill-gotten gain by casting it into the temple treasury; and finding no relief, in an agony of remorse and despair he goes and hangs himself, bearing as unequivocal and precious testimony to the truth and purity of his Master in that horrible suicide, as the other apostles bore in their cheerful sufferings and martyrdom for the love of their ascended Lord.

Judas has been strangely overlooked by the Church; no day is assigned to him in the calendar; no account is taken of his services; — yet we could have better spared a better man. We thank God for the life-record of those of the sacred college who followed closest in the footsteps of their Lord; yet while we have the Master, we might not have missed even James, or Peter, or Nathaniel. But we do need Judas, to learn what aspect the Saviour manifested to a subtle, captious, and treacherous witness, and thus to have the testimony of the vilest avarice, meanness, and malice, alongside with that of God and the holy angels, to the truth of his claims, the guilelessness of his spirit, the purity of his life.

I have thus presented the evidences of our Saviour's Divine mission and character afforded us by those of whom the Evangelist writes, "He ordained twelve, that they should be with him." In transmitting to us their testimony, he has ordained us also, that we should be with him. This is the place to which Jesus calls us and heaven invites us. Be it our place; and may it be our blessedness so to confess him in our earthly lives and before men, that we may be owned of him in heaven, before the angels of God.

II.

NOTES.

NOTE A. — PAGE 22.

"[HEROD'S] wife having discovered the agreement he had made with Herodias, and having learned it before he had notice of her knowledge of the whole design, she desired him to send her to Macherus, which was subject to her father, and so all things necessary to her journey were made ready for her by the general of Aretas's army; and by that means she soon came into Arabia, under the conduct of several generals, who carried her from one to another till she reached her father, and told him of Herod's intentions. Aretas made this the occasion of hostility against Herod, who had also some quarrel with him about their limits in the territory of Gamalitis. So they raised armies on both sides, prepared for war, and sent their generals to fight instead of themselves; and when they had joined battle, all Herod's army was destroyed by the treachery of certain fugitives, who, though they were of the tetrarchy of Philip, had joined Herod's army." — JOSEPHUS, *Jewish Antiquities*, xviii. 5. 1.

NOTE B. — PAGE 32.

Several of Justin's alleged additions to the narrative of the canonical Gospels were probably only his own amplification or exposition of that narrative. Thus, when he quotes the Jews as saying of the miracles of Christ "that they were a magical delusion," he but expresses in different words the charge, "He is casting out demons by Beelzebub, the prince of demons." Thus also, when he says, that "Christ, being regarded as a worker in wood, made, while among men, ploughs and yokes," he is simply drawing a natural inference from Christ's being called a carpenter in Mark's Gospel.

In describing the birth of Christ, he says, that "as Joseph could find no room in any inn at Bethlehem, he lodged in a cave near the village, and while they were there, Mary brought forth the Messiah, and laid him in a stall." This is not by any means inconsistent with the narrative of St. Luke, nor with probability. The (so-called) Cave of the Nativity was shown at a very early period, and the frequent use of caves as stables in the East is attested by modern travellers, as well as by several passages that might be cited from ancient writers. Such knowledge of the local fact or tradition concerning the cave needs no written authority to account for it, as Justin was not a stranger in Palestine.

In his account of the baptism of Jesus, Justin varies from the Gospels, as we read them, in two particulars. One is the statement that "when Jesus came to the river Jordan where John was baptizing, upon his entering the water, a fire was kindled in the Jordan." This must have been a very early tradition; for, though there is no reason to believe that it was put on record by the author of the first Gospel, it is found in the oldest extant manuscript of the earliest Latin version of that Gospel (Matt. iii. 15), and in one or more other old Latin manuscripts, having been, no doubt, first written in the margin of some

Greek copy, and rendered by the translator as a part of the text. It is, however, manifest that Justin derived it from unwritten tradition; for he adds: "The apostles of this same person, our Messiah, *have written* that when he came out of the water, the Holy Spirit, like a dove, alighted upon him." The other deviation from the narrative of the Gospels concerns the voice from heaven at the baptism, which Justin twice quotes as having uttered the words, "Thou art my Son, this day have I begotten thee." These words may have been in Justin's copy of St. Luke's Gospel; for they are found (Luke iii. 22) in the Cambridge Manuscript of the Greek text, — one of the oldest authorities, — and (translated) in several of the earliest Latin manuscripts extant.

Justin, while he quotes very largely from our Saviour's own words, quotes as his but one saying, not found in the Gospels, namely, "In whatever actions I apprehend you, by those will I judge you." This may have originated from a lapse of memory in quoting some one of the not unlike recorded sayings of Jesus, or it may have been one of the many utterances which were repeated as his among his disciples without being recorded by his biographers.

It is certain that Justin had in his hands the fourth and latest Gospel; for he quotes as a saying of Christ, "Unless ye be born again, ye cannot enter into the kingdom of heaven," — a text in which the common editions of the New Testament read "the kingdom of God," but which in the Sinaitic manuscript — the oldest and highest authority — (and according to several other early authorities), is written "the kingdom of heaven." (See Norton's "Evidences of the Genuineness of the Gospels," Part I. chap. ii., and Tischendorff's "Origin of the Four Gospels.")

NOTE C. — PAGE 33.

Justin's writings afford conclusive proof that what are commonly called the "Apocryphal Gospels," if already written in his time, had no authority among intelligent Christians. Had he possessed them, and regarded them as authentic, it is impossible that, with his full and minute citations of Christ's words and deeds, he should not have quoted from them. There is, indeed, no trace of their existence during the first three centuries, and in the fourth century they are expressly referred to as late compositions, by unknown persons, and of no historical value. They are not in a single instance quoted with approval within the period in which their sanction by a Christian writer could have any bearing on the question of their authenticity or early antiquity. They are, however, of great worth, as showing what kinds of traditions must have found ready circulation among the more ignorant Christians, and thus by their contrast with our canonical Gospels enhancing the presumption in favor of the latter as authentic. The Apocryphal Gospels seem to have been written by sincerely devout Christians, of large credulity and little spiritual discernment, who thought to do honor to Christ by ascribing to him marvellous acts of whatever kind, frivolous, useless, or mischievous, equally with those worthy of "a Teacher sent from God."

NOTE D. — PAGE 35.

The chapter of Eusebius with reference to Papias is so admirable a specimen of candid and cautious criticism, as to deserve to be quoted in part, in order to correct the common impression that the early Christian writers exercised no discrimination as to the testimony offered them in behalf of what they wanted to believe.

"There are said to be five Books of Papias, which bear the title 'Interpretation of our Lord's Declarations.' Irenæus makes mention of them as the only works written by him, in the following terms: 'These things are attested by Papias, who was John's hearer and the associate of Polycarp, an ancient writer. They are spoken of in his fourth Book, for he has written a work in five Books.' But Papias himself, in the preface to his discourses, by no means asserts that he was a hearer and an eye-witness of the holy apostles, but informs us that he received the doctrines of faith from their intimate friends, which he states as follows: 'I shall not regret to subjoin to my interpretations, for your benefit, whatever I have at any time accurately ascertained and treasured up in my memory, as I received it from the elders, and have recorded it in order to give additional confirmation to the truth by my testimony. For I have never, like many, delighted to hear those that tell many things, but those that teach the truth; neither those that record precepts from other sources, but those who report precepts that are given by the Lord for our faith, and that came from the Truth itself. But if I met with any one who had been a follower of the elders anywhere, I made it a point to inquire what were the declarations of the elders; what was said by Andrew, Peter, or Philip; what by Thomas, James, John, Matthew, or any other of the disciples [*i.e.*, apostles] of our Lord; what was said by Aristion, and the presbyter John, disciples of the Lord,—for I do not think that I derived so much benefit from books as from the living voice of those that were still surviving.'

"Here it is proper to observe that the name of John is twice mentioned. He first mentions John with Peter, James, and Matthew, and the other apostles, evidently meaning the evangelist. Again he ranks the other John with those not included in the number of apostles, placing Aristion before him. This man he distinguishes plainly by the name of presbyter. Thus it is here proved that the statement of those is true who assert that there were two of the same name in Asia, and that there were also two tombs at Ephesus, both of which bear the name of John even to this day, — which it is particularly necessary to observe; for it is probable that the second John — if it be not allowed that it was the first — saw the Revelation (*i.e.*, wrote the Apocalypse) ascribed to John. The same Papias, of whom we now speak, professes to have received the declarations of the apostles from those that were in company with them, and says also that he was a hearer of Aristion and the presbyter John; for, as he has often mentioned them by name, he also gives their statement in his books. . . .

"He also gives other accounts which he adds as received by him from unwritten tradition, likewise certain strange parables of our Lord, and statements of his doctrine, and some other matters rather too fabulous. In these he says that there will be a certain millennium after the resurrection, and that there will be a corporeal reign of Christ on this very earth, which things he appears to have imagined as if they were authorized by the apostolic narratives, not understanding correctly what they propounded obscurely in their representations. For he was very limited in his comprehension, as is evident from his discourses; yet he was the cause why most of the writers of the Church, relying on his having lived at so early a time, were carried away by a similar opinion; as, for instance, Irenæus, and others that adopted such sentiments. . . .

"We shall now subjoin to the extracts already given a tradition concerning Mark, who wrote the Gospel, in the following words: 'John the presbyter also said this: Mark being the interpreter of Peter, whatsoever he recorded he wrote with great accuracy, but not, however, in the order in which it was spoken or done by our Lord; for he neither heard nor followed our Lord, but, as before said, he was the companion of Peter, who gave him such instruction as was necessary, but not a full account of our Lord's discourses. Wherefore Mark has not erred in any thing, by writing things as he has recorded them; for he was careful not to omit anything that he heard, or to state anything falsely.' Such is the account of Papias respecting Mark. Of Matthew he has stated as follows: 'Matthew wrote his history in the Hebrew dialect (*i.e.*, the Syro-Chaldaic), and every one translated it as he was able.'" — EUSEBIUS, *Ecclesiastical History*, iii. 39.

It is very probable that Matthew's Gospel — designed for Jewish readers — was originally written in the then vernacular language of Palestine, and that Papias had never seen a translation of it; yet there is strong internal evidence that our present Greek Gospel of Matthew — if a translation — is nearly as old as the original; while abundant testimony, both direct and indirect, points to it as undoubtedly the oldest book in the canon of the New Testament.

NOTE E. — PAGE 67.

One of Justin's works is a Dialogue with Trypho, a Jew, — an imaginary personage, who, however, is supposed to maintain, after the fashion of his own time, the

Jewish side in the controversy with Christianity. In this, though the Jewish interlocutor does not make the charge, his opponent refers to the hypothesis of magic as the common Jewish mode of accounting for the miracles of Christ.

The Babylonian Talmud says that Jesus was condemned to death "because he dealt in sorceries, and persuaded and seduced Israel." In another passage it is said that the son of Stada (by which name Mary is called) brought enchantments from Egypt in an incision in his flesh, the native magicians being on their guard to prevent the exportation of magic books. His miracles are also ascribed to magic arts learned in Egypt, in a Jewish work of the twelfth century, which consists in great part of a running commentary on the Gospel history from the Hebrew point of view; and also in a similar work of the fifteenth century.

In a Jewish Life of Jesus, extant a century or two earlier, and regarded with high favor by the mediæval Jews, it is mentioned as the common belief that Jesus, entering the temple clandestinely, stole the stone on which was engraven the ineffable name of God, copied the name on parchment, and concealed the parchment in a hole cut by himself in his own flesh, and immediately healed by the might of that name. The author of the Life dissents from this theory, saying that without magic and incantation he could not have obtained entrance to the holy place where the sacred name was kept, whence it is manifest that all that he did was performed by the spell of an impure name and by magic art. (See Wagenseil's "Tela Ignea Satanæ.")

Note F. — Page 72.

John vii. 53–viii. 11 is wanting in the four oldest manuscripts extant, — the Sinaitic, the Alexandrine, the Vatican, and the Parisian (*Codex Ephraemi*), and indeed in all the manuscripts of an earlier date than the eighth century, except the Cambridge, which, though in some respects of high authority, shows evident tokens of a transcriber who understood his work but imperfectly. It is either wanting, or inserted in the margin, in all manuscripts of the earlier versions that can claim high antiquity or authority. No reference is made to it either by Origen or by Chrysostom, both of whom cover by their quotations almost the entire Gospels. Ambrose speaks of it as undoubtedly spurious. In many of the manuscripts in which it occurs, when not inserted in the margin, it is marked with an asterisk or an obelisk. In some it is found at the end of the Gospel, and in some between chapters xxi. and xxii. of Luke's Gospel, which it resembles in style more than it resembles John's.

There is in this short passage a designation of a place, and there is also a mode of describing certain persons, neither of which occurs elsewhere in the Gospel of John, while it frequently makes mention of that place and of those persons. The place is "the Mount of Olives," — a name belonging to a considerable tract of country in the environs of Jerusalem, which is often used by the synoptic evangelists. John never uses it, but instead of it uses the name of some one of the divisions of that district, as Gethsemane, Bethany. The persons are "the Scribes," who — so called by the synoptics — are nowhere else mentioned under that name in the fourth Gospel, though the persons so termed are often mentioned by John under the more general designation of "the Jews," which with him denotes the captious or hostile part of them. He wrote his Gospel at Ephesus, where the term *γραμματεύς* (*scribe*) bore an entirely different meaning.

The context of this passage also plainly shows that it does not belong where it is found. If we omit it, we have a connected narrative of a series of conversations held by our Saviour, on the same day, in the same place, with the same persons, and in the same tone on his part and on theirs. If we insert it, we have to suppose that those who were disputing with him went home, that he spent the night somewhere on the Mount of Olives, that the guilty woman was brought to him in the temple on the following morning, that her conscience-stricken accusers left him alone with her, that on his dismissing her a company identical with that of the preceding day gathered about him, and that he and they resumed the discussion suspended on the previous day. Moreover, the transition from the suspected passage to the next sentence is abrupt and unnatural, and supposes a series of intervening incidents of which we have not the slightest trace. The close of the doubtful passage leaves Jesus alone. The next verse begins, "Therefore (*οὖν*, E. T. *then*) spake Jesus again to them." Wherefore? to whom? why "again," if not with reference to a preceding conversation? The sentence thus beginning obviously has no connection with the suspected passage; it as obviously implies a connection with something preceding; and, unless we omit this passage, it is impossible to define the circumstances that led to the ensuing conversation. But if we omit this passage, vii. 52 and viii. 12 run together by a perfectly natural and easy connection, as successive sentences in a continuous narrative.

NOTE G. — PAGE 102.

"It must be borne in mind that there exists in the Bible an element foreign to the Aryan races, to be found neither in the books of Zoroaster, nor in Brahmanism, nor in the Veda, namely, the personality of God. Although the problem of the Divine nature does not present itself as entirely solved in the Vedic hymns, yet many of them tend strongly to pantheism. A little later, pantheism was established in India as a fundamental theory, together with Brahmanism, and it has never ceased to be the religious doctrine of the Hindoos. It is known that in Persia the highest divine person is Ormuzd, who was the Asura of the primitive age, and in the celestial hierarchy of Zoroaster was the first of the Amschaspands; but above this personal and living God, supreme agent of the creation and governor of the world, the magi, as well as the brahmins, conceived of the absolute and eternal being, in whose unity all living beings, and Ormuzd himself, are merged. There is, then, no essential difference between the metaphysic of the Persians and that of the Hindoos.

"The scholars of our day who have occupied themselves on the Semitic races, and among them M. Renan, who is an authority in these matters, have shown that Semitism, on the contrary, rests on the Divine personality, and in this respect diverges from the Aryan dogmas. We must recognize in this conception of God an element introduced into the doctrine of God by that race. It is recognized in the Bible from its very first words, and it served as a support for the entire political system of the people of Israel. If the prophets had not yielded to its influence, and had preserved in its integrity the doctrine of the Aryans, it is probable that they would have had only a very limited hold on the Jewish people, the Semitic majority of which would have had no comprehension of a metaphysic so high. The cerebral and intellectual development of the Semitic race is arrested before the age at which man is able to understand these transcendental speculations. The Aryan alone can attain to them; the history of religions and that of philosophies show us that he alone has risen high enough. What the young Idumæan cannot comprehend he will not teach to his sons; the inaptness of the race will be perpetuated by natural descent; and their God, however separate from the world, will always have the characteristics of a great man, of a mighty prince, of a king of the desert. . . .

"As to the fundamental doctrine, one can hardly be mistaken in admitting that it tends to return to its absolute [*i.e.* pantheistic] form, and that, in spite of all the modifications which transient causes may impose upon it, it persists, like the race that first conceived it, in its transparency and spontaneity. Thence comes it that when we, Aryans, give ourselves the pains to make a comparative study of the Koran, the Bible, and the Veda, we reject the first as the work of a race inferior to ours; the second astonishes at the outset, yet without having much attraction for us, as we perceive that the men concerned in it were not of the same race with ourselves and did not think as we do; in the third, all modern science recognizes its own veritable ancestry. It is thence, consequently, that the light was born, and, in spite of refracting media, has been transmitted even to us. Some of these media have let the ray pass scarcely bent; others have broken it, decomposed it, discolored it; there are those which have almost quenched it, and which have remained opaque. It is to science that it belongs to survey the routes which the religious idea, that took its departure from central Asia, has followed over the world, and to determine the causes which in every country have more or less essentially modified it. It is for science to reconstruct the primitive idea of the doctrine, and to enunciate the laws that have governed its transmission." — EMILE BURNOUF, *La Science des Religions*, Ch. XI.

These extracts indicate the views professed by a large school of continental *savants*, of which Burnouf is a fair representative. They regard belief in the divine personality as the birth of an inferior order of intellectual development, and maintain that it will yield place to pantheism with the growing ascendency of the Aryan races.

NOTE H. — PAGE 123.

Cicero in his *De Officiis* (III. 32) quotes Polybius, who was regarded as of the highest authority in his history of this war, as telling the story of one perjured soldier sent back to Hannibal in chains; and cites Acilius, another historian of approved credit, as telling a similar story of several captives, who were suffered to remain at Rome, but were degraded from citizenship. In an earlier part of the *De Officiis* (I. 13) Cicero without quoting any authority, says that ten were sent back to Rome, and staid there in degradation; and that one of those ten unsuccessfully claimed immunity for his violated oath by a "constructive return." This confusion of accounts as to the details of a well-known passage of history is to be ascribed to the fact that it was so well known, and that so intense stress was laid in the popular speech and memory on the central incident of a shameless and till then unprecedented perjury.

Note I. — Page 131.

"When I was sent by Titus Cæsar with Cerealius, and a thousand horsemen, to a certain village called Thecoa, in order to know whether it were a place for a camp, as I came back I saw many captives crucified, and I recognized three of them as among my former acquaintance. I was very much grieved at this, and went in tears to Titus, and told him of them. He immediately ordered that they should be taken down, and that every thing possible should be done for their recovery; yet two of them died under the physician's hands, while the third recovered." —*Life of Josephus*, § 75.

Note J. — Page 135.

The churches of Asia Minor seem to have celebrated the crucifixion and the resurrection on their reputed anniversaries, on whatever days of the week they might occur, and they appealed for this usage to the authority of the apostle John. Polycarp, Bishop of Smyrna, alleged that he had himself thus observed the sacred season with the apostle John. Anicetus, Bishop of Rome, also claimed apostolic authority for dissent from this practice. Both may have been in the right; for it is by no means improbable that in a matter in itself unessential a diversity of practice might have grown up under the auspices of different members of the apostolic college. The controversy, which was sometimes waged with no little acrimony in the primitive Church, is of importance only as establishing the antiquity of the celebration, and thus confirming the authenticity of the resurrection, no less than that of the crucifixion which no one doubts. (See Neander's "Church History," vol. i., section 3.)

NOTE K. — PAGE 156.

"The future world has been placed by the wisdom of God, just in that light in which it is most for our benefit that it should be placed. Were we fixed in the situation of the apostle John, were the heavenly state continually laid open to our view, religion would be no longer a voluntary service; we should be forced to attend to objects so transcendently glorious brought thus near to us. Could we distinctly hear the voices, like mighty thunderings, heard within the vail, they would render us deaf to every earthly sound: religion would be no longer matter of choice; and consequently faith would be no longer matter of virtue. The preference of present to future interests, and therefore the exercise of self-denial, would be impossible. But the Divine Being has been pleased to throw over the heavenly world a great degree of obscurity. Jesus Christ has, indeed, brought life and immortality to light by the Gospel; has raised our hopes to the highest point, by investing the future state of glory with unspeakable elevation and grandeur, but has not explicitly taught in what that state will consist. 'It doth not yet appear what we shall be.' We know enough of futurity to make it become the great object of our attention; although it does not so press upon our organs as to render us insensible to present scenes and interests." — ROBERT HALL, *Works* (Gregory's edition), vol. iii. p. 326.

"In a divine revelation, we must expect many points of information to be reserved. You send a child, for instance, on an errand to a distant street; and you give him the street's name, and the number of the crossings, and repeat to him perhaps more than once his particular business;

but you do not detain and perplex him by either a history or a panoramic exhibition of the city he visits. 'When I was a child, I spake as a child;' and the converse is also true: 'When I was a child, I was spoken to as a child: such knowledge was given to me as was proper for my childhood's estate.' And even in our manhood, and with reference to our fellow-men, there are always topics as to which we are more or less ignorant, and as to which speculative information is withheld. Thus a government sends forth a colonist; but gives him just information enough to enable him to perform his particular work. A general charges an inferior officer with a special duty; but here, too, there is silence as to whatever does not belong to this duty. To enlarge the official directions given in either case, so as to include all the knowledge the superior may possess, would perplex the agent, and withdraw his attention from that which concerned his work to that which did not concern it. And if we are to expect such silence in a parent's dealings with a child, and in a government's dealings with a subaltern, how much more reason have we to expect it in the dealings of God with man! God knows all things and endures from eternity to eternity; man comes into the world knowing nothing; lives at the best a life which endures for a few years; and in this short life is charged with the momentous question of settling his own destiny for the eternity to come. Silence, then, on all irrelevant questions is what we would expect in the revelation of an all-wise God; and of the irrelevancy, He is the sole judge." — Rev. FRANCIS WHARTON, D.D., LL.D., *The Silence of Scripture*, chap. i.

Note L. — Page 162.

"Valor, or active courage, is for the most part constitutional, and therefore can have no more claim to moral merit than wit, beauty, health, strength, or any other endowment of the mind or body; and so far is it from producing any salutary effects by introducing peace, order, or happiness into society, that it is the usual perpetrator of all the violences which from retaliated injuries distract the world with bloodshed and devastation. It is the engine by which the strong are enabled to plunder the weak, the proud to trample upon the humble, and the guilty to oppress the innocent; it is the chief instrument which ambition employs in her unjust pursuits of wealth and power, and is therefore so much extolled by her votaries. It was, indeed, congenial with the religion of pagans, whose gods were, for the most part, made out of deceased heroes, exalted to heaven as a reward for the mischiefs which they had perpetrated upon earth, and therefore with them this was the first of virtues, and had even engrossed that denomination to itself; but whatever merit it may have assumed among pagans, with Christians it can pretend to none, and few or none are the occasions in which they are permitted to exert it. They are so far from being allowed to inflict evil, that they are forbid even to resist it; they are so far from being encouraged to revenge injuries, that one of their first duties is to forgive them; so far from being incited to destroy their enemies, that they are commanded to love them, and to serve them to the utmost of their power. If Christian nations therefore were nations of Christians, all war would be impossible and unknown amongst them, and valor could be neither of use or estimation, and therefore could never have a place in the catalogue of Christian virtues, being irreconcilable with all its precepts. I object not to the praise and honors bestowed on the valiant, — they are the least tribute which can be paid them by those who enjoy safety and affluence by the intervention of their dangers and sufferings, — and assert only, that active courage can never be a Christian virtue, because a Christian can have nothing to do with it. Passive courage is indeed frequently and properly inculcated by this meek and suffering religion, under the titles of patience and resignation: a real and substantial virtue this, and a direct contrast to the former; for passive courage arises from the noblest dispositions of the human mind, from a contempt of misfortunes, pain, and death, and a confidence in the protection of the Almighty; active, from the meanest, — from passion, vanity, and self-dependence: passive courage is derived from a zeal for truth, and a perseverance in duty; active is the offspring of pride and revenge, and the parent of cruelty and injustice: in short, passive courage is the consolation of a philosopher; active, the ferocity of a savage. Nor is this more incompatible with the precepts, than with the object of this religion, which is the attainment of the kingdom of heaven; for valor is not that sort of violence by which that kingdom is to be taken; nor are the turbulent spirits of heroes and conquerors admissible into those regions of peace, subordination, and tranquillity.

"Patriotism, also, that celebrated virtue, so much practised in ancient, and so much professed in modern times, that virtue, which so long preserved the liberties of Greece, and exalted Rome to the empire of the world, — this celebrated virtue, I say, must also be excluded; because it not only falls short of, but directly counteracts, the extensive benevolence of this religion. A Christian is of no country; he is a citizen of the world; and his neighbors and countrymen are the inhabitants of the remotest regions, whenever their distresses demand his friendly assistance. Christianity enjoins us to imitate the universal benevolence of our Creator, who pours forth his blessings on every nation upon earth; patriotism, to copy the mean partiality of an English parish officer, who thinks injustice and cruelty meritorious, whenever they promote the interests of his own inconsiderable village. This has ever been a favorite virtue with mankind, because it conceals self-interest under the mask of public spirit, not only from others, but even from themselves, and gives a license to inflict wrongs and injuries, not only with impunity, but with applause; but it is so diametrically opposite to the great characteristic of this institution, that it never could have been admitted into the list of Christian virtues.

"Friendship, likewise, although more congenial to the principles of Christianity, arising from more tender and amiable dispositions, could never gain admittance amongst her benevolent precepts for the same reason; because it is so narrow and confined, and appropriates that benevolence to a single object, which is here commanded to be extended over all. Where friendships arise from similarity of sentiments, and disinterested affections, they are advantageous, agreeable, and innocent, but have little pretensions to merit; for it is justly observed, 'If ye love them which love you, what thank have ye? for sinners also love those that love them.' But if they are formed from alliances in parties, factions, and interests, or from a participation of vices, the usual parents of what are called friendships among mankind, they are then both mischievous and criminal, and consequently forbidden; but in their utmost purity deserve no recommendation from this religion." — Soame Jenyns, *Internal Evidence of the Christian Religion.*

Note M. — Page 176.

We have in the synoptic Gospels the record of but two passovers during the public portion of our Saviour's life, the last being that made memorable by his death and resurrection. We have the record of but three feasts other than passovers; namely, that of Tabernacles, that of the Dedication, and one earlier than these, not designated by name, at which occurred the cure of the infirm man at the pool of Bethesda. The fourth Gospel (vi. 4) seems to refer to another passover as near at hand at the time of the feeding of the five thousand. If this narrative holds in John's Gospel its true chronological place, he certainly describes three passovers. On the bipaschal hypothesis the narrative of the five thousand must belong in the order of time between the eleventh and twelfth chapters. To have placed it there would have separated two narratives which for æsthetic and spiritual reasons the author may have specially desired to present in close connection; namely, the raising of Lazarus, and Christ's next meeting with Lazarus and his sisters at their house in Bethany, on the first day of the crucifixion-week. This transposition of the sixth chapter brings John's chronology into harmony with that of the synoptics; and we then have no great feast that occurred during our Saviour's ministry without some record of him in connection with it. There seems to have been no unanimous tradition in the early Church as to the length of our Lord's ministry. Irenæus, however, recognized three passovers; while most of the Fathers speak of Christ's ministry as having embraced but one full year, quoting as literally applicable to it the words of the Messianic prediction, "The acceptable *year* of the Lord." Whether they drew their chronology from the single noun in the prediction, or whether they quoted that noun in confirmation of knowledge elsewhere acquired, it is impossible to say. They were entirely capable of the former.

Note N. — Page 196.

The flagitious facility and frequency of divorce in the latter days of the republic, and under the earlier emperors, cannot be overstated. The most virtuous men in the city did not regard the wanton, arbitrary repudiation of a wife as a stain on their virtue. Cato Uticensis, a man of incorruptible integrity, and deemed a paragon of excellence, did not hesitate to give his wife and the mother of his children in marriage to his friend Hortensius, so far as it appears without even asking her consent, taking her again as a wife when she became the rich widow of Hortensius. Æmilius Paulus divorced a wife whom he confessed to be blameless, without so much as giving a reason for his conduct. Cicero, after a married life of thirty years or more, divorced the mother of his children, at best, on account of a quarrel about property, — according to the statement of his less partial biographers, in order to marry the young heiress, his ward, whom he shortly afterward did marry. The divorce to which the emperor Augustus compelled Livia, that she might become his wife, is even more revolting in its circumstances than either of the above-named instances. "Cæsar cupidine formæ aufert marito, incertum nam invitam; adeo properus, ut, ne spatio quidem ad enitendum dato, Penatibus suis gravidam induxerit." — Tacitus, *Annal.*, v. 1.

Cicero, in his Oration for Cluentius, relates a case, which must even then have indicated abnormal depravity, but which was fully within the legal rights of the parties to the transaction. The mother of his client had induced her own son-in-law to repudiate his but recently married wife that she might take her daughter's place in his household. "Lectum illum genialem, quem biennio ante filiæ suæ nubenti straverit, in eadem domo sibi ornari et sterni, expulsa atque exturbata filia, jubet." — CICERO, *pro A. Cluentio Avito,* § 5.

The following passage from Seneca indicates the profligate extent to which the mania for divorce had diffused itself among the women of his time: "Pudorem rei tollit multitudo peccantium; et desinet esse probri loco commune maledictum. Numquid jam ulla repudio erubescit, postquam illustres quædam ac nobiles feminæ, non consulum numero, sed maritorum, annos suos computant, et exeunt matrimonii causa, nubunt repudii? Tamdiu illud timebatur, quamdiu rarum erat. Quia vero nulla sine divortio acta sunt, quod sæpe audiebant, facere didicerunt. Numquid jam ullus adulterii pudor est, postquam eo ventum est, ut nulla virum habeat, nisi ut aduterum irritet? Argumentum est deformitatis pudicitia." — *De Beneficiis,* iii. 16.

NOTE O. — PAGE 197.

The latest instance of the extreme exercise of the power of life and death by the father of which we have record is a case recorded by Seneca; and in this instance it would seem that public sentiment had already outgrown the law. He writes: "Within our memory the people in the forum stabbed with their *stili* Erixo, a Roman knight, who had whipped his son to death. The authority of

Augustus Cæsar hardly sufficed to rescue him from the hostile hands of fathers, no less than of sons." — *De Clementia*, i. 14.

We have no intimation that Erixo's act was illegal, nor have we proof that it would have been so at any period prior to the conversion of Constantine.

Note P. — Page 199.

The law of divorce in the Code of Theodosius annexes some similar crimes to those specified in Constantine's edict of 331. The following are its provisions as regards the wife's and the husband's right to divorce.

"Si maritum suum adulterum, aut parricidam, aut veneficum, vel certe contra nostrum imperium molientem, vel falsitatis crimine condemnatum invenerit, si sepulchrorum dissolutorem, si sacris ædibus aliquid subtrahentem, si latronem, vel latronum susceptorem, vel abactorem, aut plagiarium, vel ad contemptum sui domusve suæ ipsa inspiciente cum impudicis mulieribus (quod maxime etiam castas exasperat) cœtum ineuntem, si suæ vitæ veneno, aut gladio, aut alio simili modo insidiantem, in se verberibus (quæ ingenuis aliena sunt) afficientem probaverit, tunc repudii auxilio uti necessario permittimus libertatem, et causa dissidii, legibus comprobare."

"Vir quoque pari fine clauditur, nec licebit ei sine causis apertius designatis propriam repudiare jugalem; nec ullo modo expellat nisi adulteram, vel veneficam, aut homicidam, aut plagiariam, aut sepulchrorum dissolutricem, aut ex sacris ædibus aliquid subtrahentem, aut latronum fautricem, aut extraneorum virorum, se ignorante vel nolente, convivia appetentem; aut ipso invito sine justa et probabili causa foris scilicet pernoctantem, vel circensibus, vel theatralibus, ludis, vel arenarum spectaculis in ipsis locis, in quibus hæc adsolent celebrari, se prohibente, gaudentem, vel sibi veneno, vel gladio, aut alio simili modo insidiatricem, vel contra nostrum imperium aliquid machinantibus consciam, seu falsitatis se crimini immiscentem, invenerit, aut manus audaces sibi probaverit ingerentem, — tunc enim necessario ei discedendi permittimus facultatem, et causas dissidii legibus comprobare."

The Church from the very first adhered to the stricter evangelic law of divorce, which, with the growing ascendency of the Church, prevailed in the legislation of the empire, as it did in the codes of all Christian nations till a comparatively recent period.

NOTE Q. — PAGE 199.

The first law annulling the power of the father over the child's life is an edict of Constantine (A.D. 318), which subjects the father who kills his child to the normal punishment of the parricide; namely, being sewed up in a bag with a cock, an ape, and a viper, and thrown into the sea, or the nearest river.

With regard to infanticide, we have from Lactantius ample proof that the practice prevailed without reproach or shame until the beginning of the fourth century. In A.D. 315 we find an edict of Constantine recognizing the practice as prevalent. "Let all the cities of Italy take note of this law, which is designed to turn aside the hands of fathers from child-murder, and to inspire them with a better mind. If any father has children whom he is too poor to feed and clothe, let food and clothing be furnished without delay from our treasury and our domain; for aid to be given to new-born children does not admit of delay." [This, we believe, was the earliest poor-law in the Roman empire.] Theodosius subsequently made the exposure of children a capital crime.

In addition to the *quasi-castrense peculium*, which under Constantine was made to include the income of various offices, Constantine sanctioned by his imperial edict the *peculium adventitium*, which embraced whatever came to the son from his mother, whether by will or by inheritance. Subsequent Christian emperors enlarged this *peculium*, so as to include whatever might come by bequest, succession, or gift from the child's maternal kindred, as also gifts from the wife to the husband or from the husband to the wife; and Justinian, finally, extended it to whatever came to the child from any source other than the father himself.

NOTE R. — PAGE 204.

The following is the edict of Constantine (A.D. 312) referred to in the text: "Nec immoderate jure suo utatur [dominus]: sed tunc reus homicidii sit, si voluntate eum [servum] ictu fustis aut lapidis cæciderit; vel certe telo usus, lethale vulnus inflixerit, aut suspendi laqueo præceperit, vel jussione tetra præcipitandum esse mandaverit, aut veneni virus infuderit, vel dilaniaverit pœnis publicis corpus, ferarum unguibus latera persecando, vel exurendo oblatis ignibus membra, aut tabescentes artus atro sanguine permixta sanie defluentes, prope in ipsis adegerit cruciatibus vitam relinquere sævitia immanium Barbarorum."

INDEX.

Uniform with this Volume.

(Being the Second Course of Lectures on the "Ely Foundation" of the Union Theological Seminary, N.Y.).

CHRISTIANITY AND POSITIVISM. A Series of Lectures to the Times on Natural Theology and Apologetics. By JAMES McCOSH, D.D., LL.D., President of Princeton College. 12mo. $1.75.

"In the arena of conflict between sceptical scientists and Christian philosophers we welcome the athletic Dr. McCosh. As a practised dialectician he is a formidable opponent, and he brings to the defence of the truth a varied and extensive erudition. His recent lectures on 'Christianity and Positivism' are timely and valuable. The style is clear and strong, and, with rare exceptional sentences, it is scholarly and attractive. The author is too broad in his sympathies to be a bigot, and too liberal and progressive in his tendencies to reject a truth because it is new. He encourages a spirit of free inquiry, and fosters no jealousy of philosophy or of science. In this volume he gives three lectures on Christianity and Physical Science, four on Christianity and Mental Science, three on Christianity and Historical Investigation, and in the Appendix three articles: I. Gaps in the Theory of Development; II. Darwin's Descent of Man; III. Principles of Herbert Spencer's Philosophy." — *Congregational Monthly.*

"In the present as in preceding defences of her divine origin, Christianity finds in her ranks the men demanded by the time. Among those who have been foremost in her service Dr. McCosh holds an honorable place. A large part of his life has been devoted to the study and the discussion of the main questions involved in the debate between the Positivists and Materialism on the one side and spiritual Christianity on the other. He comes to the subjects in hand as one that deals with themes that have been long familiar, and have been considered on all sides. Nearly the whole series of his published works have, in fact, had a bearing, more or less direct, against the form of unbelief which is now developing its full strength. It is a happy circumstance that a man so armed and equipped has had the time and the courage to come to the aid of the thoughtful young men and women of our country who have been more or less perplexed by the speculations and pretensions of acute and determined opposers of revealed religion, as Dr. McCosh has done in the volume entitled 'Christianity and Positivism,' lately issued by the Carters.

"It grapples directly with the vital questions. Every reader must admire its fairness. It is all the better adapted to popular reading from having been written to be delivered to an audience. Indeed, the thinking is generally so clear, and the style so animated and luminous, that any person of average intelligence and culture may understand and enjoy the discussion; and no such person who has begun to read the work will be likely to rest satisfied till he has finished it. It is in some parts eloquent and beautiful, and is throughout forcible and effective for its end. Would that thousands of the young people of our country, and of all classes whose faith may be in peril, might read it with the attention it deserves." — *Independent.*

ROBERT CARTER & BROTHERS,

New York.

530 Broadway, New York,
February, 1875.

ROBERT CARTER & BROTHERS'

NEW BOOKS.

EXPOSITORY NOTES ON JOSHUA. By Howard Crosby, D.D. 12mo. $1.00.

An admirable book for teachers pursuing the International Series of Lessons which, on January, 1875, enter upon the book of Joshua.

THE SCOTTISH PHILOSOPHY. Biographical, Expository, and Critical. By James McCosh, D.D., LL.D., President of Princeton College. 8vo. $4.00.

From the Preface.

"The English-speaking public, British and American, has been listening to divers forms of philosophy, — to Coleridge, to Kant, to Cousin, to Hegel, to Comte, to Berkeley, — and is now inclined to a materialistic psychology. Not finding permanent satisfaction in any of these, it is surely possible that it may grant a hearing to the sober philosophy of Scotland.

"I have tried to make my work a contribution to what may be regarded as a new department of science, the history of thought, which is quite as important as the history of wars, of commerce, of literature, or of civilization."

CHRISTIAN THEOLOGY FOR THE PEOPLE. By Willis Lord, D.D., LL.D. 8vo. $4.00.

"Our theology has long needed some popular and attractive dress like this. Most of the old treatises on Systematic Theology are too long, too learned, too heavy as to style, too much in the form of lectures and sermons. Dr. Lord has steered clear of all these faults. He has produced a work comprehensive as a whole, attractive in form, brief in each particular part, sound in doctrine, true to Scripture, evangelical in spirit, beautiful in diction, which any intelligent layman, or any intelligent lady, not less than our ministers and students of divinity, might read with profit and delight. To all such, who wish to know what our theology is, we heartily commend it." — *Interior.*

CHRISTIANITY AND SCIENCE: A Series of Lectures by the Rev. A. P. Peabody, D.D., of Harvard College. 12mo. $1.75.

This volume, uniform with Dr. McCosh's "Christianity and Positivism," is, like Dr. McCosh's work, a series of lectures on the Ely Foundation of the Union Theological Seminary. At the close of the last of the lectures, Dr. John Hall (as reported in the "New York Observer") said: "I will venture to tell the young men who enjoyed these lectures that, when they wish for a type and model of calm, dispassionate argument, of transparent style through which the meaning shines, of eloquence that is not aware that it is eloquence, of beauty that does not show itself beautiful, they have only to look back, as I shall long do with pleasure, on this course by Dr. Peabody."

BY THE AUTHOR OF THE "WIDE WIDE WORLD."

A Series of Tales illustrative of the Lord's Prayer.

1. THE LITTLE CAMP ON EAGLE HILL. A Tale. Illustrating the Introduction to the Lord's Prayer. 16mo. $1.25.

"The exquisite spiritual lessons, which are mingled with the making of hemlock beds and cooking of fish, will cause some who are no longer children to linger lovingly over its pages." — *Weekly Witness.*

2. WILLOW BROOK. A Tale. Illustrative of the First Petition of the Lord's Prayer. 16mo. $1.25.

"In her own inimitable style of easy, natural, and cheery dialogue, with never-ending interest in every-day matters. 'Willow Brook' is a pleasant story that keeps up unflagging attention by its vivacity and variety, and edifies by its moral and religious tone." — *Ladies' Repository.*

3. SCEPTRES AND CROWNS. A Tale. Illustrative of the Second Petition of the Lord's Prayer. 16mo. $1.25.

"The story is simply and often sweetly told, intermingled with religious conversations that bring out the great truths of the Gospel and the lessons of personal duty, while the entertaining element is by no means wanting." — *Evangelist.*

4. THE FLAG OF TRUCE. A Tale. Illustrative of the Third Petition of the Lord's Prayer. 16mo. $1.25.

"Miss Warner's works never wait long for buyers or readers. She has won her way to so many hearts, that her successive productions are commended by all the pleasant memories they have awakened in the grateful homes they have visited." — *Christian at Work.*

A STORY OF SMALL BEGINNINGS. Containing "What She Could," "Opportunities," "House in Town," and "Trading." By the Author of the "Wide Wide World." 4 vols. In a box. $5.00.

"Miss Warner has a remarkable facility in the collection of charming little books for the young people, and the present work is no exception to the rule. She takes her heroine from a life of toil and dependence, and places her amid luxury and temptation, yet, with the Bible in her hand, she conquers them all." — *Journal.*

THE WONDER CASE. By the Rev. R. Newton, D.D. Containing:—

Bible Wonders	$1.25	Leaves from Tree of Life	$1 25
Nature's Wonders	1.25	Rills from Fountain	1.25
Jewish Tabernacle	1.25	Giants and Wonders	1.25

6 vols. In a box. $7.50.

THE JEWEL CASE. By the Same. 6 vols. In a box. $7.50.

"Dr. Newton possesses the rare faculty of writing successfully for the young. He interests, instructs, and benefits them at once. His style is clear and simple, but not childish; and it is a pleasure for children of all ages — from ten to fourscore — to read his books, which have attained such a wide popularity in this country and Europe." — *Lutheran Observer.*

GOLDEN APPLES. Fit Words for the Young. By the Rev. EDGAR WOODS. 16mo. $1.00.

"Many a mother will be pleased to possess it, that she may, by its aid, be able to make her little ones acquainted with the teachings of the Master." - *Baptist Union.*

FOLLOW THE LAMB; or, Counsels to Converts. By HORATIUS BONAR, D.D. 18mo. 40 cents.

"There is a great deal of wisdom compressed in this little book, and it would be well if a copy were placed in the hands of every beginner in the Christian life." — *Albany Evening Journal.*

EARTH'S MORNING; or, Thoughts on Genesis. By HORATIUS BONAR, D.D.

THE RENT VEIL. By HORATIUS BONAR, D.D.

CLEFTS IN THE ROCK; or, The Believer's Ground of Confidence in Christ. By the Rev. J. R. MACDUFF, D.D. 16mo. $1.50.

The author of "Memories of Bethany," and of "Morning and Night Watches," has secured for himself an honorable place among the writers of devotional books.

THE WHITE ROSE OF LANGLEY. A Tale. By EMILY SARAH HOLT. $1.50.

The author of this volume has admirable talent for grouping in charming narrative the facts of history, and this is one of her most interesting books.

BY THE SAME AUTHOR.

1. VERENA. A Tale of To-day. $1.50.

2. ISOULT BARRY, OF WYNSCOTE. A Tale of Tudor Times. By EMILY SARAH HOLT. $1.50.

3. ROBIN TREMAYNE. A Tale of the Marian Persecution. A Sequel to the above. $1.50.

"The advent of Froude, Burke, and others, as lecturers on Irish and English history, have imparted a new interest to the study of English history, especially of the period of the Tudors; and it is fortunate for American readers that there should have appeared, just at this time, two narratives of Tudor times — 'Isoult Barry, of Wynscote,' and 'Robin Tremayne' — which, in their careful record of the events of those times, their fidelity to the manners, customs, and language of the period, and their skilful limning of the prominent actors, both princes and nobles, throw more light upon the era of the Tudor dynasty than any merely historical work could possibly do." — *Educational Monthly.*

4 ASHCLIFFE HALL. A Tale of the Last Century. $1.25.

"Deserves a high place among the best books of its class. It is both well written and thoroughly entertaining from beginning to end" — *Record.*

5. THE WELL IN THE DESERT. An Old Legend of the House of Arundel. $1 25.

"A tale of the Middle Ages, showing that there were beautiful gleams of light even in those dark days. It is a touching story." — *The Christian.*

THE ARGUMENT OF THE BOOK OF JOB UNFOLDED.

By WILLIAM HENRY GREEN, D.D., of Princeton Seminary. $1.75.

Extract of a Letter from a Clergyman.

"Hitherto the Book of Job has been to me an enigma. I admired its beauties, but could not comprehend its design. Now, under Dr. Green's guidance, I understand it; and it appears, as never before, indispensable to the Sacred Canon. It solves the problem of suffering and calamity. . . . Its diction, its sentiment, its mastery of a difficult subject has captivated me."

A LAWYER ABROAD. What to See, and How to See. By

HENRY DAY, of the New York Bar. Twelve full-page illustrations. $2.00.

"We have here one of the most instructive and entertaining books of travel. The author seems to have seen every thing and to have inspected all thoroughly. The volume will make a good and valuable work for any library." — *Episcopalian.*

EXPOSITORY THOUGHTS ON THE GOSPELS. By the

Rev. J. C. RYLE. Now completed. 7 vols. In a box. $10.50. (The volumes are sold separately. Matthew, $1.50; Mark, $1.50; Luke, 2 vols., $3.00; John, 3 vols., $4.50.)

"It is honest, evangelical, instructive, — the kernels without the shells, — expressed in language adapted to the quick comprehension of all readers." — *Christian Union.*

"His wonderful power consists in seizing the *practical* import. No expositor, ancient or modern, that we have ever come in contact with, equals him in this respect." — *Southern Churchman.*

*SONGS OF THE SOUL. Gathered out of Many Lands and

Ages. By the Rev. S. IRENÆUS PRIME, D.D. Quarto, exquisitely printed on superfine paper, and superbly bound. Morocco, $9.00; cloth, gilt, $5.00.

"None but a great reader of poetry could have gleaned, as Dr. Prime has done, through all the broad fields of eighteen centuries, and none but a great lover of poetry could have harvested such full sheaves of pure, golden grain." — *Methodist Protestant.*

"The skill of the Cambridge press and of the best binders combine to make it a treasure and an ornament." — *New Englander.*

THE PERIOD OF THE REFORMATION. 1517-1648. By

Prof. LUDWIG HAUSSER. $2.50.

"The first century and a quarter from the epoch of the Reformation is described in this work with great compactness of statement and clear analysis of principles. . . . Its impartial rendering of the fruits of research give it high authority as a book of reference." — *Tribune.*

LECTURES ON THE BIBLE. Second Series. Isaiah to Acts.

By DONALD FRASER. 12mo. $2.00.

DOORS OUTWARD. A Tale. By the Author of "Win and

Wear." $1.25.

"The story of a family who were suddenly reduced from wealth to poverty, and of the failures and successes of the eldest brother and sister, upon whom the burden of their support fell. There is a charming naturalness about the sayings and doings of the children; and in Zillah's mistakes, both comic and pathetic, older sisters will find much to ponder upon." — *Advance.*

Any book on this Catalogue sent by mail, postage prepaid, on receipt of the price.

THEOLOGICAL, DEVOTIONAL,

AND

MISCELLANEOUS BOOKS,

PUBLISHED BY

ROBERT CARTER & BROTHERS,

530 Broadway, New York.

To the Trade.—The discount on books marked thus (*) is smaller than on the others.

Able to Save;
Or, Encouragements to Patient Waiting. By the author of the "Pathway of Promise." New edition. 16mo. $1.00

Abercrombie, John.
Contest and the Armor 50

Anderson, Christopher.
Annals of the English Bible. 8vo 2.50
The Family Book 1.25

Arnot, William, D.D.
The Church in the House 2.50
Life of James Hamilton, D.D. 2.50

Assembly's Shorter Catechism. Per hundred 2.00
With proofs, per hundred 5.00

Baillie, Rev. John.
Life of Captain Bate 75
Life Studies 60

Bickersteth, Rev. E. H.
Yesterday, To-day, and Forever. 12mo, $2.00; 16mo 1.25

"It is a sublime gospel poem, scholarly enough to meet the most fastidious taste, and plain enough to be understood by all; and interesting enough to hold the reader, of whatever class, to the end, and lead him to congratulate himself that he had met with such a work produced in the present century."—*Journal of Education.*

"It is truly wonderful in conception, sweet and beautiful in execution, and stirs the soul by the grand and awful revelations it brings before it. We do not hesitate to pronounce it the greatest sacred poem that has been written in modern times."—*S. S. Times.*

The Two Brothers, and Other Poems 2.00

"In this collection the author offers us some of his minor poems. . . . While differing considerably in merit, they all indicate the true poet. In some of the pieces, there is the power of conception, and the distinctness of delineation, combined with skill in coloring, which clearly reveal the hand of a master."

Bickersteth, Rev. E. H.

The Blessed Dead, and the Risen Saints. 24mo, gilt $1.00
The Spirit of Life. 12mo 1.25
Waters from the Well-spring. 16mo 1.00

Bickersteth, Edward.

On the Lord's Supper 50

Blakely, Rev. John.

Theology of Inventions 1.25

Blunt, Rev. J. J.

Coincidences, and Paley's Horæ Paulinæ. In 1 vol. 1 50

"This work should be in the library of every Bible student. It comprises one of the very strongest arguments for the veracity of the Holy Scriptures." — *S. S. Journal*

Bogatzky's

Golden Treasury. 32mo, red edges. A beautiful edition 75

Bonar, Rev. Andrew A.

Commentary on Leviticus. 12mo 1.75
" " Psalms. 8vo 2.50
Visitor's Book of Texts 1.50

Bonar, Rev. Horatius, D.D.

Bible Thoughts and Themes. In 5 vols. 10.00

Or, separately:—

1. Old Testament . . . $2.00 | 3. Acts $2.00
2. Gospels . . . . . 2.00 | 4. Lesser Epistles . . . 2.00
5. Revelation $2.00

"This is a collection of condensed riches of Bible truth. The author has walked in the fields of the Old and New Testaments, and gathered a harvest of ripe fruits, which he spreads invitingly for the Christian reader. The volumes are beautifully printed on toned paper."

Hymns of Faith and Hope. 3 vols. 18mo, gilt top 2.25
" " " " Royal edition. 8vo 3.00

"Since Watts and Newton laid down their tuneful harps there has been no sweeter singer in Israel than Horatius Bonar. . . . Few writers of sacred song, of any age, have equalled him in simple beauty of thought and language, or in the terse presentation of great truths in poetic measure." — *Albany Evening Journal.*

God's Way of Peace 50
God's Way of Holiness 60
Night of Weeping 50
Morning of Joy 60
Story of Grace 50
Eternal Day 75
Family Sermons 1.75
Life of Rev. John Milne 2 00

Bonnet, L.

Family of Bethany 60

Booth, Rev. Abraham.

Reign of Grace 1.25

Book and its Story.

By L. N. R.. . . . . 1.50

Borrow, George.

Bible and Gypsies of Spain 1.75

Boston, Rev. Thomas.

Select Works $3.00
Crook in the Lot .50
Fourfold State .75

Breckinridge, Rev. Robert J., D.D.

Knowledge of God Objectively considered 3.00
" " Subjectively " 3.50

"The plain practical Christian will be delighted with its tone of manly piety and its rich practical instruction. The man of literary taste and intellectual culture will enjoy the originality and boldness of the thought, and the profound and truly scientific spirit which characterizes it. The student of theology will rejoice in it as a real addition to theological science in this age of shams." — *Louisville Journal.*

Bridgeman, Mrs.

Daughters of China 75

Bridges, Rev. Charles.

On the Christian Ministry 2.50
An Exposition of the Proverbs. 2.50

"The most lucid and satisfactory commentary on the Book of Proverbs that we have ever met."

Exposition of CXIX. Psalm 1.75

"Imbued with the essence of scriptural truth all over, insomuch that, as one passes from sentence to sentence, he might feel, as it were, the droppings of a heavenly manna upon the heart." — *Dr. Chalmers.*

Memoir of Mary Jane Graham 1.75

Broken Bud (The);

Or, The Reminiscences of a Bereaved Mother 1.25

Brooke, Rev. John T.

On Dancing 50

Brown, Rev. David,

On the Second Advent 1.75

Brown, John.

Concordance 50
Catechism, per hundred 2.00
Explication of the Assembly's Catechism. 12mo 1 00
" " " " 18mo 20

Brown, John, D.D.,

On First Peter. 8vo 3.50

"It has resolute adherence to the very truth of the passage, unforced development of the connection, and basing of edification on the right meaning of the Scripture. We have not met with any thing that surpasses it." — *North British Review.*

On the Discourses and Sayings of Christ. 2 vols. in one . . 3.50

"We know not the book we could place beside these volumes, whether as a study and a model for the young minister, a library companion for the pastor, or a household instructor for the people of God." — *Evangelical Christendom.*

*On Romans. 8vo 2.00

"The author was distinguished for a rare union of qualities highly important to an interpreter of the Scriptures. He was a man of profound judgment and of deep piety. He had read extensively, and was particularly conversant with the best of books." — *Bibliotheca Sacra.*

Brown, John, M.D.,

ON HEALTH $0.50

Buchanan, Rev. James.

COMFORT IN AFFLICTION 60

Burns, Rev. W. C.

LIFE OF 2.50

"The most apostolic ministry, in our judgment, which the Church has seen since the apostolic days, was the ministry of William Burns. He literally went everywhere, "holding forth the word of life." He crossed oceans, learned strange languages, lived a solitary life endured hardness as a good soldier of Jesus Christ, and made full proof of his ministry. He was as little entangled with the affairs of this life as any man who ever lived. Such characters and lives are rare, but they are needful for the instruction of the Church. We hope that the biography of this apostolic man will be studied thoroughly by the Church. It is beautifully portrayed in this volume." — *Presbyterian.*

Butler, Rev. C. M.,

ON THE APOCALYPSE 1.50

Butler, Bishop.

WORKS. Complete 2.50
ANALOGY. Separate 1.50
SERMONS " 1.75

"The 'Analogy' of Bishop Butler enjoys a reputation scarcely second to any other book than the Bible. As a specimen of analogical reasoning, we suppose it has never been equalled." — *N. E. Puritan.*

*Cabell, Dr. J. L.

UNITY OF MANKIND. 12mo 1.25

Caird's, Rev. John,

SERMONS 1.50

"The language of Mr. Caird's discourses is flowing, rich, and sparkling, often rising to the higher style of eloquence." — *Rev. Dr. Fish.*

Campbell, Rev. A. J.

POWER OF CHRIST TO SAVE 75

Cecil's Works.

Chalmers, Thomas, D.D.

SERMONS. 2 vols. in one. 8vo 3.00

"So long as the eloquence of piety and truth illustrated by the loftiest powers of intellect and the largest acquisitions of learning shall have admiring students, so long will the writings of Chalmers stand in the front rank of religious literature, and be valued among the treasures of the Church of God." — *N. Y. Observer.*

LECTURES ON ROMANS. 8vo 2.50

"As a profound thinker and a powerful writer, — as an expositor of fundamental truth in divinity, — we are much deceived if he has his superior, or in all these respects his equal, among the divines of the present age and of any country." — *Boston Recorder.*

MISCELLANIES 2.50
ASTRONOMICAL AND COMMERCIAL DISCOURSES. In one vol. . . . 1.50

"His sketch of the glory of modern astronomy and its brilliant achievements is admirable, uniting the rapidity of a general survey with the precision of scientific truth." — *Albany Evening Journal.*

Chalmers, Thomas, D.D.

CHRISTIAN REVELATION. 2 vols. $2.50
NATURAL THEOLOGY. 2 vols. 2.50

Charlesworth, Miss.

THE LAST COMMAND 30

Charnock, Stephen,

ON THE ATTRIBUTES OF GOD. 8vo 3.00

"Perspicuity and depth, metaphysical subtlety and evangelical simplicity, immense learning and plain but irrefragable reasoning, conspire to render this work one of the most inestimable productions that ever did honor to the sanctified judgment and genius of a human being." — *Toplady.*

Cheever, Rev. Geo. B.

LECTURES ON BUNYAN. 12mo . . . . 2.[illegible]

"Dr. Cheever's name will go down to posterity conjoined with the immortal dreamer, in a union no less intimate, though more honorable, than that of Johnson and Boswell. As a commentator of Bunyan, he stands without peer or rival." — *Christian Chronicle.*

LECTURES ON COWPER 1.50
BIBLE IN THE COMMON SCHOOLS 1.25

Clark, John A., D.D.

WALK ABOUT ZION 1.25
GATHERED FRAGMENTS 1.50
YOUNG DISCIPLE 1.50
PASTOR'S TESTIMONY 1.25
AWAKE, THOU SLEEPER 1.25

Clarke, Samuel, D.D.

SCRIPTURE PROMISES 50

Collier, Rev. Joseph.

DAWN OF HEAVEN 1.50

Cripple of Antioch.

By the author of the "Schönberg-Cotta Family" 1.00

Cuyler, Rev. T. L.

THOUGHT-HIVES. 12mo 1.75

"Good nature, human sympathy, and Christian zeal kindle all his pages into a magnetic warmth. Genial, open-hearted, and fascinating in his style, both spoken and written, he has made for himself a land-wide reputation, and written his name everywhere as a household word" — *Evangelist.*

THE CEDAR CHRISTIAN. 16mo 90

"Many of these papers are intense, they are all clear and forcible, and some of them are replete with that grace which comes of fervor, — that soft and mellow light which the fancy throws around what the heart sees as well as the eyes." — *Brooklyn Union.*

THE EMPTY CRIB. A Book of Consolation. 24mo 1.00

"The most beautiful little gift for bereaved parents is the Rev. Mr. Cuyler's tribute to his Georgie, — the 'Empty Crib.' A saintly bunch of white lilies is it from full hands and hearts." — *Zion's Herald.*

STRAY ARROWS. 18mo 60

D'Aubigné, J. H. Merle, D.D.

THE HISTORY OF THE REFORMATION. 5 vols. 12mo $6.00
" " " " all in 1 vol. 3.00

"Without doing any violence to historical truth, he invests history with all the charms of a dignified romance. He writes as one whose own soul has been stirred by what he describes. His characters and scenes have deeply impressed his mind; and, with the enthusiasm and skill of the poet, he sketches on the historic page his fascinating, life-like pictures."

THE HISTORY OF THE REFORMATION IN THE TIME OF CALVIN. 5 vols. 10.00

"Part of a work that will live through all time. Apart from the charms of a pleasing and fluent style, pictorial diction, and intense vitality, its accurate erudition, careful statements, judicial impartiality, and eager appreciation of good in any connection, are merits entitling to immortality. It is a brilliant and powerful history of one of the greatest revolutions in human affairs and prospects." — *Christian Advocate.*

Daily Commentary

FOR FAMILY WORSHIP. By 180 Clergymen of Scotland 2.50

David's Psalms in Metre.

12mo, cloth	$1.25	18mo, cloth, gilt	$0.75
" " gilt	1.50	48mo, cloth	.30
" *Turkey morocco	4.50	" " gilt	.40
18mo, cloth	.60	" Sheep	.40
With Brown's Notes	.75		

Davies', Samuel,

SERMONS. 3 vols. 3.75

"I most sincerely wish that young ministers more especially would peruse these volumes with the deepest attention and seriousness, and endeavor to form their discourses according to the model of our author." — *Rev. Thomas Gibbons.*

Dick, Thomas, D.D.

LECTURES ON THEOLOGY. Complete in 1 volume. 8vo 3.00

"We recommend this work in the very strongest terms to the Biblical student. It is, as a whole, superior to any other system of theology in our language. As an elementary book, especially fitted for those who are commencing the study of divinity, it is unrivalled." — *Christian Journal.*

LECTURES ON THE ACTS 2.25

*Doddridge, Rev. Philip.

FAMILY EXPOSITOR ON THE NEW TESTAMENT. Royal 8vo. Sheep .

Di 'mmond, Rev. D. T. K.

T THE PARABLES. New edition. Large 12mo 1.75

*Dublin Tracts.

Per packet 1.00

Duchess of Gordon,

MEMOIR OF 1.25

Duncan, Rev. Henry.

PHILOSOPHY OF THE SEASONS. 2 vols. 3.00

Duncan, Mrs. M. G. L.

Memoir of Mary L. Duncan $1.00
Memoir of George A. Lundie 75
Waking Dream 35

Duncan, Mary B. M.

Bible Hours 1.25

East, Rev. John.

My Saviour 75

*Edwards, Jonathan.

Works. In 4 volumes, with Valuable Additions, and a copious General Index. Bevelled boards 12.00

"I consider Jonathan Edwards the greatest of the sons of men. He ranks with the brightest luminaries of the Christian Church, not excluding any country, or any age since the apostolic." — *Robert Hall.*

"That great master-mind, Jonathan Edwards, whose close-sighted observation, clear judgment, and unbending faithfulness were of the very highest order." — *Dr. Pye Smith.*

"Jonathan Edwards is a writer of great originality and piety, and with extraordinary mental powers. He, in fact, commenced a new and higher school in divinity, to which the great body of evangelical authors who have since lived have been indebted." *Rev. E. Bickersteth.*

"To theological students his works are almost indispensable. In all the branches of theology, — didactic, polemical, casuistic, experimental, and practical, — he had few equals, and perhaps no superior." — *Orme.*

"Since the days of Calvin, the world has seen no greater theologian than Jonathan Edwards." — *American Presbyterian.*

On the Will. Separate 1.50

English Pulpit.

A Series of Sermons 2.25

Erskine, Rev. Ralph.

Gospel Sonnets 75

Evidences of Christianity.

Lectures before the University of Virginia 3.00

Fairbairn, Patrick, D.D.

*The Revelation of Law in Scripture, considered with respect both to its own Nature, and its relative Place in Successive Dispensations 2.50

"Able and scholarly, and well calculated to correct the false notions regarding law in the divine administration." — *United Presbyterian.*

"The Evangelical student will find here a rich and strengthening feast, and will rise from it with increased confidence in the eternal verities of the gospel." — *Nat Baptist.*

Family Worship.

A Series of Prayers for Morning and Evening throughout the Year. By 180 Clergymen of Scotland. New Edition, at half the former price . 2.50

"This volume is a treasure of its kind. The prayers are simple, varied, and impressive, excellent in the grasp of their subjects, and fervent in the words of supplication." — *Watchman.*

Flavel, John.

ON THE ASSEMBLY'S CATECHISM $0.60

Foster, John.

ESSAY ON DECISION OF CHARACTER 1.25
" " POPULAR IGNORANCE 1.25
" " IMPROVEMENT OF TIME 1.25

"As an essayist, John Foster was a bright and shining light. As different as possible from Addison, Steele, and Johnson, he far excels them in the importance of his subjects, and in the originality, largeness, and vigor of his conceptions."

Foxe, John.

BOOK OF MARTYRS. Complete edition, royal 8vo. Illustrated. Sheep 5.00

Fresh Leaves

FROM THE BOOK AND ITS STORY. By the author of "The Book and its Story." With more than 50 illustrations. 12mo 2.00

"This is one of the books that we would be glad to see in wide circulation. It is particularly rich in its treatment of the Old Testament period, making use of the materials of recent travels, explorations, and discoveries, and illustrating it by more than fifty engravings, twelve of which are full-page. The surprising confirmations of the sacred record by the discoveries of the last few years receive full and appropriate notice. The ordinary, and even the professional reader, will find here a large amount of interesting and important information. Let our young people get it." — *Northern Christian Advocate.*

Gasparin's, Madame,

NEAR AND HEAVENLY HORIZONS. 12mo 1.50

"This is a book to be enjoyed and revelled in rather than criticised. The reader who sits down to it will have a rare literary treat." — *Scottish Guardian.*

Giberne, Agnes.

AIMÉE. A Tale of the Days of James the Second. 16mo 1.50

A powerful and well-written story, giving a graphic historical picture of a very interesting period in English history.

Gilfillan, George.

MARTYRS AND HEROES OF THE SCOTTISH COVENANT 1.00

God is Love 1.25

***Goodrich, C. A.**

BIBLE GEOGRAPHY 50

Gosse

ON LIFE IN VARIOUS FORMS 1.50

Gray, Thomas.

ELEGY, AND OTHER POEMS. Cloth, plain, $1.50; cloth, gilt 2.00

Griscom, John, Life of 1.00

Guinness' Sermons 1.50

Guthrie, William.

CHRISTIAN'S GREAT INTEREST 1.00

Guthrie, Thomas, D.D.

Works in 9 vols., in a box. $13.50.

THE GOSPEL IN EZEKIEL $1.50
THE SAINT'S INHERITANCE 1.50
THE WAY TO LIFE 1.50
ON THE PARABLES. Illustrated, with a brief Memoir 1.50
OUT OF HARNESS 1.50
SPEAKING TO THE HEART. (Enlarged edition) 1.50
STUDIES OF CHARACTER 1.50
THE CITY AND RAGGED SCHOOLS. In one volume 1.50
MAN AND THE GOSPEL AND OUR FATHER'S BUSINESS. In one volume . 1.50

"In the quiet. tender pathos which touches some of the purest emotions of the heart; in the power to make the common things around us illustrate and enforce some of the grand truths of revelation; in the appreciation of deeds of generosity and heroism; in the inculcation of high views of Christian life and duty; and in the application of the precious consolations of the Gospel, Dr. Guthrie's Works have not been surpassed in this generation."

Haldane, Alexander.

MEMOIRS OF R. AND J. A. HALDANE 2.50

Haldane, Robert,

ON ROMANS 3.00

Of this work the Edinburgh "Presbyterian Review" says: "In ingenuity, it is equal to Turretine; in theological accuracy, superior. It is at least as judicious as Scott, and more terse, pointed, and discursive. The only Commentary on the Romans that we have read that it does not excel is that of Calvin. Calvin and Haldane stand alone, the possessors, as expounders of this Epistle, of nearly equal honors."

Hall, Newman, D.D.

FOLLOW JESUS 35
QUENCH NOT THE SPIRIT 35
NOW 35

Hamilton, James, D.D.

THE ROYAL PREACHER 1.25
LESSONS FROM THE GREAT BIOGRAPHY 1.25
LIFE IN EARNEST 50
MOUNT OF OLIVES 50
HARP ON THE WILLOWS 50
EMBLEMS FROM EDEN 50
THE LAKE OF GALILEE 50
HAPPY HOME 75
LIFE OF LADY COLQUHOUN 1.00
LAMP AND LANTERN 50
THE PRODIGAL SON. Illustrated 3.00
THE PEARL OF PARABLES 1.25
LIFE OF RICHARD WILLIAMS 1.00
,, ,, JAMES WILSON 1.25
MOSES, THE MAN OF GOD 1.50
LIFE OF DR. HAMILTON. By Arnot 2.50

"In Dr. Hamilton's writings there is so quick a sympathy with the beautiful in nature and art, so inexhaustible a fertility of illustration from all departments of knowledge, so pictorial a vividness of language, that his pages move before us like some glittering summer landscape glowing in the light of a gorgeous sunset." —*Observer.*

Hammond, Captain

LIFE OF. 12mo $1.25

Hanna, Rev. William, D.D.

THE LIFE OF OUR LORD. 3 vols. 12mo 4.50

"There is no parade of learning, no distracting foot-notes, no allusions for the erudite alone. It is an unincumbered, unartificial work. We are presented with the products, and not with the processes, of reasoning; with the results of scholarship, without the display of the critical knowledge on which they are based.

"From a perusal of these volumes we believe that the sympathetic reader will carry away a more distinct image of the character and life of Christ and his relations to his contemporaries, than he can gain from the more brilliant page of Pressensé, or the more elaborate discussions of Neander." — *North British Review.*

THE WARS OF THE HUGUENOTS. 12mo 1.25

Hart, John S.

REMOVING MOUNTAINS 1.25

Haste to the Rescue 75

Havelock, General Sir Henry,

LIFE OF 75

Hawes, Rev. Erskine,

LIFE OF 1.00

Helena's Household.

A Tale of Rome in the First Century. 12mo 2.00

"The gladiatorial scenes in the amphitheatre, the burning of Rome, life in the catacombs, &c., are all depicted with a graphic pen in this powerful story."

Henry, Matthew.

*AN EXPOSITION OF THE OLD AND NEW TESTAMENTS. 5 vols. quarto. Sheep 25.00

"For some particular purposes, and in some particular respects, other commentaries may be preferable; but, taking it as a whole, and as adapted to every class of readers, this Commentary may be said to combine more excellencies than any work of the kind which was ever written in any language." — *Rev. Dr. Alexander.*

"It is the best Commentary by far from any one hand in the English language, and we may say the best in the world." — *Independent.*

"It has never been surpassed." — *Evangelist.*

COMMUNICANT'S COMPANION 60

Hervey, Rev. James.

MEDITATIONS. 12mo 1 50
" 18mo 60

Hetherington, W. M., D.D.

CHURCH OF SCOTLAND 2.50
HISTORY OF THE WESTMINSTER ASSEMBLY 1 25

"It contains the history of one of the most interesting portions of the Christian Church, and is distinguished, as well by its neat and graceful style, as by the fulness, perspicuity, and the fidelity of its statements."

www.ingramcontent.com/pod-product-compliance
Lightning Source LLC
LaVergne TN
LVHW020232110826
845151LV00003B/899

* 9 7 8 1 4 2 5 5 3 0 1 1 2 *